Honduras

INSIDE

Honduras

Kent Norsworthy with Tom Barry

Resource Center Press
Albuquerque, New Mexico

F
1503
.N6
1994

Second Edition, September 1994
ISBN 0-911213-49-X : $10.95

Production and design by John Hawley
Cover design by Aliyah Daigneaux / The Resource Center
Cover photo Copyright © Allan Hoeltje

Published by the Inter-Hemispheric Education Resource Center

**The Inter-Hemispheric Education Resource Center
Box 4506 / Albuquerque, New Mexico 87196**

Acknowledgments

Inside Honduras, like the other books in this series, represents the contributions of numerous Resource Center staff members. For research assistance, we are grateful to Felipe Montoya, Steve Whitman, and Rose Hansen. Chuck Hosking edited the book, and John Hawley and Aliyah Daigneaux managed production and design. We are grateful to David Bronkema and Phil Shepherd for carefully reading and commenting on the manuscript. Special thanks also go to the Threshold Foundation, United Church of Christ, Disciples of Christ, and Maryknoll Fathers and Brothers.

Contents

Contents

Part 5: The Environment

Part 6: Foreign Influence

Reference Notes

Bibliography

Chronology

For More Information

Figures

Honduras

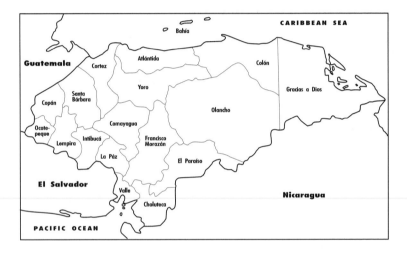

Introduction

Honduras, long relegated to the backwater of Central American politics and economy, was thrust into a new position of prominence in the 1980s. Suddenly, Hondurans heard their country being hailed as an "oasis of peace," as a "model of democratization," and as "pivotal in U.S. policy toward Central America." Centrally located on the isthmus and bordering three countries experiencing violent political conflict, Honduras was selected by Washington as a stable platform for U.S. interventionism in the region.

Short-term "stability" was indeed maintained, albeit at the cost of a mortgaged future. The gradual cessation of hostilities in neighboring countries and the drop in priority of Central America on Washington's foreign policy agenda spelled the end of what had become essentially a blank-check policy regarding U.S. aid to Honduras. Exhibiting the archetypal symptoms of dependency, Honduran leaders, who had limped their way through the 1980s resisting what they viewed as the most excessive "strings" attached to their aid allotment (particularly devaluation of the *lempira*), were suddenly faced with no alternative to the wholesale neoliberal restructuring measures "suggested" by Washington.

Beginning in 1990, the government embarked upon a new strategy of "selling" Honduras to foreign investors, promulgating a series of laws that provide lucrative incentives to those willing to bring fresh capital investment to the country. One result of this strategy was the "Asian invasion"—the large-scale arrival of *maquiladora* plants owned by investors from Taiwan, Singapore, Hong Kong, and South Korea. While a few new investors were attracted by the offer of Honduran nationality (the government offered to sell Honduran passports to foreign investors at $25,000 each), the main attraction was low wages. At 48 cents per hour in 1991, average labor costs in Honduras were the lowest in Central America.

About the size of Ohio, Honduras is largely a mountainous country of about five and one-half million inhabitants. The country has access to two oceans—through the Gulf of Fonseca on the Pacific side and via its Caribbean ports on the Atlantic side. Ethnically, the country is quite homogeneous—with nearly 90 percent of its citizens being *mestizo*.

Tegucigalpa is the capital and largest city, but San Pedro Sula is the industrial center and most prosperous city. It is the business hub of the North Coast, which since the early 1900s has been the base of the country's most dynamic agricultural and agroindustrial production. The Caribbean departments of Cortés, Atlántida, and Colón skirt the North Coast, with Puerto Cortés, Tela, La Ceiba, and Trujillo serving as the principal Caribbean ports. To the east lies the isolated department of Gracias a Dios, a frontier region inhabited mainly by Miskito Indians. The two other eastern departments are Olancho, which has a well-deserved reputation for Wild West lawlessness, and El Paraíso, the primary base of contra operations during the 1980s.

The dry and environmentally devastated department of Choluteca lies to the south and along the Gulf of Fonseca. For many years, crop failures have contributed to deepening poverty and hunger among residents of Choluteca. Nearby lie the western departments of Honduras, which border on El Salvador: Valle, La Paz, Intibucá, Lempira, and Ocotopeque. Largely isolated and characterized by steep, hilly terrain and low-grade soils, the western departments have historically been among the poorest in the country. In central-western Honduras perch the mountainous departments of Francisco Morazán (where Tegucigalpa is located), Comayagua, and Yoro. Farther west along the Guatemalan border are Santa Bárbara and Copán.

Like other Central American nations, Honduras is undergoing rapid urbanization. The arrival every month of thousands of immigrants from rural areas has swelled the population of Tegucigalpa. Thirty years ago only 72,000 people lived in the capital. Today its population is close to one million and will probably reach two million by the turn of the century if current migration and birth rates continue. Honduras sustains one of the world's highest annual population growth rates at 3.4 percent, and in rural areas the average Honduran mother gives birth to seven children.

Oil paintings by local artists present an idyllic picture of rural Honduras: a storybook land of peace and tranquility, lush with tropical colors and fruits; a world of red tile roofs, white churches, and cobblestone streets. Indeed, rural Honduras does seem a world apart from hectic urban life. But it is a benighted world lacking the most basic of services, trapped by centuries of poverty and neglect, and rejected as hopelessly backward by the forces of modernization. What peace there is comes mostly from a stillness induced by unrelenting hunger and violated expectations.

Although in the geographic center of Central America, Honduras has had the reputation of being the exception to the region's history of brutal repression. In contrast to neighboring states where class tensions and political disputes have been marked by violence, in Honduras compromise and smooth community relations have been favored over confrontation, peaceful solutions over bloodshed. This tradition was severely tested in the 1980s as Honduras was cast into the regional turmoil. Wars raged across the border in three of its neighboring states, and in two of those conflicts Honduras took an active, partisan role.

The Limits of Democracy

Soon after the Sandinistas' 1979 victory in Nicaragua, military and economic aid began to flood Honduras. Long linked to the United States through the U.S.-owned banana enclaves, Honduras cemented a new relationship with Washington in the 1980s. In exchange for use of its territory for U.S. counterrevolutionary initiatives in the region, Honduras became a favored recipient of U.S. military and economic largesse. Almost overnight the country ascended to rank as one of the world's top ten recipients of U.S. foreign aid.

Along with its newly acquired geopolitical prominence, Honduras also experienced significant internal changes. The armed forces—which had since 1956 reserved for themselves a central role in running the country—retired to their barracks, opening the Casa Rosada (the president's house in downtown Tegucigalpa) to civilian political leadership. Since 1982 four popularly elected civilian governments have administered the government. Yet even as the armed forces were ceding the reins of government to the country's two main political parties, Honduras was becoming visibly more militarized.

Unfettered by the agroexport-oligarchy links of its regional counterparts, the Honduran military had avoided the stigma of complicity in a history of brutal repression. Instead, by sharing power with intermittent civilian governments, it attained a position akin to an elder statesman, functioning as the country's final arbiter of power and the mediator of class conflicts. As such, it sponsored governments of national unity, an agrarian-reform process, and a national economic development plan that enjoyed the support of diverse social and economic sectors.

Like their counterparts in the region, the Honduran military and police have been imbued with a virulent antisocialist ideology. Nonetheless, a counterinsurgency mentality never dominated military thinking and practice to the extent it did with Honduras' neighbors. Instead of worrying principally about defense against internal leftist subversion, Honduras has historically been more caught up in fear of invasion, with a sense of military inferiority vis-à-vis its neighbors, particularly El Salvador.

Although no longer in immediate control of the government structure, the military remains the most powerful national institution. During the 1980s the country's military and police forces gained a new sense of self-importance as a result of mushrooming U.S. aid and their embrace of the imperatives of the national-security doctrine.

Under the auspices of the national-security doctrine, not only did the police and military heighten their concern about the infiltration of revolutionaries from surrounding countries, they also became engrossed in ferreting out internal dissidence. Sporadic armed actions sponsored by the tiny Honduran guerrilla groups consistently met with an overwhelming response by the armed forces. In the 1980s, while Honduras moved successfully to what some political analysts have called a "formal democracy," it also evolved into an armed camp and police state.[1] Police began checking citizen identification cards in city parks, military roadblocks sprang up, a sweeping antiterrorist law was passed, stories about basement torture chambers mounted, clandestine graves were unearthed, and disappearances and killings of popular leaders became commonplace. While the military and police were growing more repressive, they were also lavished with more and better equipment thanks to their U.S. benefactors and advisors.

Another sad irony of the 1980s, aggravated further still by the neoliberal economic policies of the early 1990s, was a boom in conspicuous consumption and luxury amid the steady decline of socioeconomic conditions. In Tegucigalpa's Central Plaza unemployed men replaced young boys in shining the shoes of the city's professionals and bureaucrats, while in the upscale part of town dollars and *lempiras* flowed freely as a new strip of luxury restaurants, U.S.-style fast-food outlets, and fancy shops prospered. Hondurans gossiped about a "rain of dollars" pouring down on the government, military, and business elite from the U.S. embassy, the Pentagon, and the U.S. Agency for International Development (AID). New restaurants and discos emerged to cater to the palates of gringo consultants, soldiers, embassy personnel, evangelical missionaries, and intelligence agents.

While droves of young boys loitering downtown or crouched in the shack-covered hills ringing Tegucigalpa lapsed into an epidemic of glue sniffing, the middle and upper classes attempted to insulate themselves from the country's surging poverty and crime. Security services became the boom business of the 1980s. Although living in more modest homes than the upper classes of El Salvador and Guatemala, the Honduran elite now employ an army of private security guards brandishing shotguns and, increasingly, automatic weapons.

Real wages fell throughout the course of the 1980s and early 1990s. Only one in ten Hondurans enjoys anything resembling a secure job. Even those holding jobs often cannot afford to meet their basic necessities since most unskilled laborers earn less than $2 a day. The cost of basic goods surged during the first half of the 1990s—so much so that even a *catracha* (beans and shredded cabbage on a *tortilla*), the standard fare of many Hondurans, has become unaffordable.

Also during the 1980s Honduras lapsed into a polarized and violent society. As a result, the country's popular sectors have grown more organized and militant. The popular movement of unions, peasant associations, and student groups—an important part of Honduran society since the mid-1950s—broadened its scope with the appearance of human rights organizations, groups representing women and indigenous people, and grassroots community organizing. At the same time, the demands of the popular movement expanded from strictly economic and sectoral concerns to broader national issues such as the environment, militarization, and foreign policy. In the early 1990s, some of the sectarianism and organizational splintering that had been prevalent during the previous decade, particularly among trade unions and peasant groups, gave way to unification efforts and coalition building.

History of Dependence and Underdevelopment

As the country was thrust into the geopolitical limelight during the 1980s, the historic flaws of the Honduran development process acquired tragic new dimensions. Characteristics of the 1980s—dependency on and subservience to the United States, paranoiac fear of its neighbors, militarization, lack of a strong national identity, absence of a dynamic entrepreneurial spirit, unprincipled and narrowly based political parties, and pervasive corruption—were not merely products of the Reagan era, but rather of deeply rooted problems that have long obstructed the political, social, and economic development of Honduras.

Long dominated by the U.S. banana giants—United Fruit and Standard Fruit—Honduras never developed a cohesive political and economic elite. Unlike most other Central American countries, the liberal reforms of the late 1800s did not spur the rise of a coffee oligarchy. It was not until the 1950s that the country began to significantly diversify its exports to include coffee, cotton, cattle, and sugar. The lack of a transportation infrastructure loomed as one obstacle to wider incorporation into the world economy. In addition, the territory's historic backwater status, lack of rich volcanic soils, isolation from world trade, and inability to form a strong national government all served as factors obstructing Honduran economic advance.

Lacking either a large indigenous population or an aristocratic coffee oligarchy, Honduras avoided the extreme stratification of its neighboring countries. There long existed an economic elite, but it never reached the heights of wealth, exclusiveness, and political power attained elsewhere in Central America. In fact, it was not until the 1950s that powerful rancher and business organizations like the Federation of Honduran Farmers and Ranchers (FENAGH) and the Honduran Council of Private Enterprise (COHEP) congealed.

Deep divisions, nonetheless, mark Honduran society, especially the traditional disjunction between rural and urban sectors. The peasantry has been relegated to the distant fringes—neglected, uneducated, and barely surviving on a diet of corn and beans. Among those who have fared well after migrating to the cities, there is a strong distaste for any manual work that smacks of their peasant legacy. At the same time, Honduran *campesinos* have been less submissive than those in highly stratified and ethnically divided societies like Guatemala. They have instead formed militant organizations to demand land, and have joined in wider coalitions and confederations with trade unions.

No other Central American country is so flagrantly corrupt. The most readily observed and experienced example of this is the venality of the police. But corruption extends far beyond the public sector deep into the core of the business community, which often seems to survive by sopping up the revenues and resources of the government and of foreign aid. Bolstered by Washington and its conservative free-market aid programs, the country's business elite has condemned government inefficiency and corruption while proclaiming its own innate economic efficiency and integrity. Yet as former Minister of Labor Gautama Fonseca lamented: "There is nothing more inefficient and corrupt in Honduras than private enterprise. They steal millions of dollars every year from the government, from the people. Now we're supposed to sell off our public enterprises at rock-bottom prices to the thieves and mafiosi who sucked the government dry to begin with." [2]

Separating business corruption from government corruption is often an impossible task in Honduras where the private sector and political elite are often indistinguishable. This was particularly the case with the Callejas administration. Elected in November 1989, Rafael Leonardo Callejas was a businessman and banker who hailed from one of the wealthiest families in the country. Before assuming his post as president, Callejas had served as a director of many state enterprises. His Cabinet was drawn largely from private-sector figures with strong ties to AID. The deceptive image of clean-cut, U.S.-educated technocrats was offset, however, by corruption reaching the highest levels of government. In early 1992, an outraged Honduran Congress announced the creation of a special commission to investigate over 70 cases of alleged corruption from the previous year against officials of the Callejas administration, including the vice-president and several Cabinet ministers.

One of the most tragic commentaries on the degree of corruption and underdevelopment in Honduras is the shadowy business of "baby trafficking." Although press reports denouncing the practice first surfaced as early as 1985, it wasn't until the early 1990s that the issue of illegal adoption was thrust onto the national agenda. According to Liberal Party Congresswoman Rosario Godoy de Osejo, unscrupulous lawyers contract with women to have children, offering $55 per month during pregnancy and an additional $370 upon delivery of the baby. The newborns are then shuttled to "fattening houses" where they are tended while the lawyers contrive through connections in the government bureaucracy to secure adoption papers. Several government agencies have been implicated in the scam, including the National Social Welfare Board (JNBS).

Also dipping generously into the public coffers and using public service to accumulate private fortunes are the military's officer corps. The influx into the country of over $1.6 billion in direct U.S. aid and hundreds of millions of dollars in contra assistance vaulted the scale of official corruption to new levels during the 1980s. Drug smuggling also became a lucrative new source of wealth during the decade. So permeated was Honduras by drug dollars that one Honduran judge dubbed the country a "narco-state." [3]

During the 1980s Honduras played the perfect foreign-policy pawn—a role for which it was richly rewarded, although the U.S. dollars that the Honduran government and military received never quite matched demands. Throughout the 1980s Honduras skillfully exploited its acquiescence to U.S. foreign-policy concerns in order to wrest continuing aid commitments from Washington while hedging on its own commitments to devaluate its currency, privatize its state enterprises, and institute harsher austerity measures. By so doing, the government managed to maintain a small measure of its historic commitment to the politics of social compromise.

During the 1980s, the country's acute internal problems were shoved into the background. The institutionalization of electoral politics combined with the anticommunist frenzy generated by the purported threat of a Nicaraguan invasion served to downplay the seriousness of Honduran underdevelopment and poverty. Meanwhile, the vast influx of U.S. dollars via economic aid, contra support, and military assistance kept the economy and government afloat while fortifying and enriching the armed forces and business elite.

But Honduras, battered by the regional turmoil of the 1980s, faces an even more uncertain and troubled future as it moves through the 1990s. As long as the United States perceives popular movements as threatening to the established order in Central America, Washington will maintain its interventionist role in the region. The continued presence of the Sandinista opposition in Nicaragua and the persistence of perceived leftist threats in El Salvador and Guatemala necessitate that Washington maintain Honduras as a close ally and platform for U.S. intervention. But U.S. budget constraints and changing foreign-policy priorities have meant that Honduras will receive less in return for its cooperation. No longer can Tegucigalpa depend on a U.S. economic bailout. The Honduran military is also being forced to scale back as U.S. military aid wanes.

Domestic tensions are likely to mount as foreign aid abates and austerity measures and free-market-oriented "reforms" take effect. Despite the election of four civilian presidents, the promise of democracy and civilian government faded between 1982 and 1994 as politicians oversaw the militarization of the country, the sale of national sovereignty, and the shelving of social reforms. As elsewhere in Latin America, a popular challenge to formal democracy in Honduras will likely characterize the country's future political arena. During the 1980s the country's unequal alliance with the United States embroiled it in the superpower's interventionist strategy for the region. During the second half of the 1990s, Hondurans may find that the acute social conflicts that have come to the forefront in surrounding countries will erupt in Honduras as well and further complicate the task of governing in this desperately poor nation.

PART 1

Politics

© Allan Hoeltje

Government

Since 1981, following 16 years of almost uninterrupted direct rule by the military, the occupants of Tegucigalpa's presidential palace have been elected civilians. In the early 1990s, a casual observer walking through the streets of the capital would notice many signs of an apparently healthy democracy. Buildings and lampposts are papered with posters from mainstream political campaigns, accented with graffiti by student groups of both the left and right. Passionate debates expressing a broad spectrum of opinion flourish in the nation's newspapers and over the radio airwaves. Labor unions and *campesino* (peasant) groups representing the poor majority press their demands and protest government policies in street demonstrations that typically meet little resistance from the authorities. Media exposés and counterattacks by competing elite factions form a constant backdrop.

But piercing this veneer of democracy are signs of a different nature. Heavily armed soldiers dressed in combat gear are routinely posted on street corners throughout the major cities. Street children brazenly enter restaurants to beg for table scraps. Military intelligence and police units zoom down the busy streets of the capital in shiny late-model cars bearing neither identification nor license plates, their faces concealed behind tinted windows. Newspapers and broadcast media exercise their freedom amid constant harassment and threats by the armed forces.

These contradictory images serve to underscore the incomplete nature of the democracy under construction in Honduras since 1980. For many Hondurans, such constraints are not measured against abstract democratic ideals, but rather against their historical experience prior to the 1980s. Seen in this light, the Liberal Party regimes of Roberto Suazo Córdova (1981-85) and José Azcona Hoyo (1985-89), followed by the National Party administration of Rafael Callejas (1989-93), have actually been less democratic in terms of the content of their policies and actions than some of the de facto regimes of the previous decades.

Between 1950 and 1980 the strategies of modernization and national development pursued by Honduran rulers often relied on notions of social compromise, limited reforms, and the politics of inclusion. Successive civilian and military governments over this period—acting sometimes under pressure from labor and *campesino* groups, sometimes in concert with them—adopted numerous reforms. These included progressive legislative changes such as a labor code and agrarian-reform laws, as well as social-protection measures like price controls, subsidies on basic goods and services, and a welfare and social security system. The reforms aimed at broadening the government's institutional base of support while seeking to avoid polarization or radicalization among the population in the face of deteriorating social and economic conditions.

Although sometimes ignored or trampled upon, the reforms nonetheless constituted important gains for the worker and peasant majorities and reflected the degree to which ruling elites were convinced of the efficacy of governing by consent and compromise. Reformist sectors in the military were particularly keen on attracting the leaders of popular organizations to the policy-formation process, and at times displayed ample flexibility in terms of incorporating their demands.

Democratization and Militarization

The upsurge of revolutionary fervor in Central America at the end of the 1970s ushered in a new period in Honduran politics. In the months following the 1979 Sandinista victory in neighboring Nicaragua, the Carter administration worked out a plan with the Honduran military to return the government to civilian hands. Since 1980 a Constituent Assembly, the National Congress, and four civilian presidencies have been established through elections. Although there had been mounting pressure inside Honduras for a transition to civilian rule, and the military itself was anxious to relinquish the business of running the government, the shift was above all a product of U.S. designs.

Carter's strategy, later expanded by Reagan, was based on bolstering the Honduran armed forces so that they could guarantee the domestic peace and stability necessary for Honduras to assume the role of a regional staging ground for counterrevolution. A civilian administration and mild reforms were essential to gaining international legitimacy for the plan. Reagan administration officials were fond of touting Honduras as a "showcase democracy."

Washington Post columnist Jack Anderson described Carter's strategy this way: "The president seems determined to add still another sorry chapter to the chronicle of Yankee imperialism in Central America. The administration apparently has chosen Honduras to be our new 'Nicaragua'—a dependable satellite bought and paid for by American military and economic largesse . . . to become the bulwark of anticommunism against the pressure of popular revolt." [1]

Since 1980, the formal reins of government have been in the hands of elected civilian leaders. But both formal and informal arrangements have assured a dominant role in the decisionmaking process for both the military and the U.S. embassy.[2] Though these three protagonists have gone to great lengths to project an image of harmonious coexistence, the relationship has been fraught with jealous infighting and power plays. As one analyst put it: "Each actor has sought greater autonomy while attempting to reduce the jurisdiction and influence of the other two. This power struggle has formed the backdrop for Honduran politics since 1980." [3]

The image of Honduran rulers reluctantly bowing to U.S. pressures, or simply selling the country in exchange for massive amounts of aid is not entirely accurate. Throughout most of the 1980s the White House was able to work with Honduran leaders because their interests and agendas were largely consistent with U.S. policies. This was particularly the case within the armed forces high command—except for a brief interlude under Gen. Walter López—which came to enjoy even greater power than under previous military governments.

Structure of Government

Honduras has succeeded in erecting a civilian state apparatus, backed up in theory by constitutional principles, responsible for carrying out policy decisions.[4] The current Honduran Constitution—the fourteenth since independence in 1838—is the product of a Constituent Assembly elected in 1980. While the Assembly worked on the document for over a year and a half, it introduced few substantial changes from the structure and pattern of government inherited from previous decades. Formal power is concentrated in a highly centralized state apparatus headed by a strong executive branch. Although in spirit the constitution subscribes to the principle of separation of powers, the executive dominates both the legislative and judicial branches. Likewise, the potential for autonomy at the local level has been blocked by centralization of authority and by the overwhelming influence of the military in outlying areas.

The executive branch, in addition to appointing and overseeing the Cabinet and the country's 18 departmental governors, presides over the state apparatus and is responsible for the assignment of posts in the public sector. This arrangement has traditionally formed the core of political patronage for the parties. By 1984 there were an estimated 70,000 employees working for the national government.

In 1993 a total of 128 representatives were elected to the unicameral National Congress where they serve four-year terms. Historically in Honduras—and the "new democracy" of the 1980s was no exception—the Congress rarely challenges executive authority. "The great problems that afflict Honduran society," lamented Christian Democratic Congressman Efraín Díaz Arrivillaga (1985-89), "namely the problems of human rights, foreign policy and the economy, are rarely debated in the Congress. The Congress legitimizes all the executive wants. Practically speaking, it is not an independent power; it does not maintain any control over the executive." [5]

The judicial system is administered by a nine-member congressionally appointed Supreme Court. The Supreme Court is empowered to intervene in cases involving questions of constitutionality. In practice, the Court's effectiveness and independence have been circumscribed by party loyalty, executive influence, widespread corruption, and continuing military impunity. New Supreme Court members are appointed with each change in government, an arrangement that further undermines the independence of the judiciary.

By the end of Callejas' presidency in early 1994, a combination of U.S. pressures, popular organizations' demands, and the general winds of change blowing through the region had resulted in increased efforts by the judiciary and the Congress to reclaim jurisdiction over matters that had been usurped by the executive branch or the military.[6]

The government structure is rounded out by 289 municipal representatives and the highly politicized National Election Board, responsible for overseeing all electoral matters. Voting is mandatory for all citizens, with the exception of active military personnel who are not allowed to vote. Only the president is elected by direct vote. Congressional and municipal seats are assigned on the basis of party slates and vote proportions. Labor unions and other popular organizations have called for democratic reforms in electoral legislation to allow voters to directly choose candidates for Congress and local posts, as opposed to the current, more restrictive system of party slates.

Political Parties and Elections

Party politics in Honduras has historically been dominated by *caudillos* (strongmen), with ideology taking a back seat to questions of personalism and influence.[7] Although recent generations of Honduran politicians have attempted to modify this tradition somewhat, the essence remains. This was especially apparent during the 1989 and 1993 presidential campaigns, which relied far more on imagery and machine politics than ideology or a programmatic platform.

The two dominant political forces—the Liberal Party (PL) and the National Party (PN)—emerged around the turn of this century. Both had close ties to U.S. fruit companies, which dominated national life and politics.

By means of highly effective repression, a complex series of legal obstacles, and traditional loyalties among the population, the Liberals and Nationals have all but made it impossible for newer parties to challenge their predominance. With the revolutionary left still in the process of emerging from years in exile or underground, and moderate or progressive forces outnumbered and marginalized, party politics remain dominated by the two big parties, whose stances on the major issues of the day do not substantially differ. As a result, since the 1950s popular organizations and trade unions have played an essential role in pressing the demands and grievances of the worker and peasant majorities.

Red and White or White and Blue?

"Vote for me, I'll be watching you on election day," proclaimed Rafael Callejas to a group of illiterate peasants in Comayagua during his 1989 presidential campaign. "I'll be the last one on the ballot, the one with glasses and no mustache, that's Callejas."[8] Four years later, voters were confronted with a contest between a red rooster (Carlos

Roberto Reina) and a blue locomotive (Oswaldo Ramos Soto). With the tradition of bipartisan politics firmly established, and few substantive issues by which to distinguish themselves, contending presidential candidates have to expend much of their campaign energies attempting to differentiate themselves in the eyes of the electorate.

For the most part, Honduran political parties operate as they did 40 to 50 years ago. From the longstanding identification by the electorate with party colors—the National's are blue and white, the Liberal's red and white—to a generational inheritance of party preferences, political traditions die hard. Similarly, a party's strength remains highly dependent upon its ability to dole out jobs in the public sector. On election day, a candidate's efforts to provide food and transportation to polling places for potentially sympathetic voters can still be decisive.[9]

The founding members of the National Party, who split from the Liberals in 1902, were closely tied to large landed interests and historically the party has allied itself with the armed forces. Today the party represents conservative elements of the business class and the state bureaucracy, and it continues to wield voting power among conservative sectors of the peasantry. By the late 1980s, the party had come under the leadership of the articulate Rafael Leonardo Callejas, who won the November 1989 elections with 52 percent of the vote. Callejas' victory broke with longstanding tradition whereby the Liberal Party scored victories in open elections, and the National Party was invited into government by de facto military rulers.

Callejas, an agricultural economist, banker, and investor schooled in the United States, expanded the traditional political machine—essentially peons voting for the landlord's party—to include a neoconservative movement. This movement is the Honduran version of a political new right, involving many young, first-time voters. Under the leadership of this Movimiento Nacionalista Rafael Callejas (MONARCA) faction, the National Party has also harnessed demographic change to its advantage by projecting an attractive, "modern" image that appeals to the rapidly growing urban population.

Although the PN led by MONARCA does not have a strong ideological definition, it is decidedly to the right of center in relation to other Honduran political formations and enjoys close ties with the ruling ARENA party in El Salvador and other rightwing forces in Central America.[10] In 1989, at a meeting in Tokyo, Callejas was elected vice-president and representative for Latin America of the International Democratic Union (IDU), an international group which brings together rightwing parties. Callejas was nominated for the position by IDU colleague Margaret Thatcher.

Under the leadership of Callejas and the banner of neoliberalism, the party moved away from its rural, autocratic origins to incorporate young technocrats and urban businesspeople.[11] Callejas' personal circle of advisors was mainly composed of young, U.S.-educated economists. After the elections, Callejas succeeded in unifying the three main factions of the National Party and contributed to disunity among the Liberal Party by appointing several Liberals to key government posts.

Traditionally, Liberals have enjoyed broader support than their National Party rivals, including a sector of conservative landowners, small farmers and the rural middle class, the more progressive urban-based professionals, and some bankers and businesspeople. Since the 1940s, the Liberal Party has advocated curbs on the military's role in national life and greater government intervention in the economy, especially through limited land reform, job creation through public investment, and expansion of social services.

In the 1980s both presidents and the majority in Congress were from the Liberal Party. But these Liberal governments broke with the party's historic image, presiding over a massive military build-up, curbing reform initiatives, and at least partially implementing harsh austerity measures demanded by the U.S. Agency for International Development and the International Monetary Fund (IMF). Progressive forces within the party were increasingly marginalized. And in the early 1990s, when military reform became an open subject for debate, Liberal deputies in Congress shied away from an opportunity to champion the cause. The prevailing sentiment among the Liberals was summed up by the party's presidential hopeful, Carlos Roberto Reina: "If you confront the military directly, you don't come to power. They won't let you." [12]

The Liberal Party remains highly factionalized. One of Honduras' most famous *caudillos*, Modesto Rodas Alvarado, leader of the party's conservative mainstream *Rodista* faction, died in 1979. Dr. Roberto Suazo Córdova took his place as leader of the faction and went on to win the presidency in 1981. Four years later, José Azcona won the support of many disaffected *Rodistas* and allied himself with the progressive, modernizing faction based among North Coast industrialists who belong to the Liberal Alliance of the People (ALIPO) faction. Another weak faction to the left of ALIPO is the Liberal Democratic Revolutionary Movement (M-LIDER). Representatives from all three factions vied for the 1989 Liberal Party nomination, with the *Rodistas'* Carlos Flores Facussé, one of the wealthiest men in the country, eventually winning. In 1993, it was ALIPO's turn, as that faction's leader Carlos Roberto Reina won the party nomination and then the presidency.

Two minority parties have managed to have representatives elected to Congress since the 1981 elections but have had no success in building a national challenge to Liberal-National dominance. In 1989, and again in 1993, their combined total amounted to less than 4 percent of the vote. One is the social democratic Innovation and Unity Party (PINU), which in 1988 affiliated itself with the Social Democratic International. Though PINU was first formed in 1970, it did not acquire legal status until 1978. As a result of the 1993 elections, PINU held onto its two seats in the National Congress. In 1991, PINU deputy Carlos Sosa was the key force behind introduction of a military-reform bill aimed at bringing the military under control of the civilian government.

The other minority party is the Christian Democrat Party of Honduras (PDCH). Garnering fewer votes in 1989 than in the previous election, the PDCH lost its two representatives in Congress. In part due to infighting among party leaders, the PDCH fared no better in 1993, leaving the organization in danger of losing its legal status.

The progressive Honduran Patriotic Front (FPH) coalition ran candidates in the 1981 and 1982 elections, but failed to win a seat. FPH organizing efforts met with intense repression, including the arrest of its candidates. The Communist Party of Honduras (PCH), which traces its roots back to the 1920s, has repeatedly been declared illegal and has never been allowed to participate directly in elections. In 1967 dissidents broke off to form a Marxist-Leninist faction, the PCH-ML.

In 1993, an umbrella group of former guerrilla organizations achieved legal status as a political organization, the Democratic Unification Party (PUD). The PUD comprised the Morazanista Liberation Party (PML), the Party for the Transformation of Honduras (PTH), the Honduran Revolutionary Party (PRH), and the Patriotic Renovation Party (PRP).

The move by the National Congress to grant party status for the PUD was largely the product of a political gesture aimed at accommodating the Honduran left as part of the Callejas administration's national reconciliation efforts. In order to facilitate legalization of the PUD, Congress waived a series of onerous requirements in the electoral law which have historically made it difficult for new parties to compete in Honduran politics. Nonetheless, PUD legalization came too late to allow the party to participate in the 1993 general elections.

Elections in the Eighties

Honduras is a prime example of the limitations of using the holding of elections as a yardstick of democracy. Under the elected civilian governments of the 1980s, Hondurans witnessed the restriction or elimination of traditional political spaces, a dramatic increase in repression and human rights abuses, and the closing of many avenues for peaceful change and reform. The policies adopted during this period—particularly in the key areas of the economy, defense, and foreign relations—were often at odds with popular sentiments on the issues. Many Hondurans remember the track record of earlier governments—both military and civilian, constituted and elected—whose sponsorship of reform initiatives provided them with greater legitimacy as "democratic" regimes than the modern-day, "cleanly elected" leaders.[13]

Throughout this period the Honduran population's confidence in elections as a vehicle for authentic democratization and empowerment eroded.[14] In 1981 Hondurans enthusiastically participated in the first direct elections for president in over 25 years. The winner, Liberal Party candidate Roberto Suazo Córdova, a country doctor and rancher, was given an overwhelming mandate based on ambitious campaign promises to meet a series of popular demands.

Four years later, a series of factors had led to widespread disenchantment with the government. Among them were Suazo's cozy relations with the military and the United States, his abandonment of proclaimed Honduran "neutrality" regarding conflicts in the region, rampant corruption, attempts to prolong his stay in office unconstitutionally, and the deteriorating economic situation. All of this contributed to the electoral victory of Liberal Party rival José Azcona under the assumption that he would break with the unpopular policies of his predecessor and return to the traditional stances of the party. Azcona also made explicit campaign promises to rid Honduras of the contra presence during his term in office. Four years later the contras were still camped in Honduras, human rights violations were again on the rise, and popular discontent over the government's economic policies had sharpened.

In 1989 the electorate once again expressed its disappointment with the incumbents, this time by voting National Party candidate Callejas into office. As a result of the 1989 elections, Callejas and his National Party counted on 71 deputies out of a total of 128 in the Congress, while the opposition Liberal Party held 55, and PINU gleaned two seats. Although voting is technically mandatory, abstention in the 1989 contest was calculated at over 23 percent of the electorate, up 6 percent from the 1985 elections—an indication of growing voter apathy.[15] Apparently many Hondurans had become skeptical about the electoral process and the nature of the democracy it represented.

Widespread irregularities in the electoral process, particularly regarding the selection of candidates within the parties and problems in voter registration, have led to both major parties incessantly exchanging charges of fraud over the years. Furthermore, periodic back-room deals between the two parties and with the military severely constrain the power of elected officials. The 1981 elections, for example, were preceded by a pact that would assure certain levels of power and influence for the military after the transition to civilian rule. Even with this agreement in hand, the campaign was marred by rumors of a military coup backed by extreme rightwing politicians and sectors of the National Party, and by calls for postponement of the elections by the centrist parties due to irregularities in voter registration lists.[16]

Similarly, the 1985 elections took place on the heels of a constitutional crisis produced when President Suazo Córdova attempted to engineer a second term in office for himself and, when that failed, to impose a hand-picked successor as the Liberal Party candidate. Anti-Suazo forces in Congress fired the pro-Suazo Supreme Court, which in turn charged the Congress with treason. Suazo retaliated by ordering the arrest of the newly appointed judges and dispatching the elite counterinsurgency Cobra forces to surround the Congress and Supreme Court buildings. Only the massive pressure brought to bear by an unprecedented ad hoc alliance of political and social groups, coupled with the mediating efforts of armed forces chief Gen. Walter López and threats by the United States to cut off aid to Honduras if its "democratic image" became tarnished, convinced Suazo to back down.[17]

Suazo's Liberal Party rival Azcona became president in 1985 in part as a result of a deal struck in the wake of the constitutional crisis. To overcome the party infighting over candidate nomination that had led to the crisis, it was agreed that any and all party factions could run candidates in the elections and the leading contender from the party with the highest combined total of votes would become president. Nine candidates eventually appeared on the ballot in November, and the National Party's Callejas garnered the lion's share with 41 percent of the votes. But because the aggregate total of Liberal Party votes for president exceeded the total for the National Party contenders, Azcona, who personally had won only 27 percent, was declared president.

Displeased with this outcome but reluctant to call for new elections, the National Party forced Azcona to share power by placing the Judicial Branch, the Ministry of Foreign Relations, and other key Cabinet posts under National Party control. The Pact of National Unity, which gave rise to the hybrid administration, underscored the fact that few political differences of importance separate the majority factions of the two parties.[18]

Once again, the 1989 elections were fraught with irregularities, uncertainties, and mutual charges of fraud.[19] This time, controversy centered on widespread irregularities in voter registration lists, including reports of tens of thousands of deceased persons and several thousand foreigners listed on the voter rolls. The U.S. Agency for International Development (AID) earmarked $4 million of its $10 million election package for voter registration activities and a purge of the electoral register, but even this intervention failed to eradicate the abnormalities.

In the days before the vote President Azcona charged that U.S. officials were meddling in the electoral process. Shortly after the elections presidential spokesman Marco Tulio Romero announced Azcona's decision not to accept the credentials of the new U.S. ambassador to Honduras, Crecensio Arcos, charging that Central Intelligence Agency (CIA) and AID agents, under the guise of "electoral advisers," had tampered with voter registration lists to ensure a Callejas victory.[20] The Liberal Party also accused AID of helping to assure an opposition victory by withholding a $70 million disbursement in previously approved aid, a move that led to visible economic difficulties for the Azcona government during the campaign period.[21]

By the early 1990s, in an effort to combat the growing problem of voter apathy and to clean up the electoral process in general, several proposals for modifying the electoral ground rules were under discussion. One proposal suggested that the two major parties hold their primary elections simultaneously to prevent the common practice of voters casting ballots in both polls. In past years, party organizations have instructed their followers to participate in the opposing party's primary, casting ballots for the candidate they think would be easiest to beat in the general election.

The 1993 elections were in many ways a repeat of 1989, with widespread popular discontent with the performance of the Callejas administration expressing itself at the ballot box in a massive repudiation of the incumbent National Party. This time, the opposition Liberal Party emerged victorious, winning the presidency by a wide margin, achieving a solid majority in the legislature, and gaining control over most municipal governments, including the important Tegucigalpa mayor's office. The huge victory margin enjoyed by Liberal party candidate Carlos Roberto Reina came as a surprise to pollsters and pundits, since nearly all pre-election public opinion polls had forecast a tight race between Reina and the National Party's Oswaldo Ramos Soto. The 1993 elections also gave the country's entrenched bipartisan tradition a shot in the arm, as a widely predicted surge by the two minority parties did not come to pass.

Reina received about 52 percent of the votes to Ramos Soto's 41 percent. The two minority parties together captured less than 4 percent. In the National Congress, the Liberal Party achieved a comfortable majority, controlling 71 seats compared to the National Party's 55, an exact reversal of the balance of forces which had prevailed since the 1989 elections. PINU retained its two seats, while the PDCH, as in 1989, failed to gain enough votes for even one seat.

Reina is an expert in international law who served as president of the Inter-American Court on Human Rights, based in Costa Rica, from 1979 to 1985. Reina became involved in politics in 1944, participating in activities against the dictatorship of Gen. Tiburcio Carías. He was subsequently jailed for opposing the dictatorship, and later went into exile in neighboring El Salvador.

Since the return to civilian rule in the 1980s, Reina struggled to modernize the Liberal Party, moving the organization away from its traditional base in *caudillismo*. Together with his brother Jorge Arturo, Carlos Roberto organized two internal party factions—the Liberal Alliance of the People (ALIPO) and the Liberal Democratic Revolutionary Movement (M-LIDER)—both of which sought to infuse greater reliance on political doctrine and ideology. Nonetheless, the Reina-led factions were largely relegated to the progressive fringe of the party throughout most of the 1980s, as the party was dominated by its conservative mainstream under the presidencies of Suazo Córdova and Azcona.

Analysts attributed Reina's unusually wide margin of victory primarily to two factors: a "punishment vote" against the incumbent National Party based on widespread discontent with the Callejas administration, and voter repudiation of the campaign tactics used by Ramos Soto.

Several analysts, including some from the National Party itself, agreed that the "punishment vote" was a key factor in the balloting. Although Reina said he would maintain the broad contours of the neoliberal economic program launched by Callejas, his campaign also promised to carry out economic and development policies "with a human face," and to launch a "moral revolution" against rampant corruption.

Meanwhile, most observers agreed that the National Party's heavy reliance in its campaign on anachronistic anti-communist themes—its main slogan was *Patria Sí Comunismo No* (Homeland Yes, Communism No)—essentially backfired, driving voters away from Ramos Soto out of fear of a return to the polarization and repression which gripped the country in the early 1980s.

In fact, both parties were widely criticized for running the dirtiest and shallowest campaigns since the return to civilian rule in 1981, the main factor cited in explaining the highest rate of voter abstention since the 1981 return to elected civilian governments, 35 percent.

Foreign Policy

The determining factor in Honduran foreign policy over the past 15 years has been the tendency of the civilian and military leadership to define national interests as a function of U.S. strategy for Central America.[22] As a result of externally imposed definitions, traditional adversaries were transformed into "allies" (El Salvador); new "enemies" emerged (Nicaragua); and a country described in 1982 as an "oasis of peace" (Honduras) was turned into a long-term base for two foreign armies (the U.S. and the contras) and a temporary training site for a third (Salvadoran). This "denationalization" of foreign policy led to a growing outcry among the public and important institutions of Honduran society, and it rendered the country an object of international ridicule.

Honduras' relations within Central America have always been influenced by the country's central geographic position on the isthmus. For centuries Honduran territory—which shares long borders with Guatemala, El Salvador, and Nicaragua—has alternately played the role of battleground, staging area, and rear guard for regional conflicts. It was in large part due to this strategic location that at the beginning of this century the theoretical cornerstone of Honduran foreign policy was defined as perpetual neutrality vis-à-vis conflicts in the rest of Central America.

Formally, the principle of neutrality has never been abandoned. But in practice it has been progressively distorted and emptied of its content by the string of military governments that have ruled during most of this century and, more recently, by increasing alignment with the United States. By the mid-1980s Honduran foreign-policy concerns had largely been reduced to mere reflections of U.S. regional strategy. With the end of the contra war and Sandinista electoral defeat in neighboring Nicaragua, and following consolidation of the peace process in El Salvador, many Hondurans were optimistic that during the 1990s the country would have an opportunity to recover authentic neutrality in foreign-policy matters.

The intermingling of U.S. and Honduran foreign-policy interests dates back to the banana empire days when the fruit companies' control over local politics ensured that the nation's foreign policy would not stray too far from the desires of U.S. political and business interests. Although more nationalist-minded sectors have since emerged in Honduras and the relationship with the United States has become much more complex, the pattern has not been broken. Honduran collaboration with the United States in the 1954 overthrow of the Arbenz government in Guatemala and in anti-Castro adventures in the 1960s find their counterparts in more recent years in the contra war and in support for the Salvadoran military's campaign against the Faribundo Martí National Liberation Front (FMLN) guerrillas.

The early 1980s accelerated a trend already under way whereby the formulation of Honduran foreign policy had been gradually shifting from the political party in power to the military and to private pressure groups. One of the conditions the military imposed as part of the 1980-81 transition to civilian government was that the armed forces would be allowed to maintain authority over the definition of key aspects of foreign policy. The military-dominated National Defense and Security Council is responsible for defining the broad contours of the nation's foreign policy (see Security Forces). The military high command often makes strategic decisions relating to foreign affairs and later presents these decisions to the president and National Congress as a *fait accompli*.[23]

Following the transition, the most influential pressure group involved in defining foreign policy was the Association for the Progress of Honduras (APROH). Formed in January 1983 with Gen. Alvarez at the helm, APROH was an alliance of far-rightwing military, business, and political elites with conservative labor and peasant groups. Described by Christian Democratic Party leader Efraín Díaz as "the center of power in Honduras," APROH operated as a think tank issuing elaborate policy proposals, particularly regarding the economy and foreign relations.

When the Kissinger Commission visited the isthmus in 1983, for example, it was APROH, not the ruling Liberal Party, that wrote the official documents for presentation to the Commission.[24] Although Alvarez and APROH have long since departed, their imprint on Honduran politics remains. In fact, several top Cabinet and advisory posts in the National Party government that emerged from the 1989 elections went to key figures from APROH, an organization in which President Callejas himself played a leading role.[25] In essence, Callejas' triumph at the polls in 1989, in tandem with the subsequent application of neoliberal tenets during the early 1990s, represented the culmination of a process initiated by APROH's appearance nearly a decade earlier. That process essentially sought to build consensus among the military, elements from the business and political elite, and at least some groups representing the worker and *campesino* majority, around a project of national transformation and modernization.

As the Central American crisis deepened during the 1980s, Honduran foreign policy evolved through several overlapping phases. Early in the decade the country was converted into the principal staging ground for the Reagan administration's regional counterrevolution. The installation of contra bases on Honduran territory, the long-term presence of U.S. troops in Honduras, and the collaboration between Honduran and Salvadoran armed forces in the war against the FMLN were the most salient manifestations of this new regional role. Beginning with the Contadora peace negotiations in 1983 and later with the Esquipulas II Peace Accords of 1987, the country's cooperation with U.S. interventionism became increasingly embarrassing and untenable. Honduras' persistent stalling tactics during the process of regional negotiations led to a deterioration of the country's image both in Central America and internationally.

By 1988 a combination of pressures forced the military and the civilian government to shift its position regarding the contra presence and to provide at least lukewarm support for efforts to demobilize the contra army. Honduras' constant vacillations about the demobilization indicate, however, that this change in policy was due more to political expediency and realpolitik than to any fundamental questioning of its overall relationship with the United States. On the one hand, by the end of the 1980s even sectors of the Honduran elite recognized the need to confront the destabilizing effect of the contra presence. On the other, both the military and the politicians became convinced that U.S. aid levels would not diminish significantly as a result of a hard-line stance in favor of contra demobilization.

The overall tendency to define foreign policy in line with U.S. concerns has not resulted in the elimination of old issues, nor has it precluded the emergence of new international actors. Some Honduran foreign-policy issues that do not fit neatly with U.S. interests hark back to the disastrous 1969 war with El Salvador. The brief armed conflict, sometimes known as the "Soccer War," erupted as a result of longstanding border tensions owing to an ill-defined demarcation, the Honduran expulsion of some 100,000 Salvadoran immigrants, and domestic political and economic pressures in both countries. The Salvadoran army invaded Honduras and advanced rapidly, while the Honduran air force retaliated with successful strikes on key Salvadoran installations. Four days later, the Organization of American States (OAS) arranged a cease-fire and international observers were sent to the zone.

Although a three-kilometer-wide demilitarized zone was formally established in 1970, negotiations remained stalled at the cease-fire level. Sporadic clashes between the two countries and an unresolved state of war persisted until 1980 when the Carter administration brokered the signing of a provisional pact, the General Peace Treaty, between the two countries. The treaty established limits on two-thirds of the territory in the disputed border *bolsones* (pockets) and, in 1986, referred the question of jurisdiction over the remaining one-third to the International Court of Justice (ICJ) at the Hague.[26]

Despite the 1980 treaty, bad blood between the two countries remained. During the war in El Salvador, the *bolsones* became *tierra de nadie* (no-man's land), where FMLN guerrillas were able to operate with relative impunity. In 1987 Honduras negotiated the purchase of advanced U.S. fighter jets partly to maintain air superiority over El Salvador. By early 1992, new flare-ups occurred in the disputed border areas with the Honduran military accusing the FMLN of settling Salvadoran families in the *bolsones*, a charge that even Salvadoran President Alfredo Cristiani denied.[27] Notwithstanding the fresh problems, both Cristiani and Callejas reiterated their earlier positions that the decision eventually handed down by the ICJ would be accepted.

In September 1992, the ICJ issued its ruling. For years, widespread anticipation had been building in both countries that the ruling would essentially favor the smaller, more densely populated El Salvador. To the surprise of many, however, Honduras emerged the clear winner in the judgment. In four of the six border *bolsones*, Honduras was awarded control of between 75 and 100 percent of the territory, while in the remaining two it received less than 50 percent.

Perhaps more important was the ICJ ruling with respect to Honduras' maritime rights in the Gulf of Fonseca. Both El Salvador and Nicaragua had advocated denying Honduras coastal status in the gulf, a position that would have left the country with no outlet to the Pacific Ocean and without rights to exploit marine resources in the gulf waters. This position was rejected by the ICJ, which instead corroborated Honduras' territorial rights in the gulf.

Thorny issues persist regarding implementation of the ICJ ruling. These include determining the fate of thousands of *campesinos* living in *bolsones* territories awarded to Honduras and who, until the court's decision, have always considered themselves Salvadorans. Nonetheless, the verdict was widely interpreted as a triumph for Honduran diplomacy.[28]

Regardless of the eventual outcome, common economic concerns propelled regional cooperation. While awaiting the court's ruling, the Callejas administration clearly did not want the bilateral dispute to get in the way of the larger, more strategic, project of regional economic integration. That project was pursued in part thanks to the active lobbying efforts of Honduras, which, early on in the process, entered into an alliance with Guatemala and El Salvador to promote the "northern triangle" free trade zone. The prominence of regional integration issues during the early 1990s was an accurate reflection of the degree to which Honduran foreign policy in general had been subordinated to the demands of a larger economic project.

Peace Process

Prior to the August 1987 Esquipulas II Peace Accords, Honduras, along with El Salvador, acted repeatedly in concert with the United States to scuttle peace initiatives in the region. Exceptions to this pattern during the post-Esquipulas II period were due to intense domestic and international pressures to demobilize the Honduras-based contra army. Regarding other aspects of the peace process, such as national dialogue and respect for human rights, Honduras made little progress since the country's leaders insisted that, as a "peaceful" country with no significant domestic problems, such clauses "do not apply to Honduras."

In the early 1980s many Honduran leaders supported contra use of Honduran territory under the assumption that it would be a short-term affair and that the occasional presence of a few bands of ex-Somoza guardsmen along the border with Nicaragua would go largely unnoticed. But by 1986 some 40,000 contras and their families, unable to establish a presence inside Nicaragua, had literally taken over a 450-square-kilometer area in south-central and south-eastern Honduras. Contra patrols at the entrance points to what they called "New Nicaragua" decided who was allowed to enter and who was not[29] (see Refugees and the Internally Displaced).

Severe military defeats suffered by contra forces inside Nicaragua during 1986 and 1987 erased any remaining hopes for a contra military victory and sent thousands of contra fighters back to their bases in Honduras. Popular pressures inside Honduras to expel the contras were reaching unmanageable levels. Anti-contra sentiments began to reach into sectors of the military, the traditional political parties, and the business elite—some of whom felt that Honduras had received far too little in U.S. aid in return for its cooperation. By the time of the Esquipulas II Peace Accords in late 1987, the Iran-contra scandal in Washington, and the waning of the Reagan years raised

Honduran anxieties that they would be left to pick up the pieces of the contra debacle.

The Honduran military, which had played a key role in supporting and safeguarding the contras' presence in the country—in part on the assumption that it would assure greater levels of U.S. military aid for the Honduran armed forces—had become increasingly alienated from the contra presence. Nationalistic sectors resented the existence of a "rival" army on national territory and feared the destabilizing consequences of thousands of contras roving through Honduras after a potential cutoff in U.S. aid. To make matters worse, when AID took over distribution of the contra aid program in 1988, the program ceased to be a lucrative source of income for the Honduran officers who had been serving as intermediaries.

Following President Azcona's August 1987 signing of the Esquipulas II Peace Accords, Honduras repeatedly vacillated with regard to its commitment to participate in the development and implementation of contra demobilization plans. It was not until the February 1989 Costa del Sol summit, after a year and a half of backpedaling and stalling, that Azcona accepted that demobilization terms would be determined by the five Central American presidents. The turnaround was due primarily to Washington's refusal to accept Honduran demands that the United States assume ultimate responsibility for the disarming and relocation of the contras.

Another round of Honduran stalling was followed by an August 1989 meeting in Tela, Honduras, at which the five presidents agreed on a concrete contra demobilization plan to be carried out by December 5 under the auspices of a UN peacekeeping force. The December deadline passed unmet, however, because of two dilemmas that rendered its demobilization commitment a difficult endeavor for Honduras to fulfill. First, the Bush administration, in open opposition to the deadlines specified in the peace accords, pressured Honduras into accepting the presence of the bulk of contra forces until after the February 25, 1990, elections in Nicaragua. The original Esquipulas II Peace Accords, as well as subsequent agreements that implied postponements of the deadline, all called for the contras to demobilize and return to Nicaragua before the elections, a position Washington tenaciously rejected. Second, the peace plan called for "voluntary" demobilization; yet most contras simply refused to leave, even in the wake of the National Opposition Union (UNO) electoral victory, after which Washington, the Sandinistas, UNO, and Honduras insisted in unison that they do so. By April 1990, with their support lines severed, most of the remaining contras began to trickle back into Nicaragua, albeit without disarming.

In the immediate aftermath of Esquipulas, there was widespread optimism in Honduras that, in addition to expulsion of the contras, the peace process would contribute to greater political openings, a drop in human rights abuses, and some form of national reconciliation to offset growing polarization. Just weeks after the August 1987 signing of the accords, the Honduran Bishops' Conference issued a declaration in support of the treaty, calling on the Azcona government to move swiftly in the formation of a treaty-mandated National Reconciliation Commission (CNR). The document affirmed that, among other issues, the CNR should promote a deepening of the democratic process through greater popular participation, ensure an end to human rights abuses, and examine the refugee situation.[30] In addition to the church, business groups, political parties, trade unions, popular organizations, and even the guerrillas made public their suggestions for a host of problems that they felt should be addressed by the CNR.

But it was not until two days before a November 5 deadline stipulated in the treaties that the government officially formed the CNR. Over the next two years, the CNR held several meetings and there was even talk of holding a broad national dialogue aimed at creating a consensus around pressing economic and political problems, but substantive accords were never reached.

Although the government's lack of enthusiasm kept the CNR from playing a more aggressive role, the process did provide a public platform for the expression of discontent over the direction of national policy in key areas such as the economy, human rights, agrarian reform, and the U.S. military presence. In August 1988, for example, the CNR presented Azcona with a list of demands including a call to abolish the police investigations unit National Investigations Division (DNI), to overhaul the judicial system, and to redesign the agrarian reform program.[31] Even the military presented a controversial communique to the CNR declaring that the economic model followed by the previous two administrations had come to a dead end, calling for a new strategy more reliant on agriculture and with greater employment-generating opportunities.[32]

What was perhaps the most significant measure in terms of Honduran compliance, amnesty for political prisoners and former guerrillas, was postponed until long after the effervescence of the regional peace process had worn off. In July 1991, Congress approved a "broad and unconditional" amnesty, which called for the release of "all persons sentenced, processed or subject to processing for political crimes and politically related common crimes." In addition to benefitting Hondurans already serving time for political crimes, the measure paved the way for the gradual return of exiled political leaders and the disbanding of Honduran guerrilla groups. The amnesty was nevertheless criticized by some human rights advocates for absolving armed forces members involved in a wide variety of crimes and abuses.

Human Rights

Honduras has the distinction of being the only Latin American country ever convicted in a court of law for the crime of disappearance. Confronted with this and other accusations of systematic human rights abuses during the 1980s—including torture, disappearances, extrajudicial executions, and widespread restrictions on civil liberties—Honduran civilian and military authorities contended that the situation in their country paled in comparison to the climate of terror that reigned in neighboring El Salvador and Guatemala. Honduran defenders of human rights counter that focusing on *numbers* of violations misses the point. Beyond the fact that the only acceptable number is zero, the real issue is that a pattern of violations continued unabated throughout the decade, and that it constituted a systematic and deliberate policy executed by the military and sanctioned by the civilian government.

The state's role in the violation of human rights has seldom been more clearly proven than in the case of Honduras. Overwhelming evidence indicates that the military—not rightwing vigilantes—commit the violations. The initial wave of abuses took place from 1982-84 when the armed forces were led by Gen. Gustavo Alvarez. As early as 1982, an Americas Watch mission to Honduras reported that "the practice of arresting individuals for political reasons, and then refusing to acknowledge their whereabouts and status, seems to have become established in Honduras." [33] The report added that many of the disappeared had been taken to clandestine prisons and tortured.

The human rights climate deteriorated rapidly under the aegis of policies implemented by Gen. Alvarez within the framework of national-security doctrine (see Security Forces). During this period, the isolated occurrences that had characterized the 1960s and 1970s—the murder and torture of trade-union and peasant organizers, arbitrary detentions, and several massacres—were replaced by a systematic policy, practiced selectively and clandestinely, of domestic repression.

By the time of his ouster in March 1984, Alvarez had presided over 214 political assassinations, 110 disappearances, and 1,947 illegal detentions.[34] To a large extent, the "dirty war" succeeded in its goal of intimidation without generating the destabilizing effects of massive repression. "Hondurans gradually submitted to collective fear and paralysis," described one observer. "The impunity with which the state's repressive forces acted made the population feel defenseless; many chose the complicity of silence, daring to share fears and opinions only with close friends."[35]

Widespread hopes that the departure of Alvarez would lead to an improvement in the situation and the prosecution of at least some of those involved in earlier abuses were short-lived. Following a brief period of relative decline in human rights violations, and in spite of intense international scrutiny and legal action, after 1986 there was a resurgence in both the frequency and intensity of abuses approaching the extreme levels experienced in the first years of the decade. Noting a shift in repression methods, independent human rights monitoring organizations reported that disappearances were largely supplanted by political assassinations.

Honduras Tried and Convicted

After years of official denials regarding human rights abuses, refusals to investigate, and simple obstructions of justice, in 1987 the violations that had occurred during the tenure of Gen. Alvarez were aired in the Inter-American Court on Human Rights (IACHR).[36] This judicial arm of the OAS, composed of seven prominent jurists—one North American and six Latin American, including one Honduran—heard three cases against Honduras in its precedent-setting trial of a member state and the first juridical treatment of the crime of political disappearance. One of the conditions for the Court's acceptance of the case was that domestic legal recourse had been exhausted.

The cases were brought to trial on behalf of the families of disappearance victims by the OAS human rights monitoring and legal action team, the Inter-American Commission on Human Rights. While the Commission prosecuted only three cases involving four individuals (two Hondurans and two Costa Ricans) "disappeared" by Honduran security forces during the 1981-84 period, to do so it had to prove that the Honduran state "conducted or tolerated the systematic practice of disappearance" during that period.

After tense and lengthy proceedings the IACHR found the Honduran state guilty in the two cases involving Hondurans (verdicts of July 29, 1988, in the Manfredo Velásquez case and January 20, 1989, in the Saul Godínez case), but was forced to dismiss the case involving the two Costa Ricans for lack of evidence. Its ruling concluded that the crimes against the two Hondurans constituted "a practice of disappearances carried out or tolerated by Honduran officials . . . between 1981 and 1984." The victims of that practice, according to the Court, numbered between 100 and 150.[37] The Court ordered the Honduran government to pay reparations to the Velásquez and Godínez families.

But the issue of the disappearance victims, and a full rendering of what actually occurred during the political repression of the 1980s, was hardly put to rest with the IACHR verdicts. Broad sectors of Honduran society incessantly pushed their demand that in order for reconciliation to occur and for the errors of the past to be overcome, it was first necessary for all to know the full truth of what had happened during this dark chapter of the nation's history.

The first big step in this direction was taken toward the end of the Callejas administration, with public release of the findings from a lengthy investigation conducted by Human Rights Ombudsman Leo Valladares. The Ombudsman's office had been established in October 1992 as a semi-autonomous body attached to the presidency.

Putting an end to years' worth of speculation, in December 1993 Valladares presented his report on the fate of nearly 200 people who were disappeared in Honduran territory during the 1980s. Valladares' landmark report constituted the first-ever direct admission by the Honduran government of official involvement in political disappearances.

For years, despite overwhelming evidence to the contrary, Honduran governments either consistently denied that any disappearances occurred or attributed them to factional infighting on the left. Valladares' report, however, was a chilling indictment of the application of national-security doctrine in Honduras beginning in the early 1980s by advisors from the United States and Argentina (see National-Security Doctrine and Militarization).

The report documents the involvement of Honduran civilian and military authorities in the disappearance of 184 individuals between 1979 and 1990 (106 Hondurans, 37 Nicaraguans, 28 Salvadorans, five Costa Ricans, four Guatemalans, one U.S. national, one Ecuadoran, one Venezuelan, and one individual whose nationality remains undetermined).

The report, titled "The Facts Speak for Themselves" (*Los hechos hablan por si mismos*), also blames U.S. and Argentinian military advisors—working with the Honduran military and the U.S.-backed contras at the time—for at least knowing of the actions and doing nothing to stop them. "Extensive testimony and many reports indicate that U.S. officials, based and operating in our country to oversee counterinsurgency activities and the contras, were aware, and at least tolerated without criticism, the disappearances of Honduran, Salvadoran, Nicaraguan and other citizens in Honduras," Valladares said.[38]

According to Valladares, the investigations which culminated with publication of the report demonstrated that "systematic, clandestine and organized" disappearances began in 1979 shortly after the arrival of Argentinian military advisors who put into practice methods already used during the Argentinian military's "dirty war" in the 1970's against leftist guerrillas. Many of the victims were abducted and taken to clandestine jail cells where they were brutally tortured during interrogation by security forces personnel. Citing testimony provided to investigators, the report provides the names of several U.S. officials who allegedly participated directly in such interrogations.

The Argentinians were brought to Honduras as part of a covert operation undertaken by the Reagan administration, a precursor to the larger U.S. campaign waged through the course of the 1980s to overthrow the Sandinista government in neighboring Nicaragua.

Among prominent Honduran officials implicated in the report were former presidents Roberto Suazo Córdova and José Azcona, several former military chiefs, and current armed forces head Gen. Luis Alonso Discua. The report also implicates some military officers currently serving in key posts in the disappearances, including the director of the National Investigations Division (DNI) Col. Marco Tulio Ayala, and Lieutenant Colonel Jordi Montanola. Discua, according to the report, was appointed in January 1984 to head the Battalion 3/16, a semi-clandestine military intelligence unit. Montanola, meanwhile, who also headed the Battalion 3/16 during the 1980s, was promoted to the rank of Lt. Col. by the armed forces in early December 1993.

In his report, Valladares included a series of specific recommendations, including:

– Honduran courts should conduct formal investigations into all individuals named in the report, concentrating on military intelligence and counterintelligence units, with the objective of prosecuting all those responsible for the disappearances. Valladares maintains that amnesty legislation put in place over the past several years does not cover individuals responsible for the disappearances.

– The military, which refused to collaborate in the investigations that laid the basis for the report, should be forced to open all files containing information relevant to the disappearance cases.

– Judicial authorities should conduct special forensic investigations at 13 clandestine cemeteries named in the report where the remains of some of the disappearance victims are thought to be buried.

– The Honduran government should form an international truth commission to oversee further investigations, similar to the UN-sponsored Truth Commission which investigated the most serious human rights abuses committed during the civil war in neighboring El Salvador.

– The Honduran government should call on the United States and Argentina to name and describe the exact duties of military advisors sent to Honduras during the 1980s.

– The government should seek from Nicaragua extradition of former contras who worked with the Honduran "death squads" and were responsible for some of the disappearances. According to Valladares, contras participated in the disappearance of Hondurans and foreigners accused of having ties with the Sandinista National Liberation Front (FSLN) and other leftist groups in the region.

The military establishment, which has traditionally denied any responsibility in the disappearances, angrily rejected the report as "biased." Top military leaders lashed out at Valladares for only investigating allegations regarding abuses comitted against leftist and progressive forces and insisted the document carries no legal weight whatsoever.

Local and international human rights groups, which had been struggling for over a decade to have the government investigate the disappearances, applauded the report. Several Honduran human rights groups announced plans to use material presented in the report to push for prosecution of several military officers involved in the disappearances, including Gen. Discua. Americas Watch, which as far back as 1982 had publicly reported the similarities of disappearances in Honduras to those which took place during the "dirty war" in Argentina, commended the job carried out by Valladares.

The task of following through on Valladares' recommendations fell to the administration of President Carlos Roberto Reina, who took office in January 1994. Reina, who in his youth was jailed and then forced into exile by the military for his political beliefs, will have to proceed cautiously if he hopes to avoid a backlash by the armed forces. The military has traditionally closed ranks around officers accused by civilians of crimes or wrongdoing, thus making a thorough purge of military personnel implicated in the disappearances unlikely. At the same time, Reina was aware that his popularity among the electorate could shrink if his administration, like its predecessors, attempted to sweep the issue of political disappearances under the rug.

Acting with Impunity

The military's continued ability to act with impunity against its perceived political enemies underscores the incomplete nature of Honduras' shift to civilian rule. Though the military touts its internal disciplinary process for demoting or discharging personnel involved in various crimes, soldiers or officers are rarely tried in civilian courts for political crimes defined as violations of human rights.

Following the ouster of Gen. Alvarez in 1984, the armed forces announced their intention to launch an internal investigation into the abuses committed under his command, but nothing ever came of the matter. When Alvarez himself returned from exile in April 1988, charges brought against him by the Committee of Families of the Detained-Disappeared (COFADEH) in the civilian courts were dropped when clerks lost the papers. During that same year, as part of the military's efforts to deflect criticism regarding human rights abuses, U.S. Methodist Minister Joe Eldridge, *New York Times* reporter James LeMoyne, and *Washington Post* reporter Julia Preston were banned from the country after writing stories critical of the military and the human rights situation.[39]

The independent monitoring organization Committee for the Defense of Human Rights (CODEH) has been the target of ongoing harassment. Formed in 1981, it has endured armed attacks on its offices, infiltration by government agents, repeated public death threats against its leaders, and the January 1988 assassination of Miguel Angel Pavón, president of CODEH's San Pedro Sula chapter. One U.S. embassy publication labels CODEH President Ramón Custodio as "a prominent Marxist ideologue," and State Department reports on human rights in Honduras dismiss many of the accusations made by CODEH and other independent monitoring groups as "politically motivated."[40]

The U.S. embassy and State Department have come under severe criticism from international human rights monitoring groups for their role in attempting to discredit organizations like CODEH whose work involves exposing and documenting abuses. Going one step further, Americas Watch has laid part of the blame for the rise in human rights violations on Washington: "Honduras is one of the countries that can most fairly be described as a U.S. client state, giving Washington a special responsibility to foster human rights improvement there. Yet U.S. behavior has fallen far short of the mark. . . . The State Department still balks at acknowledgment of past crimes by the forces the United States trained."[41]

As part of a new effort in the early 1990s by the U.S. to encourage certain reforms with regard to respect for human rights, the State Department modified its stance toward CODEH. For example, the Department's 1991 report on human rights in Honduras accepts CODEH's statistics on abuses as basically accurate and in many respects accepts CODEH's overall assessment of the human rights climate in the country.

Attempts by family members of the victims of human rights abuses to bring the perpetrators to justice have been hampered by deficiencies and a lack of will in the country's judicial system. The filing of writs of *habeas corpus* and other legal avenues rarely produce results. In part, the judicial system is paralyzed due to insufficient funding and the endemic corruption of its judges. According to the constitution, the judiciary is to receive 3 percent of the annual budget, but in 1986 and 1987 it received less than half that amount. In early 1992, about 80 judges were laid off when a $30 million AID program assisting the Supreme Court was eliminated.[42] According to the U.S. State Department's 1991 human rights report on Honduras, over 80 percent of all inmates in the country's overcrowded prisons were simply being detained awaiting sentencing. The average period for pretrial detention is 14 months.[43]

The unabated pattern of human rights violations, compounded by the inefficiency of the judicial system, have led frustrated Hondurans to form several independent organizations that aim to pressure the government and military for greater respect of human rights. CODEH is the most active and prominent. With disappearances escalating in 1982, relatives of some of the victims formed COFADEH and were instrumental in bringing the landmark IACHR case to trial in 1987. A women's group called Visitación Padilla has also included the promotion of human rights as one of its main priorities.

The Callejas government made a concerted effort to improve the country's human rights image. This included at least some attempt to investigate abuses of the past, as well as to promote reform initiatives aimed at curbing future abuses. Although human rights advocates have applauded these moves, they have cautioned that even under the rosiest of scenarios it would take years for such reforms to take hold. Meanwhile, irrespective of the motives and intentions of the government, human rights abuses persist.

In mid-1991, both Americas Watch and Amnesty International issued reports indicating that abuses, including political assassinations and torture, continued in Honduras. The U.S. State Department's 1991 report on the human rights situation in Honduras also indicated that abuses and violations, mostly committed by members of the security forces, continued. According to the report, which broke with the State Department's longstanding blind-eye approach to human rights abuses in Honduras, the main problems included "extrajudicial killings, arbitrary and incommunicado detentions, torture of detainees and the impunity of members of the armed forces who commit such violations . . . [During 1991] members of the armed forces were responsible for killing and injuring a number of civilians, apparently for personal motives." [44] The report also criticized recurrent application of the 1982 antiterrorist law against land squatters. In a clear sign of the times reflecting U.S. relations with the Honduran military, armed forces chief Gen. Luis Alonso Discua fumed that he would demand explanations from Washington regarding implications of military culpability cited in the report.

According to Ramon Custodio, during 1991 CODEH recorded a total of nine political assassinations, 72 deaths attributed to security forces personnel, 156 instances of torture, and 718 illegal detentions. "Despite multiple denunciations of continual rights violations," complained Custodio, "the government continues to play deaf and blind." [45] Custodio did credit Callejas with fulfilling his promise to eliminate the practice of political disappearance, noting that there had been no such occurrences over the previous two years. But he remarked that other types of rights abuses continued at intolerably high rates.

In particular, the early 1990s witnessed a crescendo of cases of security forces confronting *campesinos* pressuring for land. Several of these instances resulted in the shooting deaths of the *campesinos*. Reports by Americas Watch and Amnesty International affirmed that the Callejas government lacked the political will necessary to improve the human rights situation in Honduras, despite a lower level of political tensions both domestically and in the region.

Above all, however, there was one case in particular which crystallized national sentiment regarding the brutality of the armed forces and the need to put an end to military impunity.

In July 1991, the corpse of Riccy Mabel Martínez, a 17-year-old student from a Tegucigalpa teacher-training school, was found in a ravine on the outskirts of the capital. Martínez's mutilated and dismembered body was discovered two days after family members had reported her disappearance. Her captors had repeatedly raped and tortured her. According to eyewitnesses, Martínez was last seen alive on the grounds of the First Communications Battalion, located on the outskirts of Tegucigalpa, where she had been summoned for an appointment with base commander Col. Angel Castillo. Castillo had promised to assist Martínez in securing the release of her boyfriend, who had been picked up by the army one month earlier in a forced recruitment drive.

Over the ensuing two years, the military used an array of tactics—ranging from threats and intimidation to legal maneuvering and tampering with evidence—in its attempt first to cover up the crime, then to avoid having the case prosecuted in the civilian courts, and finally to have the case thrown out of court altogether. Initially, Castillo denied any connection whatsoever to the incident, while a second officer, Sgt. Santos Ilovares, openly confessed to the crime. But Ilovares later retracted his confession, claiming it had been made under pressure from his superiors.

When the civilian courts finally issued arrest warrants against Castillo and Ilovares, the military-controlled police Fuerza de Seguridad Publica (FUSEP) refused to act. FUSEP argued that the arrest warrants were invalid, since the military courts have exclusive jurisdiction in all cases against active-duty military personnel.

The army's tenacious resistance despite overwhelming evidence, plus the particularly heinous nature of the crime, helped convert the Martínez rape-murder into a test case to end impunity and to bring about military subordination to civilian authority. For many months, an unusual coalition—which included unions and popular organizations, the U.S. embassy, human rights defense groups, and some sectors within the civilian government—maintained constant pressure to resolve the case. The military eventually caved in and accepted that Castillo and Ilovares would have to stand trial. The two were unceremoniously cashiered from the armed forces to avoid a precedent-setting trial of active-duty military personnel in civilian courts.

Finally, in July 1993, judge María Mendoza brought the case to a close, sentencing Castillo to 16 and one-half years in prison on charges of rape and homicide, Ilovares to a ten-and-one-half-year term for homicide.

The prosecuting attorney in the case, Linda Rivera, as well as the victim's family members, applauded judge Mendoza's courage in upholding the verdicts despite a series of obstructionist moves by the military during the trial. CODEH President Ramon Custodio welcomed the verdicts as a crucial first step in moving toward civilian control over the military. Custodio, who played an instrumental role in pushing prosecution of the case forward, urged the government to carry out reforms to provide the Honduran judiciary with an independent office for investigations, and to enact new legal mechanisms to enforce all decisions made by the civilian courts against military personnel.

PART 2

Military

Security Forces

Following decades of intermittent direct rule by the armed forces, the army formally returned to its barracks in 1981. The deal to allow civilians to run the government turned out to be a good one for the armed forces. Behind the veneer of elected governments, and despite the fact that the country was neither at war nor facing an internal insurgency, the 1980s witnessed an unprecedented build-up of the Honduran armed forces. Between 1978 and 1984 U.S. military aid jumped more than twenty-fold while the armed forces doubled in size.[1] Equally important as this quantitative expansion, during the 1980s the military consolidated its grip on the key levers of national policy formulation and decisionmaking.[2] As one observer put it, "The military has all the power and the civilians have all the problems." [3]

But by the mid-1990s, even the well-entrenched Honduran military establishment was finding it hard to remain sheltered from the winds of change sweeping the region. As the Central American conflagration of the 1980s receded further into the background, the military's central role in Honduran society looked more and more anachronistic. Likewise, civilian politicians interested in pursuing political reforms and democratization within the Honduran state increasingly saw the longstanding tradition of military autonomy as a hindrance to their plans.

History and Structure of the Military

In Honduras, as in much of Latin America, today's military institutions trace their roots to paramilitary groups that traditionally fulfilled two essential functions. First, groups of armed men were formed and then supported by political parties, sectors of the oligarchy, and in the case of Honduras, the U.S. banana companies, with the objective of assuring the installation of favored individuals in the presidency. Second, these same groups served effectively as a police force to squelch worker and *campesino* unrest, usually on the basis of personal relations between a local barracks commander and the plantation or factory owner.

The first major efforts to transform what had started out as armed groups supporting one or another elite faction into a unified, standing military force responding to national objectives took place during the dictatorship of Gen. Tiburcio Carías (1932-48). In 1946, the Carías regime created the country's first separate armed force charged specifically with police functions—a body that eventually evolved into the Public Security Force (FUSEP). Efforts at modernization and professionalization of the emerging Honduran military, including establishment of the nation's first military academy in 1952, were further consolidated during the National Party government of Juan Manuel Gálvez (1949-54).

The process of modernizing the Honduran military was intensified after 1954 when the United States concluded a Bilateral Military Assistance Treaty and sent Army and Air Force missions to train and equip their Honduran counterparts. In the most immediate sense, the treaty was part of U.S. efforts aimed at securing Honduran assistance in the campaign to overthrow the Arbenz government in neighboring Guatemala. But in the larger picture, the treaty was but one element of a project that sought to complete the transformation of what had been a gendarme for U.S. fruit companies and the Honduran oligarchy into an autonomous, professional institution that would serve U.S. designs. On-site training and scholarships to U.S. military schools along with modest financial support characterized this relationship prior to the military expansion of the 1980s (see U.S. Military Aid).

Structurally, the armed forces are divided into four major branches: the army, the air force, the naval force, and FUSEP. All four branches are controlled by the military's Superior Council of the Armed Forces (COSUFFAA). Although the bulk of police and internal security functions reside with FUSEP and the police forces it controls, the army is also used extensively for these purposes, especially in the countryside. In any case, unlike in many countries where the police and army are institutionally separate forces, in Honduras they are merely different appendages of the same body. This means that the Honduran military has an absolute monopoly on the "legitimate" use of armed force in the country. Estimates of the total number of full-time members of the combined armed forces range from 23,700 to 30,000.[4]

The army expanded from a few thousand troops in the 1970s to an estimated 15,000 by 1989.[5] With the addition of two new brigades in 1989, one artillery and one infantry, the army now has five such units stationed around the country. Although much of Honduras is rugged, mountainous territory, the army's arsenal includes some 90 tanks.[6]

Led by a squadron of 37 combat jets out of a total fleet of 120 aircraft, the Honduran air force is considered the most powerful in Central America.[7] Washington's repeated stalling on delivery of a promised dozen F-5 supersonic jet fighters—the last being delivered in January 1990—became a longstanding point of friction between the two countries. With a smaller and less combat-hardened army than either Guatemala, El Salvador, or Nicaragua, the Honduran military regards superiority in air power as indispensable. In contrast to other Central American countries' use of air power merely to support ground-based counterinsurgency efforts, the Honduran air force is equipped and trained for offensive operations against installations in other countries.

The naval force, essentially a coast guard, is unimposing and comprises only a handful of small patrol boats. It is, however, the focus of increased attention under the aegis of the war on drugs as a key interdiction force along the country's extensive maritime coasts.

FUSEP is controlled by army officers and is subordinated to the Ministry of Defense, although it has its own general staff and a separate organizational structure. In addition to its regular police units, FUSEP controls the treasury police, the traffic police, and a counterinsurgency unit known as the Cobras. The Honduran equivalent of the FBI, the National Investigations Division (DNI), formed in 1976, was also formally under the control of FUSEP until 1993. In total, some 4,500 members of various police forces are managed by FUSEP.[8]

The intelligence section of the armed forces, known as the G-2 and functioning under the command of the Joint Chiefs of Staff, is primarily responsible for keeping tabs on political opponents and military personnel. This secret police unit in turn created and operates Battalion 3/16—the official death squad—and carries out propaganda campaigns against domestic opposition groups, critics, and dissenters. Although Battalion 3/16 is directed by intelligence officers, it recruits its operatives from numerous forces such as FUSEP, the DNI, and the immigration service. These operatives remain at their jobs as a cover to restrict knowledge of the unit's existence even within the military.

Faced with an ever-expanding crime rate during the early 1990s, many groups called on the military to scale down the size of the standing army in order to transfer personnel and budget outlays to FUSEP's police forces. Others, anxious to break the military's monopoly on the use of force, argued that FUSEP should be subordinated to the judiciary, not the armed forces. Neither proposal received much backing from the high command.

The armed forces also control several additional institutions adjunct to the military's major branches. Most important among these are the dozens of military academies and schools scattered around the country for the training of both recruits and officers. The Logistical Support Center, responsible for the storage and transportation of materials and equipment, constituted a key liaison for arms deliveries to the contras during the 1980s. The active-duty armed forces are also supplemented by stand-by and general reserve groups. The military has its own internal judicial system and, by way of a clause in the Constitution, has traditionally claimed jurisdiction over all "military matters," including crimes committed by active duty personnel against civilians.

In all branches of the military, officers tend to come from the middle classes and achieve their commissions through academies rather than by rising through the ranks. As a result, rivalries and divisions within the armed forces tend to follow lines of shared "promotions" or graduating classes more than political or ideological factors. Outside the officer corps, voluntary enlistment is rare and the military relies on crude methods of forced recruitment to press poor youths into uniform. During the early 1990s, following the drop in military activity in neighboring countries, Hondurans increasingly demanded elimination of the system of forced recruitment as an unnecessary burden. Coffee growers in the southern part of the country complained bitterly that the army's forced recruitment drives during the harvest season were a major factor behind seasonal labor shortages. Yet the armed forces hierarchy was unreceptive to such complaints. The prevailing attitude was summed up by then armed forces chief Gen. Arnulfo Cantarero: "To those who want to do away with the armed forces, I say democracy is not maintained with words or with violins, but with arms." [9] In 1993, elimination of forced recruitment was one of the main campaign promises of then-candidate Carlos Roberto Reina.

For those who enter as officers, the military is an important mechanism for social climbing. The privileges that officer status provides, along with opportunities for graft and corruption, often result in quick and dramatic fortunes. Numerous Honduran officers have acquired property or a stake in agroexport industries either through illicit appropriation of state lands or as gifts received from grateful landowners. [10] In part because being an officer in Honduras provides such attractive economic and social opportunities, the military has become top heavy, with over 300 officers above the rank of major in a force of fewer than 30 battalions.

During the 1980s, the military's direct participation in contra supply transactions and the alleged involvement in drug trafficking among some high-ranking military officers richly complemented other less-criminal avenues for moneymaking.[11] However, both of these golden pipelines eventually dried up, the former with the end of the contra war and the latter as a result of a U.S. crackdown on drug trafficking.

Although much of the military build-up of the 1980s was bankrolled by the U.S. military-assistance program (see U.S. Military Aid), defense spending consistently devoured between 20 and 30 percent of the national budget.[12] During the early 1990s, intense pressures were brought to bear on the military establishment to reduce spending. Cuts in U.S. aid levels, the prevailing atmosphere of fiscal austerity, popular pressures for demilitarization, and even direct pressure from the World Bank and the U.S. embassy constituted a powerful incentive to at least begin curbing the military appetite. Nonetheless, the high command tenaciously resisted any allocation reduction. In fact, thanks to massive lobbying by the armed forces, the 1993 budget included a small increase in military spending.

Yet even for the Honduran generals, the writing on the wall was clear. One of the strategies they pursued to assure the long-term predominance of the military establishment, and to provide a buffer from future political and economic changes, was to solidify the armed forces' roles as major economic players in their own rights. For years, the armed forces have controlled profit-making state enterprises, such as the telecommunications company (HONDUTEL) and the merchant marine. But most of the military's business holdings are owned and administered by the Military Social Security Institute (Instituto de Previsión Militar, IPM). After the IPM's major acquisitions push in the early 1990s, analysts estimated that the IPM climbed to rank among the country's top five economic investment groups. Although the IPM is not required to make public its earnings, observers say annual profits are in excess of $40 million.[13] Enterprises in which the IPM holds a controlling stake include a cement plant, a bank, investment, credit card, and insurance companies, real estate, a radio station, an advertising agency, and a funeral parlor. They also have investments in the cereal, clothing, and footwear industries.

The largest public scandal over the military's business activities took place in mid-1991 when the IPM submitted the winning bid in privatization of the state-run cement plant (INCEHSA). The private sector was outraged, arguing that selling a government industry to the military was hardly "privatization" and even trying to have the deal annulled on grounds that government revenues, in the form of salaries for military personnel, were being used to purchase INCE-HSA. Despite the protests, the deal was allowed to stand.

Faced with constant complaints like these about "unfair competition" from the IPM, military leaders have forcefully insisted that the IPM enjoys the same rights and obligations regarding the management of its pension fund portfolio as any other employee contribution-based retirement fund. In the words of armed forces inspector general Gen. Finlander Armijo, "Honduras benefits from new investments, regardless of whether they come from civilians or the military. The free market is open to all, with the goal of contributing to the development of the nation. Development cannot be achieved with weapons alone." [14]

National-Security Doctrine and Militarization

In Honduras, the process of militarization—defined not as the quantitative build-up of the armed forces and its weaponry but rather as the encroachment of military practices and control on civil daily life—stretches back many years. [15] The Constitution of 1957 eliminated civilian authority over the military, transferring ultimate control of the institution to the chief of the armed forces, who was given the right to disobey presidential orders that he considered unconstitutional. The Constitution also afforded the armed forces an active role in politics, assigning them the specific function of ultimate guardians of the constitutional order. This meant that the armed forces could step in any time they felt the Constitution was being violated. The essential elements of military autonomy from civilian authority were maintained in the 1982 Constitution.

Such formal authority provided a legal basis for the political independence and autonomous institutional development of the military and set the stage for its subsequent incursions into all areas of national affairs. This process has been facilitated by the longstanding atomization and weakness of the Honduran political parties, state, and oligarchy, and by the tradition among social and political groups of turning to the military for support. In much of the countryside, local military commanders wield more influence than civilian authorities. In many remote areas the army is the only representative of the central government. At the national level the military has long played the role of ultimate arbiter of disputes between rival political, social, and economic forces.

Shaken by its poor performance in the brief war with El Salvador in 1969, the military embarked upon a project of expansion including better training and more sophisticated weaponry, and broadened its mandate to include defense against foreign threats to national sovereignty. Revolutionary upsurges in Central America in the late 1970s, coupled with the staging-ground role chosen for Honduras by the Carter administration, thrust the militarization process into high gear.

The chief Honduran architect of this process was Gen. Gustavo Alvarez, whose tenure at the head of the armed forces officially lasted from January 1982 to March 1984. Alvarez was guided by the principles of the national-security doctrine. His exposure to these principles came during extensive training in Argentina, and through the Argentinian military advisors whom he invited to work with Honduran officers. From his post as commander in chief of the armed forces, Alvarez initiated a process of militarization that would continue unabated throughout the decade, introducing profound changes in Honduran society and politics at the same time. In essence, the Honduran conception of a national-security doctrine entailed the subordination of traditional notions of geographical and territorial enemies and borders to more overriding ideological criteria. As such, the armed forces' mandate to provide territorial defense against enemy armies, particularly the Salvadoran, was to be subordinated to a new project of ideological defense against "subversion and communism."

Internally this translated into a "preventive" war against the nascent Honduran revolutionary left, popular organizations in general, and—in the extreme—anyone considered "potentially subversive" by the security forces. In the international realm it meant collaborating with the United States in its contra war against Nicaragua and even with the traditionally adversarial Salvadoran armed forces against the FMLN.

Concretely, the military defined its defense posture for the 1980s on the basis of three distinct strategies:

– Internal preventive warfare against "subversion." This required the geographical dispersion of troops throughout the national territory, ample training in counterinsurgency techniques, a greater role in intelligence gathering and processing, and joint participation in both civic-action programs and military maneuvers with U.S. forces.

– Containment of revolutionary forces in Central America. This implied collaboration with the counterinsurgency efforts of the Salvadoran and Guatemalan military and with U.S. efforts to overthrow the Sandinista government chiefly through rear-guard support for the contras as well as the construction of military installations capable of handling a large-scale deployment of U.S. forces.

– Conventional territorial defense. While the unresolved border dispute with El Salvador took a back seat to other priorities, it by no means disappeared, and the armed forces continued to foster specific elements of the military build-up with a view toward the possibility of fighting a conventional war. A brief flare-up of border tensions in early 1992 served as a reminder of the depth of animosity between the Honduran and Salvadoran militaries.

Defense doctrines change slowly; despite the transformed regional environment of the 1990s, elements of all three of the above planks remain intact, albeit at reduced levels of importance. For the most part, the lessened need to expend energies confronting domestic and neighboring leftists has been replaced by a more prominent military role in anti-narcotics-trafficking efforts.

Some of the infrastructure necessary for waging Gen. Alvarez' proclaimed "war to the death against internal subversion and communism in Central America" was already in place in the early 1980s. Nonetheless, several institutions were devised during this period to streamline the militarization process and to allow it to be carried out beneath the veneer of an elected civilian government. One of the most important was Battalion 3/16, a clandestine paramilitary structure conceived by Alvarez in 1980 while he was head of FUSEP. This Honduran "death squad" has been singled out by defectors from among its ranks and by Honduran human rights organizations as the key unit responsible for the disappearance and extrajudicial execution of hundreds of Honduran civilians (see Human Rights). An elite counterinsurgency battalion, the Cobras, was originated as part of FUSEP in 1979. The Cobras were widely deployed in the cities to repress activities by labor unions and popular organizations, and in the countryside against guerrilla groups. The 1982 Constitution mandated creation of a National Defense and Security Council (CSN). The CSN is composed of ten of the nation's top leaders, six from the military and four civilians. The council functions without any legal or regulatory framework and its deliberations are secret. It has been referred to as a "suprapower" responsible for delineating the broad contours of national policy, particularly in the strategic areas of security and foreign relations.[16]

Gen. Alvarez was the key architect of the national-security doctrine in Honduras.[17] From his position as colonel at the head of FUSEP and the DNI in 1980, Alvarez—a staunch anticommunist and close ally of the United States—experienced a swift and dramatic rise to the heights of power in Honduras. In early 1982 Alvarez was named head of the Superior Council of the Armed Forces (COSUFFAA), the group of top officers responsible for defining military policy. In April of that year, newly elected Liberal Party President Suazo Córdova, a close personal friend of Alvarez, violated longstanding military norms and procedures to ensure the promotion of Alvarez to Brigadier General.

Alvarez quickly consolidated his hold on power by dispatching his two main rivals, Col. Leonidas Torres Arias and Col. Hubbert Bodden, to diplomatic exile in Argentina and Taiwan. Finally, in November 1982, Alvarez forced through a series of constitutional amendments transferring the role of commander in chief to himself, as head of the armed forces, while the president, who had formerly enjoyed that position, was instead given the ceremonial title of supreme chief. The country has long had a Cabinet-level post of minister of defense, but unlike elsewhere in Latin America, in Honduras it is a bureaucratic position with little authority and in any case is always awarded to a military officer, not a civilian.

The general's close relations with Suazo, and with newly arrived U.S. Ambassador John Negroponte, spun the web of a powerful triumvirate that would transform the face of the country in the short space of two years. In 1982 Honduras became the second-largest recipient of U.S. military aid in Latin America. The $31.3 million it received in that year nearly surpassed the total in military aid for the entire 1946-80 period ($32.6 million). In May 1982 Alvarez negotiated an amendment to the 1954 bilateral military agreement between Honduras and the United States, paving the way for an unprecedented string of joint military maneuvers and the rapid upgrading of Honduras' military infrastructure. New military construction during this period included dozens of airstrips, communications and radar facilities, tank traps, and port facilities. This flurry of activity, in part, allowed the Honduran armed forces to shift its focus from collaborative efforts with the Salvadoran army against the FMLN to all-out assistance of the Nicaraguan counterrevolution in its war against the Sandinistas.[18] Domestically, Alvarez presided over a rapid escalation in human rights violations as the national-security apparatus set out to decapitate incipient revolutionary organizations and stifle popular discontent stemming from an economic crisis, growing militarization, and the involvement of the country in regional conflicts (see Human Rights).

Alvarez eventually became the victim of his own excesses and was ousted in a March 1984 coup by rival military officers led by air force commander Gen. Walter López. Fueled by nationalist sentiments, discontent in the officers corps had long been brewing over issues such as Alvarez' reckless plans to invade Nicaragua, his all-too-cozy relations with the traditionally adversarial Salvadoran military symbolized by the training of Salvadoran troops on Honduran soil, the negative repercussions on the armed forces' image caused by his massive and open support for the contras, and the increasingly destabilizing nature of the repression against opposition forces. In early March, when he attempted to reduce COSUFFAA from 52 to 21 members, restrict its mandate, and virtually replace it with an eight-member Commanders Junta loyal to himself, the coup plotters sprang into action.

The new military leaders did manage to institute some changes. COSUFFAA norms and procedures, widely ignored by Alvarez, were reinstated. Coup leaders initiated a prolonged process of negotiations with Washington aimed at modifying the 1954 agreement and assuring both a greater say for Honduras in bilateral affairs and higher aid levels. In June 1985 the controversial Regional Military Training Center (CREM), installed by the United States under Alvarez to train Salvadoran troops, was officially closed down. The relationship with the contras, however, continued largely unaltered.

Some changes were also made in an effort to improve the military's human rights image. But none of the repressive structures erected under Alvarez were dismantled. Repression, which had grown increasingly generalized toward the end of Alvarez' tenure, once again became highly selective. The number of disappearances decreased dramatically, but politically motivated assassinations proliferated. Likewise, the U.S. maneuvers and military build-up continued apace.

Inside the military, the net effect of the 1984 coup was the diffusion of authority that had been concentrated in Alvarez' hands across a broader spectrum of officers, ranging from younger, more nationalist-minded ones to the more traditional rightwing sectors. For a brief period, the former began to exert pressures for substantive changes in the military's behavior. Some of these changes in particular, and the more independent course being charted for the Honduran military in general, were not looked upon favorably by Washington, however. Hope for military reform withered in February 1986 when armed forces chief Gen. Walter López, the de facto leader of this group, was forced to resign, replaced by the hard-line former navy commander Gen. Humberto Regalado.

Under Regalado the military returned to more amicable and subservient relations with the United States and generally deepened its activities aimed at squelching internal unrest and popular protest, with a consequent rise in human rights abuses.[19] Some of the repressive structures that had lain dormant since the departure of Alvarez were reactivated, and some new ones created. The military placed a new emphasis on civic-action programs chiefly aimed at creating an image of benevolence for the armed forces among the population. And the army maneuvered, mostly through the media, to portray political opponents and dissidents as common criminals and delinquents.

Amidst nagging accusations of corruption, Regalado was forced to step down as military leader in late 1989. Regalado, who belongs to the group of officers known as the Fifth Promotion, was replaced by his hand-picked successor, Col. Arnulfo Cantarero López from the Sixth Promotion. Cantarero's nomination was largely seen as a compromise aimed at avoiding further divisions or infighting within the armed forces high command.[20]

Cantarero lasted about one year in his post, resigning in December 1990 in favor of Gen. Luis Alonso Discua. President Rafael Callejas, whose ruling National Party is headed by Gen. Discua's brother Celin Discua, chose the occasion of Discua's inauguration ceremony to reiterate that as long as violence persisted in Central America, Honduras would not implement reductions in military personnel or hardware.

Nonetheless, it befell Gen. Discua to preside over the armed forces during a period when pressures for changing the military establishment's role in society reached unprecedented levels. Those pressures had been building for years, the product of a complex web of factors. As the general situation faced by the population deteriorated, it became increasingly common for attention to be focused on military abuses and excesses. According to Manuel Gamero, editor of *El Tiempo* daily newspaper: "The military is viewed here as the single most important force in the country's life. When the economy and the political system don't deliver, the military is held responsible." [21]

Discua had only been in office for six months when the case of Riccy Mabel Martínez rocked the nation and the armed forces (see Human Rights). From the outrage sparked by the brutal rape and murder, to the sentencing of two military officers charged with the crime two years later, the Martínez case came to symoblize the beginning of the end of the longstanding tradition of military impunity in Honduras. In the words of Honduran political analyst Victor Meza, the Martínez case was crucial in that it "permitted antimilitarism to become public. The army is no longer a taboo subject." [22]

Less than one month after the Martínez murder, Innovation and Unity Party (PINU) deputy Carlos Sosa introduced a bill in Congress aimed at instituting a series of reforms designed ultimately to subordinate the armed forces to the civilian government. Sosa's bill, a similar proposal discussed within the armed forces leadership, and reportedly yet another version sponsored by the U.S. embassy, all aspired to reducing the powers attached to the post of armed forces chief, transferring most of that authority to a civilian-appointed defense minister and designating the Honduran president as military commander in chief. Under these bills, COSUFFAA, the deliberative body overseeing the military in conjunction with the armed forces chief, would be reduced in size and importance. Another aspect of the proposed reforms would eliminate the current practice of budget secrecy within the armed forces, forcing the military to open its books to outside scrutiny and subjecting it to the same fiscal regulations as other elements of the Honduran state. In the words of Carlos Sosa: "Now, there is no excuse for allowing the military a hegemonic role in politics. [The proposed reforms] are basic . . . they exist in every democratic country in the world." [23]

Opposition to the reforms by the military was strong enough to virtually stall the process until early 1993 when a series of events touched off by the defection of DNI agent Josue Zúñiga combined to convince military and civilian leaders alike that the time was ripe for change. Under the protection of Human Rights Ombudsman Leo Valladares, Zúñiga described in detail the corruption, torture of detainees, and arbitrary executions which he had witnessed while working for the DNI. Faced with the growing wave of anti-military sentiment touched off by Zúñiga's declarations, the Callejas administration appointed a blue-ribbon commission, headed by Tegucigalpa Archbishop Msgr. Oscar Andres Rodriguez, to investigate the DNI and propose changes.

On April 12, 1993, the commission released its report, recommending sweeping changes in the relationship between civilian and military power in Honduras. Eight months later, the National Congress approved the legal reforms necessary for transferring authority over a series of police and intelligence functions from the armed forces to the civilian government.

First, the new laws outlined creation of a new Public Prosecutor's Office (Ministerio Público), to be headed by a civilian attorney general. Second, the laws called for dissolution of the DNI and its replacement with a new Criminal Investigations Department (DIC) operating under the direction of the civilian attorney general. In addition, all leadership posts in the Public Prosecutor's Office, including the director of the DIC, could only go to civilians. Against the tide of broad support for the legislation, the military still resisted by attempting to defend the record of the DNI and by launching a legal challenge to the ban on military personnel in the DIC leadership.

Before fully recovering from the controversy over the DNI, the armed forces soon had to come to grips with a much more far-reaching agenda for demilitarization proposed by President Carlos Roberto Reina. Military leaders had watched apprehensively during the presidential campaign as candidate Reina promised to slash defense spending—then estimated to account for about 30 percent of the national budget—and to oversee a substantial reduction in armed forces personnel.

The list of demilitarization reforms drawn up by Reina and his advisors was lengthy and ambitious. It included such items as:

– Elimination of the practice of budget secrecy by forcing the military to open its books to outside scrutiny. The armed forces would have to abide by the same fiscal regulations as other branches of the Honduran state.

– An overhaul of national defense doctrine. This would include a change in the military training regime, deemphasizing the concentration on counterinsurgency techniques in order to focus on issues such as combatting common crime, environmental protection, and defense of human rights.

– Replacement of the powerful post of armed forces chief with a civilian-appointed minister of defense.

– Transfer of control over FUSEP from the military to civilian authorities.

The Reina administration was under no illusions regarding the difficult road that lay ahead in terms of implementing military reform. After all, the military had carefully constructed—and jealously guarded—its institutional autonomy over the course of the previous 35 years. Nonetheless, Reina counted on several factors which placed him in a more advantageous position than his precedessors. First, at the national level, by 1994, there was a broad-based consensus among diverse business, political, labor, and popular organizations on the need to subordinate the military to civilian rule. By staunchly defending the status quo, the armed forces had become increasingly isolated.

Second, Reina was able to count on a powerful ally in his efforts: Ret. Gen. Walter López, one of Reina's three vice presidents. As a former armed forces chief, López was sure to add substantial weight to any civilian negotiating commission that would approach the military, a role that he was apparently looking forward to, having declared his intention early on in the administration to act as an intermediary between civilians in Reina's cabinet and senior officers in the military.

Paramilitary Groups

Most analysts agree that Honduras does not have paramilitary groups in the sense of organizations truly independent from the armed forces. The bulk of evidence relating to human rights violations reveals that units belonging to or closely linked to the military carry out the political abductions and murders, and systematically use torture on common as well as political prisoners.

The military, for its part, usually denies formal involvement with any of these groups. One exception is Battalion 3/16, the group most often referred to as a Honduran death squad[24] (see Security Forces). Originated under the jurisdiction of the intelligence branch of the

Honduran military during the tenure of Gen. Alvarez, Battalion 3/16 has been indicted by human rights monitoring organizations as the main group responsible for the wave of disappearances and extrajudicial killings occurring in the early 1980s (see Human Rights).

Guerrilla Groups

Despite conditions similar to those that gave rise to the revolutionary left in neighboring El Salvador and Guatemala, Honduras has never confronted a sustained challenge from a guerrilla insurgency. In part, this is due to the success of the relatively sophisticated and intensive repression carried out in the early 1980s, which decapitated leftwing organizations through assassinations, disappearances, and exile. Others point to the left's inability to present a coherent alternative capable of capitalizing on widespread popular discontent. Perhaps the most important factor mitigating against the possibility of a large-scale armed struggle has been the successful pursuit by the Honduran ruling class of a strategy of cooption, negotiation, and the use of limited reforms aimed at neutralizing the influence of progressive individuals and organizations.

Most of the political left's leaders who managed to escape the repression of the early 1980s fled into exile. In June 1983 five guerrilla groups announced the formation of an alliance called the National Unitary Direction of the Honduran Revolutionary Movement (DNUMRH). The primary DNU groups were:[25] the Cinchoneros Popular Liberation Movement (MPL); the Morazanista Front for the Liberation of Honduras (FMLNH); the Revolutionary Party of Central American Workers (PRTC-H); and the Lorenzo Zelaya Popular Revolutionary Forces (FPR). In late 1991, the FPR announced that it was abandoning armed struggle and would begin working within the political system, thus becoming the last of the DNU-affiliated guerrilla groups to take advantage of the government's amnesty program. By that time, nearly all of the country's exiled political leaders had returned to Honduras to engage in political work (see Political Parties and Elections).

Economy

State of the Economy

In a region already known for its poverty and underdevelopment, Honduras has traditionally been the poorest and least developed. The country's agrarian-based economy is highly dependent on export earnings from a few crops—in 1985, primary commodities accounted for a whopping 84 percent of all Honduran export earnings—and on the handful of foreign companies that dominate productive activity. Meanwhile, most Hondurans continue to survive as subsistence farmers living largely outside the market economy.

In 1980, the wealthiest 20 percent of the Honduran population received nearly 60 percent of national income, while the poorest 20 percent subsisted on just 4 percent.[1] The economic crisis of the 1980s and structural adjustment measures in the 1990s further exacerbated these income inequalities.

The last 30 years have witnessed many changes in the Honduran economy. Successive governments over this period have introduced reforms and policies aimed at modernizing the economy and guiding it onto the path to more sustainable growth. More recently, the U.S. government and international lending institutions have fostered an export-led, private-sector development strategy, heavily dependent on foreign investment, in the hope of transforming Honduras into a showcase for free-market capitalism. However, the growth model Honduras has embraced has not generated significant internal development.

Since 1990, structural adjustment policies and privatization have intensified foreign domination of the economy and aggravated existing inequalities among the population. In fact, between 1990 and 1992, the portion of the population living below the poverty line increased while exporters, a handful of industrialists, and foreign transnational corporations reaped windfall profits.[2]

Underdevelopment and Modernization

Unlike Guatemala and El Salvador, Honduras never developed a powerful agroexport-based oligarchy with its attendant extremes of wealth and poverty. Lacking rich volcanic soils and a large indigenous population to exploit as cheap labor, the country remained a backwater throughout the first half of the 1900s. Ironically, this historical lack of economic dynamism helped Honduras avoid the even more stark inequalities, polarization, and social upheavals that have characterized its neighbors.

In the absence of a strong national economy and a cohesive economic elite, Honduras was little more than a "banana republic" for most of this century. The country's politics and economy were dominated by foreign fruit and mining companies. Outside the banana enclaves of the North Coast and scattered mining centers, the economy consisted mostly of a large peasantry engaged in subsistence agriculture, a small group of ranchers, and a tiny urban commercial sector.

It was not until the 1950s and 1960s that the country's larger landowners and its nascent business class began to coalesce in an attempt to chart a new course of economic growth for Honduras. First to organize were the country's conservative cattle ranchers and large-estate owners, who in the 1950s banded together to form the Federation of Honduran Farmers and Ranchers (FENAGH). A decade later the country's emerging business class formed its own association called the Honduran Council of Private Enterprise (COHEP).

The initial goal of economic modernization was to expand commercial agricultural production beyond bananas by introducing other export crops such as coffee, cotton, and sugar. Later, in the 1960s and 1970s, Honduras began to pursue an import-substitution industrialization strategy, while becoming a partner in the Central American Common Market (CACM).

These initial modernization strategies brought mixed results. Some agricultural products, particularly coffee and beef exports, did take hold and provided the basis for limited national development. Nonetheless, to this day bananas continue to generate the bulk of export earnings. Honduran industry did develop, but it proved unable to compete with its neighbors. The 1969 border war with El Salvador and the subsequent deterioration of the CACM further undermined plans for industrial growth.

The continued domination of foreign investors also limited the benefits of economic modernization. Transnational banana corporations, for example, led much of the diversification into new agricultural products like citrus and African palm. These same banana giants initiated food processing and other industries.

Part of the modernization strategy in the 1960s and 1970s was contingent upon a new, more aggressive role for the state. Largely at the behest of international lending institutions and the U.S. Agency for International Development (AID), a host of new state and parastatal agencies assumed an active role in agriculture, banking, infrastructure construction, and labor. This elaborate state-sponsored network, however, proved to be more of a breeding ground for inefficiency and corruption than a promoter of development. Public expenditures mushroomed as private-sector elites took advantage of generous subsidies and loans. But rather than using the new money for investment and development projects, they applied it to ongoing operations, shifting their own capital into more profitable ventures or foreign bank accounts.[3]

Crisis of the Eighties

Between 1960 and 1980 Honduras experienced average annual growth rates exceeding 5 percent. But capital flight, reduced investment levels, declining terms of trade, a slump in the international economy, growing foreign debt, and unchecked budget deficits contributed to a major recession in the early 1980s. These factors, combined with an inefficient industrial sector and an agricultural sector still dependent on banana exports, crushed hopes for economic modernization. The revolutionary upsurge in neighboring countries beginning in the late 1970s, and the role played by Honduras with regard to conflicts in the region in the following years, further aggravated the economic crisis as investor confidence plummeted.

The short-term "solution" was a massive influx of foreign aid coupled with limited austerity measures. For the long term, Honduras adopted the U.S.-designed process of orienting its economy toward a greater reliance on internationally competitive nontraditional exports. An "export boom" was to be generated by new investments in enterprises in both agriculture and industry, and by the privatization of many state-run companies.

During the 1980s, the results of these diversification and privatization plans were scant, in part because successive Liberal governments were not aggressive enough in the pursuit of their objectives. During the course of the decade, economic growth rates rarely kept pace with the country's population growth. The contraction in demand for food, services, and consumer goods fostered by the lean times in turn constrained tax revenues. By the end of the decade declining export earnings, rising inflation, and diminishing foreign exchange revenues had pummeled the economy into a serious slump.

The economic ills that plagued the Honduran economy as it entered the 1990s included:

– Shortages of foreign exchange reserves. By the late 1980s the country had barely enough reserves to cover one month's worth of imports, leading to de facto import restrictions, drops in production dependent upon imported materials, and spot shortages of essential goods. The currency shortage was aggravated by a credit freeze and a cutoff of new loans from the IMF and World Bank because of debt arrearages and a failure to fully implement recommended structural adjustment measures.

– Chronic trade deficit. Honduras suffers from a chronic trade deficit, having run a trade surplus (exports over imports) in only three of the last 30 years. Despite measures taken to boost exports, the country's large trade gap narrowed only marginally over the course of the 1980s (Figure 3a).

– Lack of foreign and national investment. Despite the abundance of special privileges and incentives aimed at stimulating new export ventures, the negligible rate of foreign and national investment in the 1980s was not even enough to keep pace with factory closings and the estimated $1.5 billion in capital flight. In fact, the rate of investment as a percentage of Gross Domestic Product (GDP) declined from about 25 percent in 1980 to just over 15 percent in 1990.[4] One survey of the investment climate in 112 countries ranked Honduras number 94.[5]

– Rising foreign debt. Foreign debt, which doubled over the course of the decade, stood at $3.5 billion in 1990 and debt-service payments amounted to an average of over $1.5 million a day. Throughout the 1980s, debt-service payments burdened the economy and by 1990 the ratio of debt service to exports stood at over 50 percent.[6] During the second half of the 1980s, Honduras suspended payments on most of its debt commitments, pleading that it was simply unable to pay. Such defaults precipitated one of the lowest credit ratings in the world.

– Uncontrolled fiscal deficit. Throughout the 1980s factors like debt-service payments, massive public spending, and soaring military expenditures contributed to a growing fiscal deficit. Despite abating somewhat, by decade's end the government's fiscal deficit remained unmanageably large at nearly 10 percent of GDP.

Against this backdrop, blamed largely on the Liberal Party governments of the 1980s, voters gave an overwhelming mandate for change to opposition National Party candidate Rafael Callejas in the 1989 elections. The most pressing short-term problem for the new Callejas government was the critical shortage of foreign exchange reserves. Considering the long term, the only way for the new government to overcome Honduras' liquidity crisis was to negotiate a new agreement with the IMF to free up loans, credits, and assistance from AID and international lending institutions.

Consequently, Callejas implemented a neoliberal-inspired package of structural adjustment measures in March 1990 aimed at paving the way for negotiations on such an agreement. The president's *paquetazo* (economic-reform package) was designed to correct the

Figure 3a
Honduras' Exports and Imports

In millions of U.S. $.

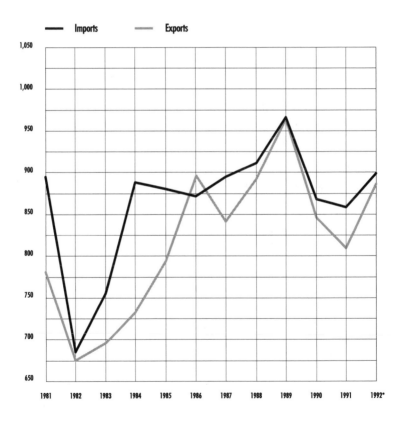

*Preliminary.

SOURCE: *Economic and Social Progress in Latin America, 1993 Report*, Inter-American Development Bank.

macroeconomic distortions that had accumulated during the 1980s, while simultaneously reorienting the economy toward export-based growth centered on the private sector. The most drastic and unpopular step in this economic shuffle was an immediate reduction in the value of the currency by half.

Other aspects of Callejas' economic-stabilization program included tax hikes on sales, leases, imports, exports, and fuel; the elimination of some tax exemptions and privileges for diplomatic missions, nongovernmental organizations (NGOs), the armed forces, cooperatives, and unions; cuts in the government budget; additional export incentives; elimination of some price controls; and the reduction or abolition of protectionist tariffs.

The program met with rapid approval by the IMF and World Bank, and soon resulted in fresh international aid commitments. Over the next two years, government compliance with the program's targets in terms of austerity and fiscal discipline earned praises for Callejas as well as additional loans and aid for the economy from international lending institutions.

To Callejas' credit, some short-term objectives of his program—such as a reduction of the budget deficit, stronger international monetary reserves, and normalization of relations with the international lenders—were indeed met. But the social costs of the program were enormous. The rapid expansion of poverty, a fully expected consequence over the short term, outpaced most forecasts and threatened to undermine the basic stability and relative social peace that Honduras had enjoyed for decades. One government response, a specially financed poverty-alleviation program—the Honduran Social Investment Fund (FHIS)—which provided public-works jobs and food handouts to impoverished nursing mothers, was widely criticized as little more than a palliative.

By the end of Callejas' term in early 1994, even the earlier gains from the structural adjustment program had vanished. Two of the chief objectives—reduction of the fiscal deficit and of the foreign debt burden—had clearly gone unfulfilled.

Below is a summary of trends for major economic indicators during this period.[7]

– Gross domestic product. Average annual growth rates during Callejas' term were significantly lower than during the 1980s (see Figure 3b). The slump was attributed, among other factors, to the high cost of imported inputs resulting from devaluation and to a drop in investments.

– Foreign trade. Following a significant trade surplus in 1989, trade deficits were posted in each of the next three years as the hoped-for "export boom" failed to materialize.

– Balance of payments. Reduced foreign aid levels, combined with the mounting cost of financing the foreign debt, produced a current account deficit during each of the years Callejas was in office.

– Public finances. According to government figures, the structural adjustment program succeeded in slashing the net budget deficit from 12.5 percent of GDP in 1989 to 2.9 percent in 1990. However, over the next three years, the deficit grew once again, reaching almost 10 percent of GDP during 1993.

Figure 3b

Change in Honduras' GDP Growth Rate, 1981-1992

In percent.

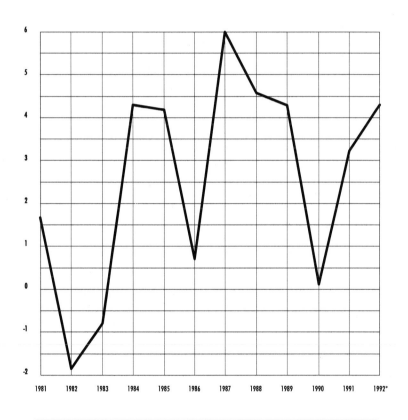

*Preliminary.
SOURCE: *Economic and Social Progress in Latin America, 1991 Report,* Inter-American Development Bank, p. 114, *1993 Report,* p. 115.

– Inflation. Elimination of price controls, the currency devaluation, and other measures led to a 23.3 percent surge in the consumer price index in 1990. The following year, inflation climbed higher still, reaching 33.9 percent, the highest annual rate in more than 40 years. By contrast, inflation never exceeded single digits between 1981 and 1989.

– Investment. 1990 saw public-sector investment slacken by 13 percent and private-sector investment erode by 10 percent. These investment contractions contributed to a drop in both employment levels and output. Devaluation and other measures resulted in windfall profits for exporters, but according to the Honduran Association of Economists, most of this easy money wound up in foreign banks rather than being reinvested in job-creating domestic enterprises.

– Employment and wages. A trend under way since the 1980s intensified as workers continued to be shunted from jobs in the formal sector to informal economic activities. According to the Honduran Association of Economists, open unemployment— defined as those lacking a steady, full-time job— jumped from 70.3 percent in 1989 to 80.8 percent in 1990.[8] Average real wages have shrunk every year since 1981, and purchasing power for wage earners plummeted with the implementation of Callejas' *paquetazo*.[9]

Throughout the 1980s the Honduran government had been under pressure from AID, the IMF, and the World Bank to adopt a structural adjustment program. Yet in Washington, Honduras' strategic importance took precedence over demands for devaluation and austerity measures. Although elements of the proposed structural adjustment program were instituted, Liberal Party governments feared that implementation of the entire program would lead to social upheaval. By 1990, however, the prospect of declining U.S. economic aid levels and the desperate need for injections of World Bank and IMF loans persuaded the National Party government to accede to international and domestic pressures for a full-blown program of structural adjustment.

There was little doubt that a serious economic restructuring was in order. The currency was overvalued, exports had stagnated, local industry was inefficient, the treasury was bare, and state enterprises had been pillaged by government, military, and business figures. Callejas' economic program promised to remedy these and other problems, but several structural weaknesses in the economy were not addressed by the *paquetazo*. In fact, the structural adjustment program tended to tighten the hold of transnational corporations over the economy and to aggravate existing class tensions. Adjustment measures emphasizing exports further discouraged production of food and goods for the local market. The strategy also failed to spur significant new investment and export production, outside of a few enclaves.

A further bone of contention among those critical of the structural adjustment program revolved around the country's foreign-debt burden. Hondurans were being cajoled into making sacrifices in order to pay off a massive debt, part of which had been squandered years earlier by the same people in charge of administering the current program. In late 1990, a bishop from the Honduran Catholic Church accused the Callejas government of employing "thieves," insisting that some of the president's closest advisors were responsible for pocketing over half of the $600 million in foreign loans contracted by the scandal-ridden state development corporation CONADI.[10] Adding salt to the wound, the structural adjustment program itself, at least in the short term, renders Honduras even more dependent on loans and aid. In 1991, for example, "successful" negotiations for $600 million in fresh loan agreements bloated the country's foreign debt by another 20 percent.

Nontraditionals and Privatization

To some extent, the strategies of exporting nontraditional agricultural products and privatizing state businesses, ostensibly designed to "solve" the Honduran economic crisis, serve only to exacerbate existing problems of poverty and inequality. Most of the profits generated by ambitious export strategies adopted since the mid-1980s have either accrued to foreign companies, which continue to dominate the economy, or have enriched the handful of Honduran entrepreneurs willing to take the investment risks.

A case in point is an ambitious program of incentives for nontraditional exports—including such diverse items as melons, cucumbers, cigars, cardamom, jam, and softballs—pursued with vigorous government support since the early 1980s. Several laws passed during this period attempted to stimulate investments in export projects, particularly in nontraditionals. These included exemptions from duties and tariffs on imported goods, tax reductions on exports, and in some cases an exemption for up to ten years on all taxes derived from profits on exports. In an effort to streamline the cumbersome bureaucratic procedures formerly constraining exports, the Ministry of Economy set up a one-stop exports facility at the Investment Promotion Office, centralizing all requirements.

Although these generous incentives did spark some advances, overall results of the export-promotion strategy have been slow in coming and far below early expectations.[11] In the agricultural sphere, the ultimate effect of growth among nontraditional exports has been to aggravate existing inequalities. Considered high-risk due to rapid fluctuations in international market prices, nontraditionals have tended to reinforce the power of the clique of modern agroexport producers, further marginalizing the majority of Honduran *campesinos* from the market economy.

In addition to normal export-promotion measures, bonus incentives have been devised specifically to attract foreign investors. In general, not only are foreign firms granted the same rights and privileges as domestic investors, but Honduras also imposes no formal limits on their profit remittances. Specific export taxes exist for bananas, shrimp, lobster, meat, and coffee. Regarding ownership, foreign investors are granted relatively free rein, although majority Honduran control is required in broadcasting, distributorships, airlines, lumber, wood, and fishing, while one-third local control is obliged in petroleum production. In addition, foreign investors are prohibited from owning property within 40 kilometers of either national borders or the coastline, except in urban areas.

Extensive foreign-investment incentives are especially aimed at promoting expansion of fruit and vegetable exports, petroleum exploration, mining, tourism, fisheries, wood products, metalworking, electronics assembly, and apparel assembly. Under the aegis of the Caribbean Basin Initiative (CBI) and other U.S. government programs, companies producing for export to U.S. markets can access credit and marketing assistance through either the Foundation for Investment and Export Development (FIDE) or the National Council to Promote Exports and Investment (CONAFEXI). The most visible success of this export-promotion strategy has been the emergence of an incipient *maquiladora* sector, composed chiefly of Asian firms located in duty-free parks on the North Coast (see Industry and Finance).

The growing trend toward privatization—spurred by passage of congressional legislation regulating privatization in early 1989 and again in 1992 also favors private investors. By 1990 ten state businesses (worth about $27 million) had been sold to private investors[12] and another 47 companies, including those linked to CONADI and the Forestry Development Corporation of Honduras (COHDEFOR), were up for sale. Observers noted that the majority were likely to wind up in foreign hands as few Honduran entrepreneurs had the capital necessary to buy or operate them, and the handful who did have such funds were unlikely to make risky investments.[13]

Many companies are sold to foreign enterprises at a fraction of their market value in order to cover debts. In 1989, for example, debt-equity swaps financed the takeover of an abandoned paper plant by the Costa Rica-based company Scott Paper, while the Nelsin Group of

Seattle bargained for a foundry and Wellington Hall purchased a furniture factory. Despite longstanding pressure from the private sector, privatization of services including water, electricity, and communications has been stalled.

Honduras Pushes Free Trade Agenda

Another plank in the government's platform for long-term transformation of the Honduran economy was regional integration, a process in which the Callejas administration attempted to play a leading role. At a Central American presidential summit in 1990, the five leaders agreed to reactivate the Central American Common Market (CACM). At a subsequent summit held in December 1991 in Honduras, it was further agreed to unite the CACM with the Caribbean trade bloc, CARICOM.[14]

In February 1992 the first phase of the new regional free-trade bloc took effect among the five Central American countries with the implementation of a duty-free list of 1,600 products, including raw materials and manufactured goods. Over the next several years, tariffs were to be removed on remaining products and nontariff trade barriers eliminated. By 1997 the five nations propose expanding free trade by implementing accords with Mexico, Venezuela, and the United States.

As part of a broader strategy designed to accelerate the pace of regional integration efforts, in early 1992 Honduras signed separate bilateral free-trade accords with neighbors El Salvador and Guatemala. Then in May, the presidents of all three countries signed a trilateral free trade accord, to take effect January 1, 1993, covering 7,000 products. The trilateral accord also authorizes coordination of customs procedures, currency exchange, and monetary and banking policies; integration of stock exchanges; and sharing of port facilities.

Most Honduran businesspeople, accustomed to years of protectionism and aware that many Honduran-made goods are not regionally competitive, do not share the government's enthusiasm for regional trade-liberalization initiatives. In any case, as of the early 1990s only about 3 percent of Honduran exports were destined for other Central American countries and it was widely agreed that achieving a significant increase in this figure was at best a long-term prospect (Figure 3c). COHEP leaders, asserting that the country was ill-prepared for competition with its neighbors, insisted that the only way for Honduras to survive regional integration was by a thorough program of industrial conversion.

Figure 3c

Direction of Trade, 1985 and 1993

In percent.

Foreign Suppliers	1985	1993*
United States	36.1	62.9
Japan	4.5	8.2
Mexico	4.3	3.2
Guatemala	7.2	2.4
Germany	3.4	1.4
Brazil	1.2	1.3
Costa Rica	4.2	1.3
Panama	4.6	1.3
United Kingdom	1.9	1.3
France	2.8	1.1
Venezuela	10.2	.73
Trinidad and Tobago	4.4	.29
Netherlands	2.2	.20
Others	13.2	14.57
Foreign Markets	**1985**	**1993***
United States	55.1	68.2
Germany	5.3	7.2
Japan	6.0	5.7
Belgium/Luxemburg	3.9	2.2
Spain	2.7	1.7
Italy	2.2	1.0
Guatemala	4.3	.75
Netherlands	2.2	.50
Others	16.1	12.7

SOURCE: IMF, *Direction of Trade Statistics Yearbook* (Washington, DC, 1994).
* Estimate

Agriculture

As in most of Central America, the agricultural sector in Honduras is at the heart of the national economy. It is the single most important generator of export earnings and employment, accounting for over one-fourth of the GDP (Figures 3d and 3e). Although over the past 20 years hard times for farmers have induced steady rural-urban migration, the majority of the population still lives in the countryside.[15]

Overall, Honduras enjoys a relatively low population density. But this is deceptive, since less than one-fifth of the country's land is suitable for agriculture (Figure 3f). The bulk of the good land—low-lying valleys and coastal plains—is owned either by large Honduran agro-export farmers or by transnational companies. Food for local consumption is generally produced by peasants with small plots of lower-quality land, usually on marginal, steep, and rocky mountainsides. The agricultural sector is characterized by low yields owing to inefficiencies at all levels. Only one in five farms in Honduras is worked by its owner; the rest are tilled by a variety of farm workers ranging from sharecroppers, to renters, to squatters.[16]

Although the concentration of land and wealth is less extreme than in neighboring Guatemala or El Salvador, both land ownership and rural income are highly skewed in Honduras. Approximately half of the rural population is considered essentially landless, and many of those who do own land inhabit plots too small or with such poor soils that they are unable to meet even subsistence needs. A full 55 percent of the farming population work plots smaller than five acres, each generating a net per capita income of less than $70 a year. At the other extreme, a mere 510 people own farms larger than 1,700 acres with a corresponding annual per capita income of almost $15,000.[17] Some 60 percent of all the country's arable land is either in the hands of the government or of the two main transnationals, United Brands and Castle & Cooke.[18]

Another major factor that has inhibited development in Honduran agriculture is the difficulty in obtaining credit, particularly for basic grain production or for small, family-based farms. About half of all bank loans to farmers are handled through the government's National Agriculture Development Bank (BANDESA) with the remainder channeled through 15 private banks. In 1991, liberalization measures in the agricultural sector mandated hiking official interest rates on farm loans from 11 percent to 23 percent. Over half of all loans provided to agricultural producers, however, come through informal credit sources. In many cases, such loans involve unscrupulous middlemen who provide cash, farm tools, and inputs in exchange for exorbitant commitments on future harvests.

Figure 3d
Honduras' GDP by Economic Sector

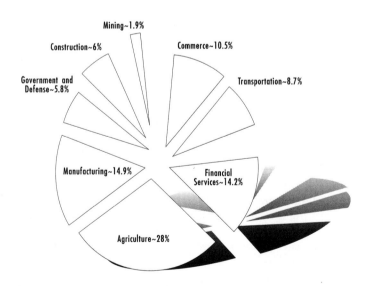

SOURCE: The Economist Intelligence Unit, *Country Report,* 4th Quarter, 1993.

Agroexport Production

Honduran agricultural exports remained fairly steady throughout the 1980s and early 1990s. Bananas provided between one-third and one half of the country's total export revenues, followed by coffee, which accounted for approximately one-fifth. The next three most important items—seafood, zinc, and beef—each contributed less than 10 percent of export earnings. Honduras continues to be one of the largest exporters of bananas in the world—with "yellow gold" accounting for a whopping 42.7 percent of the country's earnings from exported goods in 1991. In 1989-90, Honduras was the world's third ranked producer, behind Ecuador and Costa Rica (Figure 3g).

Since the early 1900s bananas have been the country's chief export item. Little profit, however, remains in Honduran hands since transnational companies maintain control over commercialization of the fruit, where most profits are generated. According to one study,

Figure 3e
Employment in Honduras by Economic Sector

Total economically active population: 1.3 million.

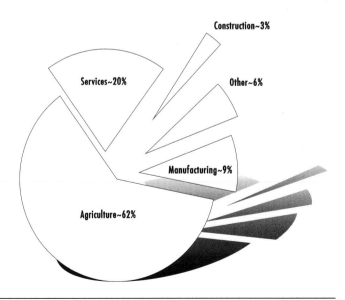

SOURCE: CIA, *The World Factbook* (Washington, DC, 1993).

only 16 percent of the profit from the production and sale of bananas is retained by producer countries.[19] In 1989, about one third of all bananas exported by United Brands' subsidiary Tela Railroad Company, which markets under the Chiquita label, were produced by members of CAGSA, a cooperative that represents about 90 independent Honduran growers. Between 1982 and 1990, Tela marketed almost 70 percent of all Honduran-produced bananas.

After Tela enjoyed a privileged position in Honduras for nearly 80 years, it came as little surprise that Tela retaliated with a "banana war" in 1990 when a British-based consortium headed by Fyffes arranged to purchase fruit directly from independent producers at over three times the price being paid by Tela. In the words of one British diplomat: "I don't understand the Americans. They proclaim the existence of economic liberalism in Honduras, but when they see com-

Figure 3f
Land Use in Honduras

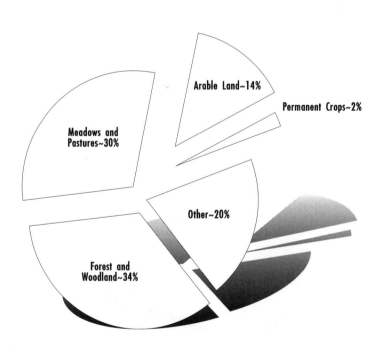

Arable Land~14%

Permanent Crops~2%

Meadows and Pastures~30%

Other~20%

Forest and Woodland~34%

SOURCE: CIA, *The World Factbook* (Washington, DC, 1993).

petition appear, they run, considering this country as if it was their exclusive turf." [20]

Three months after the contract dispute began, a deal brokered by the European Economic Community and the Honduran government brought the conflict to an end.[21] The affair, complete with sabotage actions including derailed boxcars full of fruit and millions of dollars' worth of rotten, warehouse-bound bananas, served to underscore the continued centrality of bananas to the economy.

In 1991 Honduras rejoined UPEB, the cartel of banana-exporting countries, following a two-year absence. Officially, the absence was due to Honduran nonpayment of membership dues, but analysts assert that the administration of then-President José Azcona was pressured by the Tela Railroad Company to withdraw from UPEB.

In the early 1990s, the government launched a series of efforts to stimulate banana production in order to compensate for declining income from coffee exports. In mid-1991, Congress approved legislation providing incentives for new investments in bananas. These include a three-year exemption from export taxes on bananas grown in newly cultivated areas, followed by a reduced tax rate for the following three years. A separate tax-break scheme applies to producers who rehabilitate banana plantations affected by natural disasters. In addition, a trust fund was formed to provide low-interest loans for independent and cooperative producers cultivating bananas in new areas, and a new National Banana Council was established to promote banana production, marketing, and exports.

Banana transnationals in Honduras have been successful in securing fiscal policies relatively favorable to their operations. Growers

Figure 3g
Principal Exports, 1991

Bananas	42.7%
Nontraditionals	22.6%
Coffee	18.7%
Shrimp	4.1%
Zinc	4.0%
Beef	3.7%
Wood	1.9%
Sugar	1.2%
Silver and Lead	0.9%
Tobacco	0.3%

SOURCE: ECLAC, *Economic Survey of Latin America and the Caribbean*, 1991.

must pay a 12 percent tax on export profits. But the tax paid by transnational buyers is calculated on a per-pound basis, diminishing as the volume of exports increases. The sliding scale starts at $1 per pound, but based on average annual exports of between 44 and 48 million boxes per year, the transnationals actually wind up paying less than a penny per pound of bananas exported.[22]

Unlike bananas, production of and income from coffee remain in Honduran hands, and most of the country's 50,000 producers are small growers. Officially, it is estimated that about 88 percent of all coffee producers own small- or medium-size farms. Although coffee has played an important role as a source of employment and has been prioritized as an alternative to dependence on bananas, minimal levels of technical assistance and credit contribute to Honduras achieving the lowest productivity and yields in the region. Fluctuating international market prices and unfavorable export quotas have rendered coffee production increasingly risky. Export revenues have fallen each year since 1986 despite rising volume. Collapse of the International Coffee Agreement in July 1989 led to even sharper downturns in revenues from coffee exports.

Faced with these difficulties, in early 1992 the Honduran Coffee Producers Association (AHPROCAFE) urged the government to annul the existing 7 percent tax on coffee exports, deregulate the exchange rate, and eliminate price controls on domestic coffee sales. About 92 percent of Honduran coffee is exported, with the lower grade beans remaining on the domestic market. According to AHPROCAFE, the artificially low official price for coffee on the domestic market has resulted in large-scale smuggling of locally produced beans to neighboring El Salvador, Nicaragua, and Guatemala, where the product is sold at prices effectively subsidized by Honduran producers. Marketing and technical assistance for coffee producers are coordinated through the state Honduran Coffee Institute (IHCAFE).

Beef production also waned during the 1980s, in large part due to low world-market prices. Both production volume and export revenues rebounded after 1988, however, climbing steadily during the following three years. For the most part, cattle raising is practiced in traditional fashion, dependent on rain and grass pasture, resulting in low yields. Most ranching in Honduras is managed by a small group of powerful landowners who control over 25 percent of Honduras' agricultural land, including some of the highest-quality farmlands, thereby excluding more productive use of this scarce resource.

Seafood holds the promise of becoming one of Honduras' most lucrative agroindustries. Export earnings from fishing—mainly shrimp and lobster—are substantial and growing. Lobster exports in 1991 reached $32 million. The best prospects, however, lie in shrimp farming. Cultivated shrimp export earnings reached $19 million in 1988, jumped to $46 million in 1990, and then topped $73 million in 1991, accounting for nearly 10 percent of all export revenues that year. Shrimp farming occurs primarily in the Gulf of Fonseca, which borders on Nicaragua and El Salvador. Most of the foreign investment comes from the United States, Ecuador, and Taiwan. Attempts have been made to get small farmers into the shrimp-cultivation business, but large-scale, high-tech projects predominate. One such project on the North Coast is part of a debt-equity swap between Chase Manhattan Bank and the Honduran government.[23]

Part of the effort to break dependency on the longstanding big earners like bananas and coffee has been the promotion of nontraditional exports. In agriculture, these include goods such as pineapples, melons, cucumbers, cardamom, black pepper, and ornamental flowers. Despite the myriad incentives available to prospective producers, as of the early 1990s nontraditional agricultural exports had failed to live up to expectations.

Food Security

The other side of the agroexport thrust is the slumping per capita production of basic grains and mounting food imports.[24] Between 1950 and 1985, per capita production of basic grains tumbled by 31 percent. Honduras, once self-sufficient in food production, is now forced to import basic foodstuffs each year. Between 1974 and 1985, cereal imports vaulted by 90 percent, while food aid in cereals skyrocketed by 280 percent.[25]

Noting that Honduras is producing less basic foods and that *campesinos* are abandoning the countryside, Juan Antonio Aguirre of the Interamerican Institute of Agricultural Sciences cautions that Honduras faces a "terrifying future" if corrective measures are not taken. He warned that the country's current agricultural crisis could become truly catastrophic during the 1990s.[26]

During the 1980s the true dimensions of the agricultural crisis were somewhat hidden and distorted by the large U.S. food-assistance program. Through the PL480 Title I program, Honduras received $10 to $18 million annually between 1983 and 1989 in food imports. The program eased the country's balance-of-payments crisis by allowing it to increase grain imports without having to expend scarce foreign exchange. It also helped ease urban unrest by maintaining the availability and relatively low price of wheat-flour products.[27]

The food-aid program, though temporarily disguising the severity of the agricultural crisis, has seriously impacted local food production.

The influx of relatively cheap foodstuffs has resulted in disincentives for local grain producers and has redirected consumption patterns. An AID-contracted study revealed that wheat imports (95 percent of which are included under the food-aid program) have undermined the market price of corn for farmers, who, as a result, are curtailing corn production.[28] Because wheat has become relatively cheaper and often more readily available, Hondurans have changed their diet to include more wheat products. For example, in 1988 only 65 percent of the population consumed corn as a daily staple, down from about 95 percent 20 years previous.[29] In many cases, families have simply replaced their daily fare of *tortillas*, made from Honduran corn, with bread and pastry fashioned from wheat imported from the United States. According to nutritionist Moisés Sánchez: "We're seeing a subtle process of nutritional acculturation, and unless there is an adequate production of food, the country runs the risk of becoming dependent even for its daily bread." [30]

Part of the country's food-security problem is the result of relegating food production to small subsistence farms located on the lowest-quality agricultural lands. The issue is exacerbated by government policies aimed at stimulating private investment in production of nontraditional export crops.

AID is a major promoter, if not the prime engineer, of current Honduran agricultural policy, pumping millions of dollars into programs that seek to boost production of nontraditionals for export, in many cases on farmland previously used to grow basic grains. AID has also pressured the government to terminate all programs designed to protect small-scale grain farmers. According to AID's development philosophy, the economics of comparative advantage and the free world market should guide the country's agricultural policies, rather than any commitment to national food security. In practice, this means further opening up the country to U.S. grain imports paid for with the proceeds from Honduran agroexports.

Agricultural credit policy has been one of the major instruments used to reorient Honduran agriculture. Between 1980 and 1986, of credits to producers disbursed by the Central Bank, only 2 percent was allocated to encourage production of basic grains, the rest going for support of export crops. Similarly, between 1982 and 1986, despite existence of a pronounced government policy touting national food self-sufficiency, the amount of loans provided by the National Agricultural Development Bank for basic grain production declined by 20 percent.[31]

The dangers of dependency on the United States as a primary source of food imports and chief outlet for exports are highlighted during periods of depressed world-market prices for Honduran export crops. Drops in international-market prices for coffee, sugar, and bananas, combined with the expansion of nontraditionals, have convinced many Honduran *campesinos* that agriculture has become too high-risk a venture. Some have restricted planting, while others have chosen to migrate to the cities in search of more stable opportunities.

Land Reform

Offering hope against the harsh poverty and inequitable distribution of land and wealth in the Honduran countryside, the mere existence of land-reform programs has been a major stabilizing factor since the early 1960s.[32] Nonetheless, during the 1980s even these modest reform efforts ground to a halt, and in early 1992 the government gutted existing land reform legislation with passage of a new Agricultural Modernization Law.

Under the Liberal government of Ramón Villeda Morales, in 1961 the National Agrarian Institute (INA) was created to organize rural cooperatives, propose colonization projects, and administer land distribution. International pressure to "democratize" production—one of the main thrusts of the Alliance for Progress—coincided with domestic pressures, and in 1962 the country's first Agrarian Reform Law was passed.

Although in reality very little land was distributed—under 4,000 acres—the program did serve to appease some *campesino* demands. Since most of the land targeted for redistribution belonged to the state, those who backed the reform expected little opposition from the landed oligarchy. Similarly, the transnational fruit companies actually stood to gain from the process, as it facilitated their goal of transferring some production costs and risks onto small farmers. Nonetheless, with a myopia reminiscent of Guatemala a decade earlier, the oligarchy and fruit companies considered Villeda's reforms too radical, and together with conservative sectors in the military conspired to overthrow his government.

In the wake of the resulting military coup INA's budget was drastically cut and its personnel completely replaced. The ensuing period of repression of *campesino* activism led many groups to resort to the illegal land occupations that proliferated in the early 1970s.

Responding to growing pressure from the peasantry, the government changed tactics and adopted a decidedly reformist stance. New, more comprehensive agrarian-reform laws passed in 1972 and 1975 placed ceilings on landholdings and required cattle ranchers to intensify their production. The measures attempted to stimulate more productive use of farmland and to address *campesino* demands through the distribution of idle or underutilized properties. But the ceilings were generously high and all lands planted in export crops, including transnational holdings, were exempted from the law. Between 1972 and 1975, the most dynamic years of the agrarian reform, about 300,000 acres were distributed to some 35,000 families, only one-fourth of the amount demanded by the National Front of United Peasants and far short even of the official government goal.

In 1975 conservative military leaders acceded to pressures from the oligarchy and put an end to the reform experiment. Since then, despite promises by the civilian governments of the 1980s, agrarian reform has slowed to a trickle, the victim of a marked lack of political will, cumbersome bureaucratic obstacles, and corruption and inefficiency at INA.

Finding all other avenues closed, the well-organized peasantry has responded with direct action in the form of renewed land occupations. During the 1980s, most occupations took place on idle lands that fell within the bounds of the existing agrarian-reform legislation. Hundreds of small-scale occupations occurred spontaneously in farming communities throughout the country. There were also several nationally coordinated actions designed to pressure the government into resuscitating its own agrarian-reform law. One of the largest such actions took place in May 1989, when some 400 *campesino* groups—affiliated with the COCOCH peasant umbrella organization—staged land invasions on about 50,000 acres at locations around the country.[33]

The state has responded ambiguously to these land invasions. On occasions, it has simply turned a blind eye or politely invited *campesino* leaders to negotiate settlements of claims through INA. But the most common response has been to send in the army. Many peasants participating in such actions have been jailed, tortured, or killed either by the military or by the landowners' private guards. Since 1982, those implicated in land invasions can be prosecuted under the terms of harsh antiterrorist laws.

With genuine land reform on ice in the 1980s, the government proffered a land-titling program. Many *campesino* organizations saw this AID-sponsored program as a way of dividing the peasantry. Its major thrust was providing legal claim to lands that farmers had been working for years, in some cases generations, as a way to facilitate access to credit. Title holders also gained the right to sell their land. The program thus completely failed to address the most pressing problem in the countryside—the utter landlessness of tens of thousands of *campesino* families.

Then in March 1992, agrarian-reform legislation was put to rest altogether with congressional passage of the new Agricultural Modernization Law. Originally drafted by AID, the law has three principal objectives: to eliminate all forms of state intervention in the agrarian sector; to further limit expropriations and bolster guarantees for private ownership of land; and to promote new foreign and domestic investment in agriculture.[34] Essentially, the new law replaces the previous notion of agricultural resources fulfilling a "social function" with regulations following the laws of supply and demand. The government touts the legislation as "the most comprehensive agricultural policy law in Latin America."

Much of the land that had been subject to expropriation under prior agrarian-reform legislation is now exempt. This includes land held under joint ownership, rented land, and land that is inefficiently exploited. Large landowners with extensive undercultivated tracts can now lease these lands. Likewise, landowners may now leave their farmland fallow for up to 24 months without risking expropriation.

On the other end of the spectrum, previously existing provisions aimed at discouraging consolidation of the *minifundio*—due to a five-hectare minimum limit on land eligible for titling—have been eliminated. The legislation also obliges INA to accelerate the land-titling process. Now, even holders of tiny parcels of land can receive title, thereby achieving the "right" to use their property as collateral on agricultural loans.

When the new law eliminated price controls on agricultural goods and recommended the privatization of IHMA grain storage facilities, the role of the state-run Honduran Agriculture Marketing Institute (IHMA) was reduced to providing technical assistance to farmers. Likewise, under terms of the legislation, the National Agriculture Development Bank (BANDESA) was to become a commercial bank operating with private funds. Previously, BANDESA had operated as a public trust providing low-interest loans to *campesinos*.

The legislation also alters the legal status of the country's 2,800 agricultural cooperatives, providing coop members with individual, negotiable shareholdings. Coop members will thus be allowed to apportion the farms into personal units, or simply to parcel and sell their land. During 1991, under pressure to redeem their accumulated bank debts, at least ten cooperatives sold their land—some of it to Standard Fruit or Tela Railroad Company—even before passage of the law. In 1992, more than 50 cooperatives sold part or all of the land they had received under the agrarian reform.

The law further provides for formation of a state land bank and recommends that future reform beneficiaries—for the first time including women in their own right—receive grants of seed capital. But given that expropriation criteria have been eased, and recalling the snail's pace of distribution under previous legislation, many *campesinos* were skeptical of the law's lofty promises.

Former president of the government's National Agrarian Institute (INA) Juan Ramón Martínez, who resigned his post in opposition to the law, bemoaned that the new legislation is "fundamentally a counteragrarian reform designed to halt land access by *campesinos,* derailing the capacity to develop their organizations either as unions or economically, and passes the management of the agrarian conflict from the government to private individuals."[35]

Rafael Alegría, president of the Coordinating Committee of Peasant Organizations (COCOCH), charged that the new law was unconstitutional and that it would quickly reverse even the minimal gains made by *campesinos* over the previous three decades. Alegía predicted that by eliminating the basis for hope for thousands of landless agricultural workers, the legislation was bound to lead to new upheavals in the Honduran countryside.[36]

The mere existence of reform legislation and occasional attempts to rent, grant, or provide title to land did contribute to avoiding the outbreak of widespread rural violence. Nonetheless, the agrarian reform never really managed to address the problem of landlessness. According to Martínez, as of early 1991, after nearly three decades of agrarian reform in Honduras, an estimated 180,000 families were still landless.[37] Between 1962 and 1987, about 768,000 acres had been distributed to some 70,000 families.[38] In contrast, a mere ten years of agrarian reform in neighboring Nicaragua allotted almost seven times as much land to 120,000 families.[39]

But numbers do not tell the whole story. Though there are some examples of cooperatives receiving good land and generous levels of credit and technical assistance, most *campesinos* affected by the reform were assigned land only marginally suited for agriculture. Likewise, the government's credit policy overwhelmingly favors large, private farms producing export crops. Furthermore, a lack of marketing outlets forces most peasants to sell their excess production to unscrupulous middlemen.[40] As a result of these limitations, INA estimates that as many as one of every four *campesinos* who received land from the agrarian-reform process has since abandoned it.

As in El Salvador and Guatemala, the overriding factor impeding efforts toward land reform in Honduras is the absence of political will on the part of the country's rulers. Much of Honduras' best agricultural lands, currently in the hands of big private growers or transnational corporations, is underutilized or lies idle. Although pressure from the landless can be expected to mount, the new Agricultural Modernization Law will tend to reinforce factors that exacerbate the concentration of landholdings.

Despite this panorama of growing hardships and polarization in the countryside, some Hondurans remain confident that a judicious mix of repression, cooption, and limited handout programs will continue to be effective in containing peasant unrest. Others, such as former Labor Minister Gautama Fonseca, are less optimistic:

> We'd be fooling ourselves if we said the future looked bright. Most of the *campesinos* are poor and illiterate. Our schools and universities are appalling, so we're not turning out qualified technicians. As bad as our production levels are now, they will undoubtedly decline even further. Add to that a dominant class which has no interest in solving the problems of the poor and you've got a time bomb. I have no doubt that the future of Honduras will be the same as that of Guatemala, El Salvador, and Nicaragua—that of great social upheaval and civil war.[41]

Industry and Finance

Honduras has the smallest industrial sector in Central America. Little of its industrial output is marketed outside the region except for the textiles and other products assembled in the country's maquiladoras. The manufacturing sector employs less than 10 percent of Honduran workers and accounts for under 15 percent of the GDP. Mining, forestry, tourism, and construction are all relatively marginal activities in economic terms.

Part of the government's plans for attracting new foreign investment in the 1990s include expanding exploration and extraction activities in forestry (see Environment), petroleum, and mining. During 1991, U.S.-based Cambria True Oil Company, and Venezuela's Maraven, were both awarded concessions for petroleum exploration projects in the Mosquitia region of Honduras. U.S.-based Texaco, which operates the country's only petroleum refinery (located in Puerto Cortés), also signed a four-year exploration and production agreement with the government in late 1991. The accord covers a 4,000-square-kilometer area in the Mosquitia, encompassing the continental shelf adjacent to Gracias a Dios department. Hoping to cash in on the country's considerable reserves of silver, gold, lead, zinc, tin, iron, copper, and coal, the government has expended additional resources on geological surveys of the country. Honduran mining laws offer several incentives for foreign companies that invest in mining enterprises.

The manufacturing sector consists essentially of three branches. There are the relatively long-established enterprises that produce processed food, beverages, tobacco, clothing, and footwear for the domestic market. After these are the agroindustrial firms linked to domestic agriculture and forestry, such as meat packers, sugar mills, paper and pulp plants, and furniture producers. Most recent on the scene are the maquiladoras.

More than half of all manufacturing enterprises are small, family-owned shops with fewer than ten employees. A full 40 percent of Hondurans employed in manufacturing are classified as artisans, not factory workers. The country's large, modern factories are in the hands of foreign companies or the Honduran business elite. Among the largest manufacturers are the country's two major banana companies: Castle & Cooke produces soap, plastic products, cans, boxes, and cement, while United Brands churns out rubber, plastics, margarine, and vegetable oil.

The protected regional markets erected under provisions of the Central American Common Market did stimulate significant growth of Honduran industry in the 1960s, but the boom years did not last long. With the onset of recession in the early 1980s, industry began a decline from which it has still not recovered. Virtually all manufacturing subsectors stagnated or declined during the 1980s as a result of contracting internal demand, a stifling of regional export markets, a tightening of credit, and rising import prices. Subsequently, structural adjustment programs that liberalized foreign trade and dismantled tariff barriers placed most local industries in a difficult position vis-à-vis competition with foreign products.

Maquiladoras and the "Asian Invasion"

Although the local manufacturing sector is stagnating, there has been some growth in export-oriented manufacturing.[42] In 1976 the government opened the doors to the Puerto Cortés Free Zone as part of its policy to attract foreign investment in industry. Enterprises investing in space at the industrial park, managed by the National Port Authority, may import raw materials and semi-finished products without tariffs or duties. They may subsequently freely re-export finished goods, and their profits are exempt from taxation.

As of the early 1990s, with the Puerto Cortés zone full, another five government-sponsored free zones had been created: Omoa, Choloma, Tela, La Ceiba, and Amapala. Manufacturing establishments may be installed anywhere in these towns and enjoy duty-free status. In addition, the private sector offers its own duty-free regions, known as Export Processing Zones, which provide the same preferential treatment as the public-sector zones. A private zone is essentially an industrial park built by a local developer with its space leased to foreign investors, free of state control. As of 1991 five private zones had been formed in the San Pedro Sula area directed by local consortiums, including the Continental Group and the Canahuati family.

Legislation regulating operations within the duty-free zones provides for incentives including a 100 percent exemption from import, export, local sales, excise, and profit taxes; unrestricted withdrawal of profits and capital at any time; the right to hold dollar-denominated accounts in Honduran banks; and special status in order to streamline customs clearance.

Incentives exist for firms operating outside of the duty-free zones as well. For example, the Temporary Import Law covers production facilities located anywhere in the country for companies that export 100 percent of their output to destinations outside Central America. These firms are given a ten year exemption on corporate income tax, and are allowed duty-free import of machinery, equipment, and materials.

U.S.-based companies that have set up shop in Honduras under provisions of the duty-free incentives include Warners, Best Form, Sara Lee, and Osh Kosh B'Gosh. But U.S firms have been far outpaced by their Asian rivals. As of 1992, 19 Korean investors, including Sunny Industries and the Dong Bang Corporation, had established operations in Honduras. Smaller numbers of plants were initiated by companies from Singapore, Hong Kong, and Taiwan. The bulk of the Asian *maquila* plants have settled in the North Coast industrial belt, dubbed the "Asian enclave."

Most of the fresh investment in the *maquiladora* sector is the result of low-wage, labor-intensive industries rendered uncompetitive in their countries of origin as local work forces in Asia become increasingly accustomed to better wages and highly skilled jobs. But there is also a growing trend transcending simple garment-assembly operations to more advanced manufacturing. During 1991, for example, investors from Hong Kong announced plans to construct both a textile factory and a plastics facility in Honduras, expressing interest in building bicycle and motorcycle assembly plants as well. South Korea's Hanil Group has proposed construction of a $40 million textile-weaving factory in Honduras. Other South Korean firms have also reportedly been exploring the possibility of shifting some of their Asia-based electronics and automobile assembly operations to Honduras. In 1992 the Lempira Group, comprising Hong Kong Chinese who accepted the Honduran offer of nationality ($25,000 per passport for foreign investors), announced plans to invest about $100 million in plantain and banana plantations, as well as footwear and textile plants.[43]

In addition to the government incentives, during the late 1980s and early 1990s investors in *maquiladora* plants looked favorably on Honduras for its low wages, regionally competitive rents, proximity to U.S. markets, and favorable U.S. import quotas. Following the 1990 devaluation, wages stood at $0.48 per hour (in dollar terms)—among the lowest in the Western Hemisphere.

The elaborate government incentive system has been criticized by some as an overly generous giveaway. In the words of FIDE promotions manager Moises Reyes: "Basically, all they (*maquilas*) pay are utilities and labor costs." But the Honduran government remains convinced that such reassembly-for-export ventures hold promise and thus has launched an aggressive campaign aimed at attracting new investors. The government hopes to attract investment to the industrial parks from 160 firms and to generate 30,000 jobs between 1990 and 1995.[44] But even if this ambitious goal were met, it would cover only a small portion of the employment needs generated by tens of thousands of Hondurans who join the labor force each year as a result of population growth.

Despite the official optimism, it is not clear what, if anything, the *maquiladoras* contribute to the national economy, other than low-wage jobs. The *maquilas* have been sharply criticized on several grounds. In general, the sector is poorly integrated with the rest of the national economy, and due to generous incentive programs, *maquilas* do little to bolster the national tax base. *Maquiladora* investments tend to be unstable—in the best of cases, plants remain in operation for a few years; in the worst, Hondurans have been the victims of deceptive promises and scams. In addition to labor problems over wage disputes and denial of organizing rights, complaints lodged by *maquila* workers have ranged from attempts by management to impose forced sterilization on women to unsafe workplace conditions.

Social Forces and Institutions

© Bill Barrett

Popular Organizing

Prior to the 1950s, Honduran society was perceived as the least organized in Central America. This lack of social organization paralleled the country's historic absence of political, economic, and even geographical unity. Only after World War II did Honduras gel as a national state with a professional army, Central Bank, transportation network, and diversified economy. Until 1950 the country's two main cities—Tegucigalpa and San Pedro Sula—were not even linked by a paved road. At that time there were no private-sector organizations with a national reach, and the few popular organizations were concentrated in isolated pockets.

The "Great Banana Strike" of 1954

The banana strike on the North Coast in 1954 proved to be the watershed for subsequent popular organizing in Honduras. This historic strike erupted from a foundation of worker organizing dating back to the 1920s when the Honduran Labor Federation, associated with the Honduras Communist Party, began to organize banana and mine workers. These early organizers faced constant repression by both company and government police. Often forced to operate clandestinely, they made little headway in forming labor unions or in bringing other popular sectors into their fight against the dictatorship of Tiburcio Carías Andino (1932-48) and other unsympathetic government leaders.

The long years of organizing among the banana estates of Standard Fruit and United Fruit were not wasted, however. This committed labor organizing by leftist unionists in the first half of the 1900s formed the base of a very successful strike in 1954 against the banana companies. The 1954 strike against United Fruit soon spread throughout the country, eventually shutting down 60 percent of the national economy.

The crisis caught the attention of American Federation of Labor (AFL) President George Meany and the closely associated Interamerican Regional Organization of Workers (ORIT). The U.S. labor hierarchy, working closely with the State Department, was concerned about the leading role of Communist Party organizers in the strike. In the interests of heading off the creation of a strong anti-imperialist workers' movement, Meany urged United Fruit to reach a settlement with the less militant workers and to grant union recognition.[1]

The AFL, CIO, and ORIT pledged funds for an effort to take the initiative away from the more militant strike leaders and to forge an anticommunist union movement. AFL representative Serafino Romualdi succeeded in persuading the country's archbishop to circulate a pastoral letter urging workers to join the AFL/ORIT-affiliated unions and encouraging the government to enact labor legislation. After the arrest of key strike leaders and their replacement with a more conciliatory Central Strike Committee, United Fruit agreed to negotiate. The strike settlement gave ORIT and its U.S. backers an important inroad into the Honduran labor movement—one that continues today among the country's labor unions and peasant associations.[2] The 1954 strike was, nonetheless, a major victory for Honduran workers. It opened the way for labor and peasant organizing throughout the entire country and revealed for the first time the tremendous power of the country's popular sectors.

The Social Christian Movement

Before the 1960s the Catholic Church had little to do with social justice issues, confining its social work to charitable programs (see Religion). But beginning in 1961 the church emerged as a major influence in the development of popular organizing in Honduras. It established new social service organizations and popular-education programs, while encouraging the formation of peasant leagues.

Running parallel to and sometimes closely integrated with the church's various programs in social assistance and development was the Social Christian movement. This new popular movement received financial support from Christian Democratic and Christian Socialist organizations in Europe. It stressed the importance of addressing social justice issues within the context of capitalism and guided by Christian teachings.[3]

In the 1960s and early 1970s the Social Christian movement gave birth to numerous private organizations, peasant associations, and unions. Among the organizations established with Social Christian inspiration were: Popular Cultural Action of Honduras (ACPH, 1961), Social Christian Peasant Association (ACASCH, 1963), Social Christian University Front (FRESC, 1963), Human Promotion Association (APRHU, 1965), Honduran Development Foundation (FUNHDESA, 1969), Pre-Federation of Consumer Cooperatives, and the Institute of Social-Economic Investigations (IISE, 1973). The Social Christian movement organized politically in 1968 as the Christian Democratic Movement of Honduras (MDCH).

In 1971 the social-promotion organizations of the Catholic Church and those of the Social Christian movement coalesced under a new umbrella organization called CONCORDE (Coordinating Council for Development). CONCORDE's main role was to provide assistance in various forms to affiliated groups. Named as the first CONCORDE executive secretary was Rodolfo Sorto Romero, the ex-director of CARITAS, an MDCH supporter, and an adherent of the theology of liberation. The founding organizations of CONCORDE were: Catholic Relief Services (CRS), CARITAS, the Catholic Church's social communication division (which included four radio stations and one weekly newspaper), the church's nine peasant-training centers, Federation of Savings and Credit Cooperatives (FACACH), FUNHDESA, and APRHU.

External to but closely associated with many CONCORDE members was the General Workers Central (CGT), the union federation supported by the international and local Social Christian movement. The CGT's most prominent member group has historically been the National Campesino Union (UNC), whose leaders were largely the product of the Catholic Church's training and organizing programs.

The close alliance between the Catholic Church and the MDCH was short-lived. A year after CONCORDE was founded, the church hierarchy began pulling its organizations out of the umbrella group. Prelates were concerned that the church's own social-promotion program was becoming too secularized and too closely associated with militant popular organizations. They also felt that the MDCH was using the church for its own political ambitions.

The institutional church's split from CONCORDE marked the beginning of the hierarchy's attempt to distance itself from rural land struggles and other militant expressions of the popular movement for social justice. The church was concerned that by aligning itself too closely with secular political and popular movements it was endangering its own institutional stability and its traditional place in the Honduran power structure.[4]

Peasant Organizing

The first peasant organizations, like the country's first unions, resulted largely from the work of organizers associated with the Honduras Communist Party. One of the first peasant associations was the Central Committee of Peasant Unity, founded in the mid-1950s and later reorganized as the National Federation of Honduran Peasants (FENACH). From the beginning, FENACH was targeted by the security forces. In 1963, after the military coup that overthrew the Villeda government, FENACH's offices were destroyed and its leaders imprisoned.

Along with the military and the church, the AFL-CIO and ORIT were also disturbed by FENACH's leftist activism. In 1962 the National Association of Honduran Peasants (ANACH) was formed to counteract the influence of FENACH within the peasantry and to assert "democratic" control over the incipient peasant movement. Traditionally ANACH, a member of the Confederation of Honduran Workers (CTH), has exerted a conservative influence, but during the economic crisis of the 1980s the organization began adopting some of the more confrontational tactics of other peasant groups and joined in coalitions with leftist union federations. Its longtime president, Julín Méndez, has served as a congressional deputy with the social-democratic Innovation and Unity Party (PINU). ANACH claims to have about 80,000 members.

The National Campesino Union (UNC), founded in 1970, has also been a strong influence among the Honduran peasantry. Building upon its roots within the Social Christian movement, the UNC emerged from the Social Christian Peasant Association (ACASCH) and became a member of the General Workers Central (CGT). Its major figure has been Marcial Caballero, who during the 1980s gradually assumed a position of collaboration with the government, political parties, and the army. Splits between conservative and progressive factions subsequently led to divisions within the UNC, with the Caballero faction maintaining control of the association's finances and institutional apparatus. Like the CGT, the UNC has become closely associated with the National Party.[5] It has also alienated itself from other forces within the peasant movement by cutting separate deals with the National Agrarian Institute (INA). At one point in the early 1980s elements within the armed forces suspected the UNC of being a guerrilla front. But a joint corn-production project with the military in Olancho, launched in 1989, assuaged their concerns and witnessed how far the UNC had moved from its former combative stance.

The most dynamic and progressive peasant federation is the National Union of Rural Workers (CNTC), founded in 1985 mainly by defectors from ANACH and the UNC. This peasant confederation includes: National Union of Peasant Cooperatives (UNACOOPH), National Authentic Union of Honduran Peasants (UNCAH), Unitary Federation of Peasant Cooperatives (FUNACH), and Front of Independent Honduran Peasants (FRENACHINH). Although the U.S. embassy charges the CNTC with a marxist bent because of its working relationship with the leftist Unitary Federation of Honduran Workers (FUTH) labor federation, its politics would more aptly be described as progressive social-democratic.[6]

Splintering continues to plague peasant organizing in Honduras. The Federation of Honduran Agrarian Reform Cooperatives (FECORAH), founded in 1970, finds kinship with the government's National Agrarian Institute and is generally conservative. On the other hand, the July 1989 formation of the Honduran Peasant Organization (OCH) split off another sector from the embattled UNC. The Coordinating Committee of Peasant Organizations (COCOCH), which includes the CNTC, ANACH, UNC, and FECORAH, is the latest attempt to unify the divided peasant movement.

Another group formed in the late 1980s is the Association for Development of the Western Region (ADRO), comprising about 3,500 affiliated peasants. ADRO President Eusebio Ramos, summarizing the frustrations of most Honduran peasants, grumbled: "For years the government has been coming into our villages and giving us promises. Either there is no action at all, or all the money is wasted on a few cars and on salaries for people who don't do anything." [7] The independence of peasant associations from government is a major concern in Honduras, where both the government and the military have a long history of intervening in and controlling the popular movement so as to neutralize protests and isolate more militant elements.[8]

There are numerous organizations of peasant women in Honduras, including the Honduran Federation of Peasant Women (FEHMUC), the Council for Integrated Development of Peasant Women (CODIMCA), and the National Association of Peasant Women (ANAMUC), an auxiliary of ANACH (see Women and Feminism).

Expanding Popular Movement

Before the 1980s the popular movement was largely limited to worker, peasant, and student groups. These groups played a key roll in supporting the reformist military governments of the 1970s. During the ensuing decade, the popular movement gained broader dimensions with the formation of human rights groups, ethnic and Amerindian organizations, a major research center, women's organizations, and new popular coalitions.

The strength and integrity of popular organizations in Honduras have long been limited by entanglements with the major political parties, government institutions, the armed forces, and foreign funding organizations. Other weaknesses of the popular movement include myopia and opportunism—demands are often limited to the economic realm and leaders are frequently ready to collaborate with the government and armed forces in pursuit of short-term goals. Likewise, frequent personality conflicts among the leadership of different groups, often tied to internal power struggles, have provided fertile ground for attempts by the government and the military to divide the movement.

The longstanding tradition of collaboration and compromise has reaped certain rewards for the popular movement over the years. Recognizing the disruptive potential of the popular movement, the political parties and military have, on repeated occasions, responded to worker and peasant demands. Specific achievements since the 1950s include adoption of a labor code, institution of an agrarian-reform program, and implementation of legislation regarding social security, price controls, and a minimum wage. Yet despite this history of social compromise, the Honduran population remains among the poorest and most downtrodden in Latin America.

In response to the worsening economic conditions and intensifying repression of the 1980s, the popular movement gathered new strength and unity. It is still too weak, divided, and unsure of its political direction to present a serious challenge to either the national-security doctrine of the armed forces or the economic policies of the political elite and oligarchy. But there are clear signs that the popular sectors may be able to build upon past strengths and develop a national movement capable of mounting such a challenge in the 1990s.

In addition to the peasant organizations already enumerated, Honduras now counts several women's organizations (see Women and Feminism), human rights organizations (see Human Rights), combative student associations (see Schools and Students), and a strong labor movement (see Labor and Unions). The two small political parties—Christian Democrat Party of Honduras (PDCH) and the Innovation and Unity Party (PINU)—play an important role in the expanding popular movement, while the more leftist Honduran Patriotic Front (FPH) is reviving earlier organizing efforts (see Politics). In recent years Honduras has also experienced the emergence of community groups that have mounted militant demonstrations demanding better government services and lower prices for basic goods.

Although the popular sectors have taken some steps to form coalitions, these efforts have repeatedly been undermined by political sectarianism, personality differences, police infiltration, and internecine violence. These and other factors have long obstructed achievement of the degree of unity necessary to confront repression and deteriorating socioeconomic conditions.

In 1989, however, several of the country's major popular organizations were successful in a unification effort that resulted in the formation of the "Plataforma de Lucha para la Democratización de Honduras." The Plataforma was officially launched in October 1989, following the release of a document with the same name, signed by representatives of the country's four major *campesino* federations (all members of COCOCH), four labor federations (CTH, FUTH, CGT, and FITH), the federation of cooperatives (CHC), and several professional groups. The immediate objective of the groups that participated in elaborating the Plataforma was to produce a document that could be used to influence the presidential candidates in the 1989 general elections. But the Plataforma went on to play an important role long after the elections.

Emergence of the Plataforma was important for two reasons. First, given the notorious levels of sectarianism that had for years divided the popular movement, plus the severity of the onslaught faced by constituent groups as a result of neoliberal economic policies, any trend toward unity in action among the myriad groups was considered a step forward. Second, by 1991, despite widespread organizing efforts by leftist and progressive political party, labor, *campesino*, and other groups, aimed at stemming the excesses of neoliberalism, the Plataforma stood alone in offering a comprehensive alternative program.

According to Plataforma coordinator Marco Orlando Iriarte, the coalition made no pretensions to achieve organizational unity among the ideologically diverse member groups. "We are seeking *coincidencias* (points of agreement). Right now," he explained, "[the Plataforma] is the only instrument we have to engage in debate with the government." [9]

The Plataforma founding document espouses wide-ranging reforms in Honduran politics, economy, foreign relations, education, etc. It denounces the current Honduran economic system as "neocolonial capitalism" and proposes a series of transformations that would restructure the economy to function for the needs of the majority. These include expansion of the cooperative sector, an extensive agrarian-reform program that would eliminate unproductive *minifundios* and *latifundios*, strengthening of domestic industry, tighter integration of agriculture and industry in order to generate more highly processed items, fiscal reform, and drastic cuts in military spending. The document also calls for radical changes in income distribution through higher wages and benefits, and a greater degree of participation by workers at all stages of the production process.

In the political realm, the Plataforma demands reform of the electoral system to allow for individual votes for posts at all levels, rather than the current, more restrictive, practice of party slates. It further proposes simplifying the requirements for registration of new political parties and for running independent candidates in elections. Significantly, the document also urges reforms within the popular movement itself, including the expansion of internal democratic practices and a call to resist intervention in internal affairs by the government, political parties, the military, or employers.

During 1990 and 1991, the Plataforma succeeded in projecting itself as a powerful force in national politics, clearly demonstrating the importance of unity among the popular organizations. Nonetheless, its effectiveness was clearly mitigated by two factors. First, given the diverse nature of its constituent groups, unity at the level of discourse and agreement in principle was much more easily achieved than unity in practice and action. The more Plataforma was forced to adopt concrete stances in relation to actual struggles and to rally coalition affiliates to support those stances, the more likely divisions were to appear. Second, faced with a barrage of government attempts to divide and weaken the popular movement and to coopt certain sectors through the offering of short-term benefits, the Plataforma was repeatedly confronted with the dilemma of just how far to go in terms of legitimizing the government through participation in negotiations as opposed to remaining "on the sidelines" with more radical proposals.

Labor and Unions

Since the landmark strikes of 1954 the Honduran union movement has been deemed the region's largest and strongest.[10] Currently about 15 percent of the total work force—and some 40 percent of urban workers—belong to unions. Union organizing encompasses three broad sectors of the economy: tens of thousands of Hondurans employed by the state, wage earners in agriculture, and the relatively small industrial work force.

Honduran unions and peasant organizations have struggled for their position as influential actors on the national political scene; few governments over the past 30 years have attempted to ride roughshod over their demands, and several have tried to integrate them into broad coalitions. But persistent attempts to divide the movement, internal sectarian practices, and opportunistic leadership have often diluted its strengths. In addition, despite legal gains wrested by unions—such as a progressive labor code and minimum-wage legislation—enforcement has largely paralleled the government and private-sector's ability to pay, and has been limited to the small, modern wing of the economy that employs skilled labor. Particularly since the onset of the economic crisis of the 1980s there has been widespread noncompliance, and the brunt of the burden of structural adjustment of the economy has been shifted to wage earners, who have watched their purchasing power wane since 1981.

Predictably, imposition of neoliberal economic policies under the Callejas administration led to acrimonious battles between the government and organized labor. On more than one occasion, after lengthy strikes and labor disputes persisted, the government resorted to its age-old tactic: calling in the army. The early 1990s also witnessed mounting efforts aimed at displacing militant union forces, including firings, arrests, and the imposition of *solidarista* associations (see *Solidarismo*).

Origins and Rise of Unions

Labor organizing got its start in Honduras amid the U.S. mining and banana enclaves soon after the turn of the century. Harsh economic conditions and the antilabor policies of the foreign companies—which often called in the Honduran army to help quell worker unrest—offered fertile ground for the growth of militant union activity.

After a long period of clandestine and relatively isolated activities, a major turning point revitalized Honduran trade unions when a strike erupted in 1954 on the banana plantations (see Popular Organizing). Workers in related labor sectors—such as railroads, ports, and mines—soon joined in solidarity and the strike eventually encompassed some 50,000 workers. The 1954 strike cast the union movement onto center stage as a force to be reckoned with. The government soon instituted the country's first national labor code, including complete union legalization and recognition of the rights to strike, to organize, and to demand a minimum wage. A revised labor code, passed in 1958, provided for paid vacations and severance pay.

But the unprecedented show of worker solidarity in 1954 provoked other responses as well. In an effort to defuse the growing militancy and to channel organizing sentiments into more acceptable paths, the American Institute for Free Labor Development (AIFLD) and ORIT began assisting the creation of passive, alternative unions. In the space of a few years, Honduras became the headquarters for this type of U.S.-sponsored union activity in Latin America. By 1960 compliant ORIT-linked unions installed on the banana plantations had acceded to a 50 percent reduction in the work force by both United Fruit and Standard Fruit Companies.

In 1964 most pro-ORIT federations—including the most powerful of the banana workers' unions and the largest peasant organization, the National Association of Honduran Peasants (ANACH)—assembled to form the Confederation of Honduran Workers (CTH). The CTH dominated legal union activities throughout most of the 1960s and 1970s and, despite challenges by newer groups, remains the largest confederation in Honduras, claiming 160,000 workers. CTH-affiliated unions pervade almost all sectors of the economy.

The CTH describes itself as social-democratic. Although the confederation has no formal links with any political party, several members from its leadership council have run in national elections as PINU candidates. The CTH is affiliated with the International Confederation of Free Trade Unions (ICFTU) and with ORIT; it receives aid from AIFLD, from Germany's Friedrich Ebert Foundation, and from ORIT. Notwithstanding ample diversity among member unions, the CTH as a whole has collaborated with the government and for the most part has confined its activities to the search for immediate worker benefits.

A second national confederation, the General Workers Central (CGT), was founded in 1970 but was refused legal recognition until 1984. Originally linked to the more conservative sectors of the Christian Democratic Party, conflicts over strategy and patronage have divided both the leadership and the base of the CGT since its founding. The CGT enjoys close ties with the National Party. In fact, several of the confederation's leaders stepped down in order to run for office on the National Party slate in 1989, including one of Callejas' three vice-presidential designates, Marco Tulio Cruz. Several CGT leaders were elected to Congress in 1989 on the National Party ticket; others were appointed by Callejas to high government posts. The CGT leaders-turned-politicians have endorsed Callejas' strategy of "selling" Honduras to foreign investors, billing it as the only way to create new jobs.

The CGT base has adopted a more critical stance and was instrumental in pressuring the leadership to include the organization in the progressive Plataforma de Lucha coalition. The CGT claims to represent 120,000 members, two-thirds of them from the peasant groups affiliated with the National Campesino Union (UNC). Internationally, the CGT is affiliated with the Latin American Workers Central (CLAT) and the World Federation of Labor (WCL). During the 1980s CGT unions received assistance from several Western European Social and Christian Democratic foundations.

The more radical Unitary Federation of Honduran Workers (FUTH), originated in 1978 and awarded legal status in 1989, counts 30,000 workers. Although far smaller than the two major national confederations, FUTH's vocal stances on burning political issues—combined with its strategic concentration in workers from the Central Bank, the National University, electricity and water companies, and construction—have afforded the group a high profile.

Sometimes allied with the more conservative CGT, and occasionally even with the CTH, FUTH has promoted a broad agenda among labor, advocating opposition to the contra and U.S. military presence and respect for human rights. Several FUTH leaders have been assassinated or disappeared, allegedly by the security forces.

The latest addition among the labor confederations is the Independent Federation of Honduran Workers (FITH), established in 1985. Based in San Pedro Sula, FITH member unions include municipal workers and small industrial unions, comprising about 13,000 workers.

Divisions and infighting—in some cases over legitimate political and ideological differences, in others the product of deliberate policies pursued by management and the government—continue to characterize the Honduran union movement. The four confederations stand worlds apart on many issues. Nonetheless growing hardships induced by the economic crisis and austerity policies have led to deeper levels of programmatic unity within the movement.

Concretely, since the early 1980s, three key battlegrounds precipitated the waging of several major strikes and a heightened degree of unity within the union movement: 1) coordinated pressure for a raise in the minimum wage in the face of ever-declining purchasing power; 2) the fight against large-scale layoffs, as cutbacks or closures in factories, farms, and in the state sector increasingly outpaced the creation of jobs through new investments; and 3) efforts to prevent the penetration of *solidarismo*.

In another expression of the growing tendency toward trade union collaboration, the country's four major federations—CTH, CGT, FUTH, and FITH—promoted a series of common demands during the International Workers Day celebrations May 1st, 1989. Six months later, the four further solidified their budding unity by joining the Plataforma de Lucha. Subsequent collaboration was evidenced when the four confederations threatened to launch a nationwide general strike. But despite these unification efforts, and their embodiment in the programmatic alternatives advocated by the Plataforma, the labor movement has had a difficult time resisting the imposition of neoliberal policies, particularly wage controls, layoffs in the state sector, and privatization. Thus during the early 1990s, many workers watched the gains of previous decades fritter away. Unprecedented numbers of strikes did take place in 1990 and 1991, including lengthy union-management battles in the cases of banana-plantation workers, miners, and state employees. But by and large, these struggles were at best aimed at retarding or attenuating the advances of neoliberalism.

Solidarismo

Both transnational firms and Honduran businesspeople have embraced *solidarismo* as an effective way of undermining traditional trade unionism and of assuring a more compliant work force. Well-established in Costa Rica, the *solidarismo* movement seeks to replace existing unions with worker-owner financial associations. Under solidarity agreements, workers lose their rights to collective bargaining, strikes, and usually to all grievance procedures.

Efforts to impose solidarity associations in Honduras have surfaced in industry, on the banana plantations, and in the mines, moving to displace existing unions affiliated with the major federations. These takeover attempts have achieved mixed results. In mid-1988 the leaders of the CTH, CGT, and FUTH jointly petitioned Congress for a reform of the labor code to effectively bar solidarity associations. In December of that year, *solidarismo* was dealt a severe blow when striking workers from the country's most powerful union, SITRATERCO at the United Brands-owned Tela Railroad Company, won their demand that management renounce its efforts to establish a parallel workers organization.[11] As of 1991, an estimated 10,000 workers belonged to solidarity associations.[12]

Schools and Students

Until the late 1950s education in Honduras was the exclusive privilege of those among the middle and upper classes who could afford to send their children to private schools. The reformist government of Ramón Villeda Morales (1957-63) introduced the concept of public education and began an ambitious school construction program. According to the Honduran Constitution, primary education (ages 7 to 14) is obligatory and free. Despite this constitutional guarantee, education remains a privilege in Honduras because of the lack of schools, the poor quality of public education, and the prohibitive cost of educational materials.

Illiteracy is widespread in Honduras, affecting more than 27 percent of the total population and 84 percent in rural areas.[13] A third of Hondurans have not received any formal schooling.[14] In many isolated areas of Honduras there are no accessible schools or, if available, instruction extends only through the third grade.

Of every ten children entering first grade, seven drop out by sixth grade. And of every 100 entering first grade, 19 drop out, 34 "fail" and have to repeat, and only 47 are allowed to move on to second grade. Of those 47, only 14 in rural areas (19 in the cities) actually finish primary school in the normal six years. Secondary education offers two tracks: *ciclo común*, vocational education, and *ciclo diversificado*, preparation for higher education. Only 30 percent of Honduran children who enter first grade eventually attend secondary schools, and of those only 8 percent continue to postsecondary institutions.[15]

Even when educational opportunities do exist, the quality of instruction is poor due to inadequate teacher training, low pay for teachers, outdated teaching methods, corrupt and unqualified administration, and lack of adequate buildings and teaching materials. The Honduran teachers' union has raised demands for a 400 percent increase in salary. Some teachers are not even paid regular wages but instead receive food as part of government food-for-work programs. Memorization is the chief (and often the only) form of instruction.

The National Autonomous University of Honduras (UNAH) is the cardinal higher-educational institution in the country. Founded in 1847, UNAH caters to some 30,000 students. University branches in San Pedro Sula and La Ceiba form the University Center of the North (CURLA). There are three private universities: the tiny José Cecilio del Valle University, established in Tegucigalpa in 1978; the Central American Technological University (UNITEC), founded in 1987 in Tegucigalpa; and the University of San Pedro Sula (USPS).

The U.S. Agency for International Development (AID) began funding USPS in the 1980s in order to "provide a political counterweight to the traditionally leftist-dominated National University." Through its grants, AID is shaping USPS as a business-oriented university with "curriculum emphasis in the skills areas most needed for improving Honduras' competitiveness in world markets: management, finance, international marketing, business law, and the physical and agricultural sciences." AID is also exploring the possibility of arranging a joint program with a U.S. university that "could also act as a 'brain trust' for Honduran industry through consulting work and research." [16] This support for USPS is consistent with other AID programs that promote the privatization of basic services like education and health.

In an evaluation of AID projects in Honduras, Philip Shepherd of Florida International University referred to the USPS project as "probably one of the worst, most politically charged and interventionist projects contemplated by AID at the present." Shepherd branded the project an "attempt to create, subsidize, and develop private university education for elites in Honduras" and added that "various AID project descriptions ooze with ethnocentric contempt for Latin American public university traditions of open admissions, free public higher education, and student-faculty activism." [17]

Privatization of Education

The new influence of private university education is intended to complement the key role of private schools in primary and secondary education. According to one estimate, the more than 800 private educational institutes in the country served 5 percent of primary school students, 50 percent of secondary students, and 3 percent of university students.[18]

The proliferation of private educational institutes is due in large part to the deficiencies and unavailability of public education. Although the private schools do fill the gap created by lack of government attention to education, these institutions have problems of their own. Private education is often viewed simply as a profit-making venture with little attention to quality or accessibility. Teachers at these schools are often paid a pittance while the directors and owners rake in large incomes from high student fees.

In late 1989 the Azcona administration introduced a measure in the National Congress that would allow the government to regulate the level of teachers' salaries and the monthly tuition of students. The proposed law met with strong resistance from the associations of private schools (FENIEPH) and Catholic schools (FENCEPCH), both of which denounced it as an infringement on free enterprise and an attempt to subject education to totalitarian rule. They were joined in their opposition by the Honduran Council of Private Enterprise (COHEP). Supporting the proposal was the COLPROSUMAH teachers' union, which argued that all teachers should receive a base salary and that they should be hired according to their qualifications, a bone of contention with private schools.

Student Organizing

Student organizing at UNAH is highly ideological, extremely divisive, and often violent. Until the early 1980s, leftist activists exercised strong influence over the student organizations and university council. The Reformist University Front (FRU) lost its influence after having become dogmatic and sectarian, eventually splitting into a pro-Moscow line (*los gordos*) and a maoist tendency (*los flacos*). The military, at that time under the command of Gen. Alvarez, also played an important role in fostering divisions and in precipitating the eventual downfall of FRU. As the influence of FRU declined, the void was filled by the Democratic University United Front (FUUD), a rightwing student organization with close ties to the new, conservative university administration. Appointed as university rector in the early 1980s was Oswaldo Ramos Soto, an associate of Gen. Alvarez and the secretary of the rightwing APROH (Association for the Progress of Honduras) coalition[19] (see Military). Ramos Soto, who served as FUUD coordinator until he resigned as UNAH rector in late 1987, was succeeded by Omar Casco, a rightwing ideologue linked by some popular organizations to death squads.[20]

Student elections at UNAH have long been vigorously contested; in the late 1980s they often degenerated into shooting and rock-throwing matches, with Molotov cocktails, tear gas, and grenades exchanged in confrontations among the polarized student factions. Leftist student organizations, FRU and the United Revolutionary Force (FUR), accused FUUD of electoral fraud and the use of armed force to maintain its hold on the university's official student bodies like the Federation of University Students (FEUH). In 1989 FUR's presidential candidate was seriously wounded by gunfire.[21] Leftist students however, have not, been the only victims of political violence at the national university. In mid-1989 a rightwing student leader was assassinated and a bomb destroyed FUUD headquarters. In late 1991, FUUD leader Raul Suazo was assassinated in an attack for which Honduran guerrillas later claimed responsibility, charging that Suazo was an informant working for the police. Revolutionary and progressive student groups have also fought among themselves. Nor has political violence been limited to the national university. Other educational institutions, like Francisco Morazán Superior Teachers School, have also been torn by conflicts between rightwing student leadership and leftist challengers.

An important progressive force at UNAH is the university's Workers Union (SITRAUNAH). The union has denounced repression at the university and maintains close ties with the CODEH human rights organization.

Communications Media

Francisco Morazán, the national hero of Honduras, is credited with having introduced the first printing press into the country in 1829 to publish his newspaper *La Gaceta*. Today the country has four daily newspapers, six television channels (only one broadcasts nationwide), and 152 radio stations.

The Electronic Media

Because of the high illiteracy and low income of the population, radio is the medium with the greatest outreach. There are over one million radios in the country with some 3.5 million weekly listeners.[22] The first radio station in the country was established in 1929 by the United Fruit Company in Tela. The two largest radio networks are both privately owned: HRN—The Voice of Honduras, by Emisoras Unidas of the Ferrary-Villeda family; and Radio América, a station often broadcasting news about worker and peasant issues, by the leader of the PINU political party. Both the Catholic Church and the evangelical community operate radio stations. Unlike the evangelical station, Radio Católica has little religious programming. Radio Honduras is the government station.

All television stations are privately owned and based either in San Pedro Sula or Tegucigalpa. Television was introduced in 1959, and about one-quarter of Hondurans own television sets. Emisoras Unidas dominates television broadcasting, as proprietor of channels 3, 5, and 7 in Tegucigalpa and channels 4 and 7 in San Pedro Sula. On the upswing are the channels of Vica Televisión ("Voz e Imagen de Centro América"), owned by the Sikaffy family and other business investors in San Pedro Sula.[23]

The Print Media

Tiempo, arguably the country's most influential daily in the urban areas, is owned by Jaime Rosenthal, a banker and a controversial vice-president during the Azcona government. Based in San Pedro Sula, *Tiempo* has a circulation of 32,000 and is the country's most liberal newspaper. Unlike the other papers, *Tiempo* has often criticized the military and police, and regularly publishes liberal opinion articles. Its editor, Manuel Gamero, has on occasion been jailed for his critiques of the military and police. Conservatives and military hardliners have branded the paper "communist." Even though *Tiempo* does regularly criticize the government and armed forces, its reporting still shows signs of self-censorship.

La Prensa (circulation 42,000) is also based in San Pedro Sula and has close links with the commercial and industrial interests of that city. Its editorial bent is conservative. Jorge Larach is the president and editor.

El Heraldo, based in Tegucigalpa and distributing 37,000 papers daily, is also owned by the Larach family. It too is conservative and often closely reflects the opinions of the military and the National Party.

La Tribuna, also based in the capital and with a circulation of 38,000, is owned by the Flores Facussé family and is linked to the new industrial sector of Tegucigalpa. *La Tribuna* reflects the opinions of the orthodox Liberal Party and is considered moderate and nationalistic in its editorial direction.

A variety of smaller periodicals round out the print media selection. For English speakers there is a weekly called *Tegucigalpa This Week*. AVANCE, a business group funded by the U.S. Agency for International Development (AID), publishes *El Agricultor*, a tabloid aimed at the peasant population. The Honduras Documentation Center (CEDOH), founded in 1980 and directed by Victor Meza, publishes a valuable monthly news bulletin called *Boletín Informativo* as well as a more lengthy magazine with analytical works, *Puntos de Vista*. The Committee for the Defense of Human Rights disseminates a monthly bulletin on human rights issues called *Boletín CODEH*. Honduras also produces several magazines, including the progressive *Presente*, the progressive literary review *Tragaluz*, the centrist business magazine *Cambio*, and the centrist review *Prisma*. The government publishes official decrees and speeches in *La Gaceta*.

Quality of the News

Repression, self-censorship, dependence on U.S. sources and programming, an environment of corruption and payoffs, poor technical quality, and control of the media by oligarchic interests all help explain the relatively poor state of news reporting in Honduras. The widespread practice of self-censorship was described this way by Honduran poet Roberto Sosa: "In Honduras open censorship does not exist, but rather a more subtle form of censorship: self-censorship. Honduran reporters have not actually disappeared. But they have disappeared as thinking and inquisitive journalists, and this is worse. They are like zombies." [24]

Media owners and journalists are careful not to cross an invisible line of what can and cannot be reported, especially about the military. Of the major media, *Tiempo* has been the most daring in treading the fine line between what is permissible and not permissible. One ex-columnist for *Tiempo* described this invisible line: "Every reporter knows the limit of the truth of the owners and has to write within those limits. It is a very sophisticated system and the hardest part is to see it. It is more difficult than official censorship, although the results are the same." [25] *Tiempo's* Gamero elucidated: "Honduras isn't like Guatemala or El Salvador where the repression is of a different magnitude. In our country, the methods of repression are tolerable, relatively speaking. The problem that exists is that there is much manipulation of the press by the government and the private sector. Neither of those sectors believes that the public has the right to be informed." [26]

When journalists do cross the line they are subject to arrest, harassment, blacklisting, violence, and, in the case of foreign reporters, deportation. After Rodrigo Wong Arevalo, the director of Radio América, aired a series of editorials opposing the contras in 1986, a car bomb exploded outside his house. Other Honduran reporters have been arrested and threatened by military intelligence. But the most common forms of punishment are firing or blacklisting. According to the Council on Hemispheric Affairs: "Virtually every news organization as well as the *Colegio de Periodistas* (association of reporters) has yielded to government pressure to adhere to an official blacklist of journalists, preventing dissident members of the press from practicing their craft." [27] During the 1980s, several foreign journalists were deported or denied permission to enter the country, usually for having published material critical of the military.

Low pay for journalists contributes to a corrupt system in which reporters regularly receive gifts and bribes from government, businesses, and other institutions seeking favorable reporting. Beginning reporters receive only $250 monthly, while veterans may earn twice as much. Gratuities and payoffs from the government are quite common. This does not preclude occasional criticism of the government, but rather ensures very little follow-up or investigative reporting.[28]

The pervasive U.S. influence in the Honduran media is a product not only of heavy reliance on U.S. news services and television programming but also of the United States Information Service (USIS). Operating at the U.S. embassy, the USIS disseminates a daily array of wireless file material and radio and television programming. Included among its information services are five weekly half-hour programs for 23 radio stations.[29]

The State of Health

The country's deadening poverty is reflected in its deteriorating state of health (Figure 4a). According to the Pan American Health Organization (PAHO), health conditions in Honduras are among the worst in the hemisphere, and a 1989 study by the United Nations Children's Fund (UNICEF) revealed that malnutrition among Honduran children has deteriorated even further in the last two decades.[30] It is estimated that at least 12,000 Honduran children die each year—about 33 daily—from preventable illnesses. The UNICEF study determined that 25 percent of Honduran families suffer from protein deficiency, 70 percent experience inadequate iron intake, and 62 percent exhibit calorie deficiency.[31]

Widespread malnutrition and the lack of access to potable water and sanitation facilities are the main factors in the country's low life expectancy (66 years) and high infant mortality (59 per 1,000 live births according to official estimates,[32] and 157 per thousand in rural areas according to a January 1989 report by the country's teaching hospital).[33] Only one-third of Hondurans have easy access to potable water and 50 percent do not have even the most rudimentary system for human waste disposal.[34]

So widespread is malnutrition that the main public hospital in Tegucigalpa accepts only third-degree or severe cases. In the malnutrition ward at that hospital, between 10 and 15 children die each month. "And you have to realize," deplored Judith Castigo, in charge of the ward, "that the most desperate children never make it to the hospital. Those are the ones whose families don't have the bus fare to get to the capital, or the 50 cents for the doctor's visit. They die quietly in their homes." [35] According to a survey conducted by the Ministry of Health, a full 63 percent of all Hondurans suffer some degree of malnutrition.[36]

In several areas of the country, severe malnutrition affects a quarter of the children entering first grade.[37] In rural areas 77 percent of the population simply cannot afford the food necessary to provide itself with minimal nutritional requirements.[38] Malnutrition, which had subsided in the 1960s and 1970s, climbed again in the 1980s. Dr. Fidel Barahona, a Ministry of Public Health official, warned in 1988 that rising malnutrition would cause coming generations of Hondurans to be mentally and physically less developed.[39]

Figure 4a
Social Indicators

Demographics

Population (1992)	5.5 million[a]
Fertility rate (1993)	4.9 children born per woman[c]
Population density (per sq km)	48.7[a]
Population living in urban areas (1992)	45% (1990)[d]
Population under 16 years old (1991)	51% (1990)[d]

Health

Infant mortality rate (1993)	59 per 1,000[c]
Maternal mortality per 100,000 live births	220[d]
Life expectancy (1993)	66 years[c]
Population growth rate (1993)	2.9%[c]
Children less than five years old underweight (1990)	19.8%[d]
Infants underweight at birth (1990)	9%[d]

Education

Adult literacy (1990)	76% (males); 71% (females)[d]

Poverty

Population living in poverty (1990)	73% (urban); 79% (rural)[b]
Population without access to safe water (1988-90)	44% (urban); 51% (rural)[d]
Population without access to health facilities (1987-90)	38%[d]

SOURCES: [a] Inter-American Development Bank, "Basic Socio-Economic Data," January 1994. [b] Comisión Económica para América Latina y el Caribe (CEPAL), "Bases para la transformación productiva y generación de ingresos de la población pobre de los países del istmo centroamericano," January 1992. [c] U.S. A.I.D., *Latin America and the Caribbean: Selected Economic and Social Data,* Washington, DC, 1993. [d] Bread for the World, *Hunger 1994: Transforming the Politics of Hunger,* Silver Spring, MD, 1993 [e] Honduran Health Ministry, cited in "Central America Report," February 15, 1991. [f] *Regional Surveys of the World: South America, Central America and the Caribbean, 1991* (London: Europa Publications Limited, 1990). [g] The Economist Intelligence Unit, "Country Profile: Guatemala, El Salvador, Honduras, 1991-92."

Infectious and parasitic diseases are the leading causes of death in Honduras. According to the Ministry of Health, gastritis, enteritis, and tuberculosis are the country's main health problems. Health care is out of financial or geographic reach for most Hondurans. In the most isolated rural areas there are no doctors or nurses. Although government health clinics do exist, they are often little more than empty buildings without medicines or medical equipment. The government's Health Ministry recognizes that it is only able to reach about 60 percent of its targeted population with primary health care.[40] According to one report, only 5 percent of Honduran women have had Pap smears—and of these 90 percent registered some abnormality.[41]

Alcoholism and drug addiction are major health concerns in Honduras. At least 6,000 Hondurans belong to a narrow category of alcoholics (known as *pachangueros*) who drink a dangerous mixture of water and straight alcohol. Thousands of Honduran youth are glue addicts. According to a government mental health doctor, as many as 150 children die each year from inhaling a widely advertised brand of glue called Resistol.

The first known Honduran victim of AIDS died in May 1985, and the death toll as of May 1992 stood at 551. By mid-1992 over 1,800 cases of the disease had been registered, and health authorities estimate that as many as 70,000 Hondurans are HIV carriers. An estimated 40 percent of all AIDS cases in Honduras, representing about one-fourth of all cases in Central America, have been registered in San Pedro Sula.

Most AIDS cases reported thus far have been among heterosexuals. Many Hondurans place the blame for the spread of AIDS on the influx of U.S. soldiers. Although prostitution has boomed around Soto Cano Air Base (formerly Palmerola) where U.S. troops are stationed, the country's poor health conditions and lack of education are probably the primary reasons for the rapid spread of the fatal infection. As Dr. José Enrique Zelaya, chairperson of the National AIDS Commission, explained: "Problems related to poverty and lack of health maintenance mean AIDS is hitting a population that is already weak." [42] According to PAHO statistics, Honduras—with an average AIDS incidence of 99.8 per million—exhibits a rate over four times that of the rest of Latin America.[43]

Another factor in the spread of AIDS may be the repeated use of disposable needles. Rather than going to a doctor, poor Hondurans often pay 50 cents to those advertising "Injections Applied." Nurses and hospital aides are known to collect disposable syringes and needles from hospital trash baskets to take home to use in their moonlighting businesses.[44]

A cholera epidemic hit Honduras in late 1991, and by mid-1992 over 100 people had been diagnosed with the disease. Due to generally poor sanitation conditions, officials feared that the disease would eventually take root and spread nationwide.

Honduras suffers at once from both a proliferation and a shortage of medicines. Estimates by the Ministry of Public Health show that over 17,000 medicines are available in the country, but a random sampling by a research team at the national university found that only 61 percent of the medicines encountered at pharmacies were of any value. The report concluded that the Honduran market was flooded with ineffective and unapproved products dumped by U.S. and European producers. According to the World Health Organization, 300 drugs are sufficient to treat most health problems. The flood of foreign medicines often induces pharmacists into prescribing drugs that are untested and potentially harmful.[45]

A more pressing problem, however, is the lack of medicines in public health facilities. The ever-worsening foreign-exchange crisis combined with austerity measures have resulted in less money available to import needed drugs. Even when hospitals do have medical supplies, they quickly disappear due to the widespread practice of stealing drugs from government health care facilities to sell to private drugstores.[46]

The most acute health concerns include the lack of access to medical services and the limited reach of social security. The Ministry of Health has concluded that only 11 percent of the population is protected by the Honduran Institute of Social Security—despite constitutional guarantees of health care and social security services.[47]

Religion

The Roman Catholic Church is the oldest and most powerful religious institution in Honduras. The arrival in 1521 of Franciscan missionaries beside the Spanish conquistadores won the church its early foothold.[48] Although the Catholic Church has enjoyed more than four and a half centuries in Honduras, it has never developed into an indigenous institution. Instead, it is one of the most foreign-dependent churches in Latin America. A symptom of this external dependence is the large number of expatriate clerics—of the some 292 priests working in Honduras, only about 70 are natives.[49]

The first major challenge to the church's institutional power arose from the country's emergent political forces in 1821—the year the region won independence from Spain.[50] Tense relations persisted until a rapprochement in 1838 eased tensions between the church and the political elite. But by the 1880s the church was once again under attack. The Liberal Party, gaining momentum throughout Central America, set out to dismantle the feudal-like power of the Catholic Church by stripping away its traditional economic and social privileges and by establishing the legal separation of church and state. While substantially weakened, Catholicism nonetheless remained the semiofficial religion of Honduras.

For the Catholic Church, the last three decades have been a time of rapid change and constant challenge. In the late 1950s the Catholic hierarchy, encouraged by the Vatican, launched a concerted effort to consolidate and strengthen the institutional church. In 1959 the church hierarchy called for an ambitious evangelization campaign to transform into practicing Catholics the large number of Hondurans until then only culturally tied to the Catholic faith.

The plea emanated from the Vatican to churches throughout the world to send missionaries and financial assistance to Honduras. Priests, brothers, and nuns from the United States, Spain, Canada, and France arrived in Honduras to perform this mission of church-building and evangelization. By the late 1960s the number of dioceses had tripled, most of them presided over by foreign-born bishops. The new missionaries discovered a nation of deeply religious people, but for most Hondurans, superstition and magic were at least as important to their faith as externally imposed church dogma.

Prior to the call to evangelize, the social assistance programs of the Catholic Church were disjointed and not linked to any broad vision of social change. Local parishes did sponsor various charitable programs, but there was no institutional commitment to social assistance and community welfare programs. Catholic Social Action handled individual charity cases but did little to address the structural causes of poverty and hunger.

When the church expanded into rural areas, it found a sea of illiteracy, poverty, and disease. As part of its evangelism, the church tackled these tough socioeconomic problems with reading and social service programs. To a large extent, the church's interest in improving *campesino* literacy was a direct outgrowth of its attempt to teach its catechism to the rural poor.

Social Welfare and Anticommunism

The rising interest of the Catholic Church in social assistance programs coincided with the installation in Tegucigalpa of the reformist government of President Ramón Villeda Morales (1957-63). Although humanitarian concerns certainly constituted a large part of this new church and government interest in social welfare, anticommunism was the main motivating factor. Economic growth and unprecedented popular organizing in the 1950s and early 1960s indicated that Honduran society was changing rapidly. Those sitting in the traditional seats of power wanted to be sure not to lose control of the social situation. Both the church and the government regarded social reforms and community development programs as doses of preventive medicine against the disease of communism.

The progressive government of Jacobo Arbenz in Guatemala and the 1954 strike against United Fruit sparked fears of the possible rise of a leftist-inspired revolution in Honduras. Worries among the church hierarchy about the advance of communism in Central America were heightened by the triumph of Castro's guerrilla forces in Cuba in 1959. Encouraged by the Vatican, the bishops resolved to combat both this perceived communist threat and the growing secularization of society. Programs were thus established to lure workers and peasants back into a revitalized church.

In the 1960s the Catholic Church and the incipient Social Christian movement began wooing the poor with messages of liberal reform, social betterment, and anticommunism. In 1961 the church began to play a prominent role in the promotion of *campesino* leagues, community development cooperatives, and other nongovernmental groups. The church hierarchy established such organizations as CARITAS, the Popular Cultural Action of Honduras (ACPH), and Radio Católica.

Foreign missionaries had enabled the hierarchy to establish new dioceses and parishes, but the shortage of indigenous clergy persisted. To fill this gap, the church turned to lay workers; many new lay societies like the Legion of Mary and the Christian Family Movement were established in the 1960s. A lay catechist movement called the Celebrants of the Word was formed to spread the dogma of the Catholic Church to communities seldom visited by clergy.

Although the church hierarchy did become acutely concerned about socioeconomic issues, prelates always tried to keep the social programs closely linked to religious agendas. Institutional stability and growth were always among their paramount objectives.

Three Trends: The Institutional, Developmentalist, and Prophetic Church

The Catholic Church is not a monolithic institution. Within the church are numerous ideological tendencies and geographical divisions. Gustavo Blanco and Jaime Valverde in their book *Honduras: Iglesia y Cambio Social* describe three major tendencies that have evolved within the Catholic Church since the late 1950s: the hierarchical church, the developmentalist church, and the prophetic or socially committed church. While each tendency or sector is distinct, none is exclusive, and each of the three trends has gone through periods of dominance and decline.[51]

The hierarchical or institutional church aims to consolidate itself as a strong institution tied to the international church based in Rome. During the 1960s and early 1970s the developmentalist and prophetic tendencies within the church became more dominant.

The developmentalist sector was heavily influenced by the political and economic vision of President Kennedy's Alliance for Progress and by reformist factions within the Honduran military. Within the church, developmentalist lay workers and clergy not only tended to the spiritual needs of their congregations but also assisted them materially by promoting self-help organizations such as cooperatives and housewives' clubs.

Although poor Hondurans were the focus of church-related development programs, poverty in Honduras was perceived to be more a result of lack of education and opportunity than the result of rigid class divisions and unjust social structures. To improve the underdeveloped state of rural communities, the developmentalists advocated such nonconfrontational and legal measures as the formation of savings cooperatives, better education, technical assistance, improved government social services, enforcement of agrarian-reform laws, and frontier settlement programs for the landless. The salient characteristics of this developmentalism were foreign aid, community organizing, and adherence to Christian principles.

Not all developmentalists, however, were satisfied with this reformist approach to social problems. Within the church's developmentalist sector, many *campesino* leaders and clergy adopted a more radical focus. They perceived the limits of developmentalism and felt that more profound changes were needed in order to produce true economic and social development in Honduras. They defined the country's problems in terms of institutionalized class rule by the wealthy, and they enthusiastically adopted the findings of the Medellín Bishops Conference in 1968, which advocated the church's "option for the poor." In doing so, this segment of the church—known in Honduras and elsewhere in Central America as the prophetic church—became closely committed to the demands of *campesino* and worker organizations. The prophetic church was also characterized by its strong denunciations of both military repression and economic exploitation of the poor. The prophetic tendency (at its zenith in the 1967-75 period) was closely identified with the theology of liberation and spurred the growth of the *iglesia popular* (popular church), centered around Christian base communities and such activist clergy as Father Guadalupe Carney. The popular church in Honduras, however, never achieved the size or influence of its counterparts in neighboring Nicaragua or El Salvador.

The "Shock of Olancho"

The contradictions among the three different tendencies of the church—hierarchical, developmentalist, and prophetic—were most clearly revealed in the department of Olancho. Tended by a North American bishop, the Olancho diocese was the paragon of the church's commitment to an "option for the poor." It was in Olancho, as well, that the private-sector elite mounted its strongest opposition to the growing popular movement.

The 1972 military slaying of six *campesinos* participating in a UNC land takeover signaled the beginning of the repression against the popular movement and the prophetic church. Three years later, in May 1975, the large landowners and their vigilantes lashed out with unprecedented brutality at the local church and *campesino* movement, leaving ten *campesinos*, two female students, and two priests dead.

For the military government and FENAGH (Federation of Honduran Farmers and Ranchers), the "shock of Olancho" achieved the desired effect. While the church hierarchy did denounce the repression in Olancho, it also reduced its commitment to social justice issues after 1975. The 1975 massacre was a severe blow to the budding popular church and to the growing popular organizations in Olancho and other parts of the country. The attacks were not isolated incidents but formed part of a mounting, calculated repression against the popular church. Foreign priests were expelled, others were arrested, and Catholic radio stations and *campesino* centers were forced to close.

The "shock of Olancho" not only undermined the prophetic or socially committed sector of the church but also debilitated the developmentalist faction by intimidating it from engaging in even the most nonconfrontational type of social action. After 1975 the church hierarchy pulled back from its former commitment to such social justice issues as land reform. It also retracted its commitment to lay organizations affiliated with the institutional church, like the Celebrants of the Word. At the same time that it was disavowing socially active lay groups, the hierarchy was revitalizing spiritualist lay organizations like the Charismatic Renewal Movement and the Movement of the New Catacombs. To a large degree, these retreats were defensive measures adopted to protect the institution in the face of growing persecution. But the church hierarchy also capitalized on the incidents in Olancho as a way to isolate the popular church and its more radical vision of social change.

After the Olancho massacre the institutional church emphasized its moderating role in Honduran society and shied away from endorsing the causes of popular organizations. It sought once again to establish cordial relations with the state in the interests of its own stability and standing within society. The years 1975 to 1981 witnessed the fading of the prophetic tendency among church leaders and the suppression of the popular church. It was a time, too, when social reforms were throttled by military governments more concerned about promoting economic growth and aiding the private sector than about dealing with pressing social issues.

The church also withdrew from the aggressive developmentalism that had characterized some of its more prominent social programs. Gone were the demands for structural change in Honduran society and the emphasis on popular community organization. Developmentalism remained a part of the church in the 1980s, but its community development programs often resembled the small-business and productive-enterprise programs promoted by AID and other international donors. After Olancho, the institutional church retreated to the safe and paternalistic handout programs sponsored by CARITAS and the Christian Family Movement.

A Voice for Social Justice

As social circumstances degenerated in Honduras in the late 1980s and early 1990s, the church revived its criticisms of the government. Once again there were signs that the prophetic or socially committed faction was on the upswing within the Catholic Church.

Although the church hierarchy has generally adopted a conciliatory role, it was spurred to more critical positions in the 1980s. An early break with the Suazo government was precipitated by the emergence of APROH (Association for the Progress of Honduras), an organization dedicated to creating a new rightwing ideological front in Honduras to support U.S. foreign economic and military policy. APROH was headed by military strongman Gen. Alvarez Martínez and received funds and other assistance from CAUSA, a political arm of Reverend Sun Myung Moon's Unification Church. The government's acceptance of this new private organization and the role of the Unification Church greatly angered Catholic bishops.

Another factor prompting the Catholic Church to assume a more critical posture was the arrival of refugees from Guatemala and El Salvador. The diocese of Santa Rosa de Copán denounced the Honduran military's repression of this refugee population, and the local bishop assumed part of the responsibility of caring for the Salvadoran refugees, with CARITAS providing food and other services. The Refugee Committee of the diocese played a key role in focusing national and international attention on the situation. The killing of two CARITAS workers by the Honduran security forces drove the national church hierarchy to condemn the repressive conditions in the country.

The slumping economic conditions in the country, a renewed militarism fueled by the United States, and the failure of the Suazo and Azcona governments to address the needs of the nation's poor were other factors inciting the institutional church to become more outspoken about social issues in the 1980s. The creation of groups within the church like the Christian Movement for Justice and the continuing experience of the clergy in rural areas also nudged the church into assuming a more socially committed role in Honduran society.

Gradually, during the 1980s, the bishops escalated their denunciations of the government and military—but always as diplomatically as possible. At the same time, though, the bishops denounced purported links between the popular church and marxists, a posture that tended to fortify the military's own campaign against leftist dissidents. Although critical of the growing repression in Honduran society, the institutional church was careful always to align itself with anticommunism.

Foreign clergy and financing, both from the United States and Europe, have been essential in the rise of the developmentalist and socially committed church in Honduras. Jesuit priests in Yoro and Colón, for example, have played a critical role in popular-education efforts. Accountable to their own vicariate, these foreign clergy (from Spain and the United States) have enjoyed some measure of autonomy from the generally more conservative Honduran hierarchy. Foreign clergy in Honduras, however, have occasionally found themselves subject to deportation by the military. Progressive and popular priests, both foreign and native, have been increasingly targeted for transfers outside the country or to other more conservative or less politically volatile areas.

Protestant Churches and the New Evangelicals

In the 1980s evangelical churches and organizations emerged not only as a major religious sector but also as the sponsors of many social service programs. Evangelical groups, most of which receive U.S. supplies and financing, have also exerted a significant conservative political influence within Honduras.

Among the first evangelical missionaries in the country were Anglicans of the Society of the Gospel in Foreign Parts, who began preaching on the North Coast in the 1870s. During the 19th century, Protestant missionary efforts focused on the English-speaking inhabitants of the North Coast, La Mosquitia, and the Bay Islands. The British influence along the Atlantic Coast facilitated the development of Protestant churches in this region, as did the expanding banana trade with the United States around the turn of the century.

Eventually the traditional Protestant churches extended their mission to the country's interior, though maintaining their strongest bases on the Atlantic side of Honduras. Faith missions from the United States like the Central American Mission helped spread evangelical beliefs of a fundamentalist character throughout Honduras. On a national level, it was not until the 1950s and the 1960s that the evangelical church community began to gain a foothold in this Catholic country.

The rise of evangelicalism presents a major threat to the stability and growth of the Catholic Church. To a certain extent, renewed

Catholic emphasis on lay organizations with a spiritual focus constitutes an effort to counteract the growing appeal of the evangelical churches. Catholic charismatics and spiritualist groups highlight the personal relationship of man to God and the key role of the Holy Spirit. This stress on individualistic faith and salvation resembles that of the evangelical churches.

Occasionally, the bishops excoriate the *evangélicos* (Protestants) for their simplistic approach to religious faith and for their reactionary politics. But in doing so they often lump all evangelicals together—both mainline and pentecostal—thereby exhibiting a superficial understanding of the Protestant community. The failure of the Catholic Church to address its own weaknesses contributes to its apparent inability to respond adequately to challenges presented by the evangelical movement in Honduras.

Hurricane Fifi in 1974 ushered in a new wave of evangelical missionaries, mostly from the United States. Until then, the evangelical community consisted largely of traditional Protestant denominations like the Baptists, the Adventists, and fundamentalist mission churches. The membership of Pentecostal churches like the Assemblies of God and Church of God swelled in the 1970s, and the country began receiving an influx of neopentecostal missionaries, churches, and organizations. Since 1980, pentecostals have set the direction and pace of the evangelical movement. Jimmy Swaggart and Pat Robertson—both of whom have visited Honduras several times—have contributed greatly to evangelical growth through their teleministries.

Between 1978 and 1985 the number of evangelicals in Honduras doubled, and as of 1988 approximately 12 percent of Hondurans professed to be evangelicals.[52] Only a small number of these belong to mainline liturgical Protestant denominations like the Lutherans. Most adhere to fundamentalist evangelical bodies like the Church of God and the Assemblies of God or are members of evangelical pentecostal denominations. The balance of the non-Catholic Christian community belongs to religious groups like the Adventists and the Quakers.

Today the largest evangelical congregations in the country are the Assemblies of God, the Southern Baptists, and the Central American Mission. Most evangelical churches in Honduras are closely linked to U.S. denominations and groups, although churches based in Guatemala and El Salvador are also quickly gaining influence.

Free Food and Bibles

Evangelical churches usually operate social-assistance programs in conjunction with their religious ministries. Most efforts involve education, medical care, and food distribution. These programs are part of what many evangelicals call integral evangelism—the combination of material assistance and spiritual guidance. Humanitarian assistance by evangelicals normally comes hand in hand with Bibles. This assistance—medicine, used clothes, food, toys, and vitamins—flows from a wide variety of evangelical relief organizations including Larry Jones' Ministries, MAP International, World Concern, World Opportunities International, Friends of the Americas, and Pat Robertson's Operation Blessing. This evangelical humanitarian aid is generally shipped to Honduras on banana boats (courtesy of Standard Fruit and United Brands) or on U.S. military planes (according to the provisions of the Denton Amendment, which allows humanitarian assistance to be shipped on military aircraft on a space-available basis).

World Vision plays a key role in fomenting the growth of evangelical churches and in integrating social work with evangelizing. The group recognizes the close link between evangelical growth and the ability of evangelical organizations to respond in some fashion to the weighty socioeconomic realities of Honduras. In a recent analysis of the country, World Vision concluded that Honduras remained poor and underdeveloped because of the self-interested behavior of large landowners, business elites, and political bureaucrats.[53] It encourages evangelical churches to become more politically and socially active, noting the resistance of many evangelicals to involve themselves in secular affairs. This call by World Vision for more social and political involvement by evangelicals is part of a regional trend. Rather than isolating themselves from political issues, many evangelicals are setting up programs for displaced persons and even forming political parties. The sudden emergence in Guatemala of an evangelical chief of state in 1982 fueled this trend.

There seems to be little real interest, however, in addressing structural economic problems in the society. The common belief among most evangelicals is that the serious social and economic problems in Honduras are the work of Satan. During his Honduras crusade, Jimmy Swaggart blamed that "shadowy entity" for guerrilla war and poverty in Central America. "Sin is the cause of your problems," he harangued the listening multitude, "Sin is the cause of your pain." Instead of attacking the social causes of Honduran poverty and injustice, evangelical churches try to allay the symptoms with handout programs while preaching their message of personal salvation.

Most churches conduct their own assistance programs, and many also rely on teams of evangelical health workers and other religious volunteers to implement their charitable works. Politically sensitive areas like La Mosquitia are saturated with such volunteer teams, most of whose members have minimal language skills or experience in third world countries. Evangelical teams from the United States also build churches, lead crusades, and direct seminars throughout Honduras.

There is, however, a sector of progressive evangelical organizations concerned about social justice issues and advocating ecumenism. The Christian Development Commission (CCD), for example, has a reputation for effective, community-based development work. It is also true that although the hierarchy of most evangelical churches is very conservative, evangelical pastors on the local level are more concerned about social justice issues.

Nongovernmental Organizations

Largely because of the country's strategic role in U.S. foreign policy in the 1980s, there was a rapid rise in nongovernmental organizations (NGOs) involved in development, refugee relief, business promotion, and social service operations. Between 1980 and 1990, the number of NGOs in Honduras tripled, and most of this flood was composed of U.S. private and church organizations funded by the U.S. government.[54] Nowhere in Central America was the U.S.-linked boom of NGOs so pronounced as in Honduras during the 1980s.

This upsurge in private groups is most noticeable in Tegucigalpa. Green-and-black *Misión Internacional* license plates abound, expatriates frequent a new strip of high-priced clubs and restaurants along Morazán Boulevard, and English-speaking evangelicals are propagating missions in poor and rich neighborhoods alike.

Until 1975 most NGOs were linked to the Catholic Church or the Social Christian movement and provided education or training for organized community groups and mass organizations. These few (but highly influential) organizations largely shared a common understanding that poor Hondurans suffered from structural injustices in society. Solutions were sought not via charity but through community organizing.

In the 1960s and early 1970s several NGOs financed by the U.S. Agency for International Development (AID) also began operating in Honduras. These organizations were mostly involved in providing technical assistance, channeling credit, distributing food, or in the case of the American Institute for Free Labor Development (AIFLD) trying to establish a strong, conservative, pro-U.S. labor sector. Starting in 1962, AIFLD worked through the National Association of Honduran Peasants (ANACH) and the Confederation of Honduran Workers (CTH). Later, AID funds were also channeled to the Federation of Honduran Agrarian Reform Cooperatives (FECORAH) and to the National Campesino Union (UNC), historically one of the more militant of rural organizations.

AID-Funded Boom

The meteoric rise in the number of NGOs operating in Honduras during the 1980s was largely attributable to AID. In fact, it is now difficult to find Honduran NGOs that do not receive AID funds. Dozens of local groups have been created with AID funding, while many U.S.-based NGOs have also opened offices in Honduras. Additional AID support for private voluntary organizations (PVOs) in the 1980s mirrored the agency's stated commitment to the privatization of development work.

AID contends that it supports NGOs because they are a way to promote pluralism in Honduran society and because private groups are more efficient than government agencies. One common concern in Honduras is that AID itself is defining the boundaries of this pluralism. Most AID development funds flow to groups that focus on entrepreneurship, export production, or paternalistic community development. Excluded from AID's funding programs are grassroots peasant associations, militant trade unions, progressive development organizations, and human rights groups. In fact, many of these popular organizations, which receive most of their funding from Europe, would reject AID support even if it were offered because of their sharp disagreements with AID's political and economic objectives.

AID does direct some money to rural cooperatives, mostly earmarked for programs designed to increase export-oriented production and to improve administrative capabilities. In one case near Tela, AID encouraged a group of small farmers associated with ANACH to grow chili peppers for export. Promised by AID that markets were available, the small growers toiled at chili production for two years only to discover upon attempting to export their locally unmarketable crop that there were no foreign buyers.

Since 1980 AID has been responsible for the creation of at least ten organizations designed to promote the interests of the private business sector, particularly those entrepreneurs and investors involved in export production. AID also funds established business chambers like the Honduran-American Chamber of Commerce (see U.S. Economic Aid). The agency also contracts with U.S. organizations like Winrock International and the National Rural Electric Cooperative Association for technical assistance to the Honduran government and other NGOs.

Although most of AID's support for private groups flows to business organizations and chambers of commerce, AID has also directed funds to an array of service and development groups. AID dollars have resulted in the rapid expansion of a small umbrella organization for Honduran NGOs called FOPRIDEH (Federation of Private Development Organizations of Honduras). Most AID funding for FOPRIDEH is apportioned to projects that assist microentrepreneurs. Although Honduran NGOs attempt to maintain some degree of independence, AID's control over FOPRIDEH's finances ties these NGOs to Washington's apron strings and aligns them with AID's development philosophy.

It is difficult to escape the web of financing spun by AID. Known as the bountiful "*Señora Aida*" by some NGOs, the agency disburses money to most government agencies and almost all NGOs. The military also receives AID funds through civic-action programs and through the Permanent National Emergency Committee's (COPEN) disaster-assistance program. In many cases, government agencies and NGOs do not even know they are using AID money because it comes in the form of *lempiras* channeled through the government's Central Bank. "Everywhere you go you are offered funds which turn out to be Economic Support Funds local currency," exclaimed one NGO director. Independence vis-à-vis AID is a concern among some NGOs. A director of one of the few NGOs not accepting AID funds put it this way: "Our country is very weak now. We are being manipulated by the United States, and find ourselves just waiting for gifts from the outside." Another NGO representative asserted that the paternalistic and handout nature of AID assistance is not working: "Each day the poverty and underdevelopment are getting worse. The aid is not even keeping up with the growth in poverty and unemployment. The problem is that AID is not interested in funding groups that want to change the system in Honduras; they just want to hand out pills to deaden the pain." [55]

Significantly, it is generally only those NGOs that do not receive AID money that have maintained ties to and work closely with the more progressive and independent peasant, worker, and community organizations. These NGOs rely mostly on funding from Europe, Canada, or nongovernmental groups in the U.S. and they insist that development work must be done in association with self-organized poor people's organizations.

The direction of development projects sponsored by NGOs in the 1980s correlated closely with their independence from the government and AID. Only a small number of NGOs in Honduras still espouse the development priorities prominent in the 1960s and 1970s. Instead of pressing for peasant leadership training, cooperative formation, and integral popular education, during the 1980s most NGOs in Honduras tended to stress such values as profitability, competitiveness, individual enterprise, and marketability.

Women and Feminism

Throughout Central and South America, women are generally consigned to inferior status and Honduras is no exception. Statistics reveal the severity of this social discrimination. Only 44 percent of children in primary school are female, and about 40 percent of Honduran women have received no schooling.[56] Of high school and university graduates, only 25 percent are women. Only 25 percent of the paid work force is female—yet almost half of all children are born to single mothers who head households.[57] As of the 1989 elections, women occupy only 9.4 percent of seats in Congress and only 6.2 percent of all mayorships. Of the top 54 Cabinet posts in the Callejas administration, only two were alloted to women, and only one of eight Supreme Court justices was a woman.[58]

Then there is another reality not adequately portrayed by statistics. In a society pervaded by base *machismo*, women are often regarded as little more than sexual prey and cheap labor. The daily newspapers feature pin-ups to help sales, and the political parties show seminude women dancing to help promote their candidates. Sexual abuse and rape of young girls by male family members and neighbors is common. Indeed in many poor urban *barrios* few girls make it beyond their early teens without becoming sexual victims.

Activist Elvia Alvarado depicts the lot of rural Honduran women: "We women work even harder than the men. We get up before they do to grind the corn and make *tortillas* and coffee for their breakfast. Then we work all day—taking care of the kids, washing clothes, ironing, mending our husbands' old rags, cleaning the house. We hike to the mountains looking for wood for cutting. We walk to the stream or the well to get water. We make lunch and bring it to the men in the field. And we often grab a hoe and help in the fields. We never sit still one minute." [59]

Irresponsible paternity is a common problem in Honduran society, particularly in rural areas. A study by the Overseas Education

Fund found that 41 percent of the homes in 29 Tegucigalpa neighborhoods were headed by women.[60] In rural Honduras, few women and men formally marry owing to the inordinate expense and the male-dominated culture. Peasant men commonly leave their wives and children to start new families elsewhere and only rarely feel responsible for the sustenance of all their offspring.

Fertility is the third highest in Latin America, and at least half of Honduran children are born out of wedlock.[61] Contraceptive use is low—practiced by only about one-third of the population—and abortion is illegal (as it is throughout Latin America with the exception of Cuba). Illegal abortions are available, but many poor women must resort to self-inflicted abortions.[62] Complications resulting from a botched abortion represent one of the five leading causes of female mortality in Honduras.[63] According to one report, 40 percent of all maternal deaths in Honduras are linked to medical problems arising from clandestine abortions.[64] One of the most common means of birth control is sterilization—which many women undergo without consulting their mates.

Legal protections against sex discrimination are not well-developed and only rarely enforced in Honduras, the last Latin American country to grant women the right to vote (in 1954). Single childless women have no adjudicative land rights, whereas all males over 16 years of age enjoy such rights. When a landowner dies, his land passes directly to his oldest son—not to his widow—unless otherwise arranged. The country's penal code exempts a husband of culpability in cases of assault, battery, and even murder if his wife is caught in an adulterous act.[65] Only in 1984 did the country's Family Code extend rights to children born out of wedlock, an important step in enforcing paternal responsibility.

Women's Organizing

Honduras has a long and proud history of women organizing for their rights.[66] The Women's Culture Society, founded in 1923, was the nation's first women's organization. With close links to the communist-led Honduran Union Federation, the society led the fight for political and economic rights for Honduran women, with a special focus on the families of banana and mine workers. It sponsored educational seminars and published the *Cultura de la Mujer* magazine. Visitación Padilla and Graciela García, the society's two leading figures, were among the country's major popular activists. García, a Salvadoran, lived in Honduras until her expulsion in 1944 for her long history of opposing the Carías dictatorship (1932-48).[67]

The Federation of Honduran Women's Associations was initiated in 1950 to lead the fight for women's suffrage. Largely an organization of middle-class and professional women, the federation was instrumental in securing the country's Family Code and operates a social service program to promote organizing projects by poor women.

The Honduran Federation of Peasant Women (FEHMUC), formed in 1978, is one of the few female peasant organizations in Latin America. FEHMUC evolved jointly from members of the rural Housewives' Clubs (CAC) within CARITAS, the Catholic Church's social service organization, and from the Social Christian peasant movement. Inspired by the "preferential option for the poor" tendency within the church, the CAC movement grew increasingly active in social justice issues. After the 1975 Olancho massacre and amidst mounting pressure against activist clergy, the Catholic Church retracted from many of its more committed social programs. At the same time, the more politically aware activists with the CAC were prodding their community organizations to sever ties with the Catholic Church and affiliate with the National Campesino Union (UNC), since many of them were wives of UNC members.[68]

At a 1978 conference organized by ex-CAC leaders, FEHMUC was conceived, and by the late 1980s comprised 294 women's groups in 13 of the 18 Honduran departments. Its purpose is to integrate peasant women into the social, economic, and political life of the nation. In support of its social service and educational programs, FEHMUC has received aid from the United Nations Voluntary Fund for Women (UNIFEM), the Inter-American Foundation (IAF), European foundations, CARE, and (most recently) AID.

Charging that FEHMUC was becoming increasingly conservative and classist, a left-leaning faction split off in 1987 and established the Council for Integrated Development of Peasant Women (CODIMCA). CODIMCA, which receives funding from progressive organizations in Europe, comprises some 100 women's groups engaged in small development and social service projects in Lempira and other departments. Among other things, the group promotes the use of traditional herbal medicine.[69]

Another women's organization, the Visitación Padilla Women's Peace Committee, is named after the founder of the Women's Culture Society. Padilla, a leftist peace activist in the 1920s, co-founded the *National Defense Bulletin*, which sparked popular opposition to the intervention of U.S. Marines in Honduras in 1924.[70] The committee protested the U.S. military build-up and contra presence in Honduras during the 1980s, and has petitioned the National Congress to enact legislation delineating legal penalties for violence and discrimination against women and children.

Several other women's groups are also active in Honduras. The League of Patriotic Honduran Women (LIMUPH), launched in 1988, works in the poor urban *barrios*. The Center for Women's Studies—Honduras (CEM-H), a university-based group, sponsors research on issues affecting women and publishes a bulletin called *Mujer*. An association of professional women called the Committee for the Defense of Women's Rights (CLADEM); an umbrella organization for about 25 women's groups known as the Federation of Honduran Women's Organizations (FAFH); and the Association of University Women all add their contribution to the overall effort by females to make their voices heard in a male-dominated society.

Ethnic Groups and Native People

To a large degree Honduras is an ethnically homogeneous society—the population being about 86 percent *mestizo*, or mixed indian and Spanish. Only 10 percent of Hondurans are pure indian, 2 percent are black, and 2 percent are Caucasian (Figure 4b). Spanish is the national language, although English creole, Carib, and Mayan dialects are also spoken. In the Bay Islands, La Ceiba, and other areas along the Atlantic Coast there is a small, black population that speaks either English or English creole. The main settlements on the island of Roatan, for example, are predominantly black. The Bay Islands are also inhabited by whites, some of whom claim to be descendants of Henry Morgan and other English pirates. These Antillean whites migrated to the Bay Islands in the 1830s from other Caribbean islands. There are also small communities of Arabs and Lebanese (deprecatingly called *turcos*), who play a major role in the country's business and industry.

The Garifuna or Black Caribs

Honduras has two different black ethnic groups. The Antillean blacks, who live on the Atlantic Coast and the Bay Islands, are descendants of laborers imported from Belize, the Cayman Islands, and Jamaica to work in the banana plantations. Sprinkled along the Atlantic Coast and among the Bay Islands are communities of Garifuna, formerly known as Black Caribs. They are the descendants of a mixture of African and Carib peoples on the island of St. Vincent in the Lesser Antilles. Resistance to British encroachment of their land base led to the Carib War of 1795. After the British prevailed, the entire Black Carib population was deported to Roatan Island, off the coast of Honduras.

The British had hoped that the nearly 1,700 Black Caribs who landed at Roatan would form a garrison to enhance British interests in the region, but the entire population "defected" to the Spanish and moved to the nearby port of Trujillo on the mainland. They soon established settlements along the coast from Belize to Cabo de Gracias a Dios in the Miskito and Sumu territory, where they engaged primarily in subsistence farming and fishing activities.[71]

The Garifuna avoided plantation labor during the banana boom of the 1930s, though many held good jobs as stevedores in the ports. During World War II, many Garifuna served in the merchant marine—evidence of their high reputation as seamen. Some parts of the Atlantic Coast of Honduras are still accessible primarily by Garifuna canoes, now equipped with outboard motors. Fishing and farming have been waning as sources of income, with most Garifuna dependent on wage labor, remittances from family members who have migrated to the United States, or merchant marine pensions.[72] There are approximately 70,000 Garifuna in Honduras, most of them quite poor.[73] A growing ethnic pride and consciousness, especially among young, educated Garifuna, is reflected in the emergence of OFRANEH, the Black Fraternal Organization of Honduras, which struggles to overcome racial prejudice and class bias against the Garifuna and other blacks in Honduras. Most Garifuna, however, are not active in either social movements or political parties.[74]

The Amerindians

The indigenous population at the time of the Spanish conquest has been calculated at about 800,000, although other estimates range to 1.4 million or more.[75] Even before the conquest, the Mayan civilization was waning. The magnificent Copán religious and political center, for example, had been abandoned before the Spanish arrived. Estimates of the current Amerindian population in Honduras range from 157,000 to 450,000.[76]

Disease, massacres, debilitating work in the mines, and the Spanish slave trade were among the leading causes for the rapid decline of the native population. Some 30,000 to 50,000 indians were killed during the conquest, and tens of thousands later died from disease.[77] Leading the main resistance to the Spanish incursion was Lenca Chief Lempira, who was finally killed in 1539.

As many as 150,000 indians, particularly those living along the coast, were enslaved and exported to estates and mines in Guatemala, the Caribbean islands, Nicaragua, Panama, and Peru. Wishing to avoid this fate for their children, indians apparently induced miscarriages and practiced infanticide as well as abstention from sexual intercourse.

There are two general groups of Honduran indians: the settled agricultural communities of the West and the aboriginal indians of the northern lowlands. Of the former group, the most important tribe is the Lenca, the others being the Chorti, Chorotega, and Pipil. Although most speak Spanish, they still retain cultural and religious traits that set them apart from the dominant *mestizo* population.[78] The Pipils, living mainly in the isolated northern region of La Mosquitia and in parts of Olancho and Yoro, are sometimes called the forest indians. They include the Miskito, Pech (Paya), Rama, Sumu, and Jicaque (Torpán) tribes. Because they are so isolated they are less acculturated than those living in western Honduras.

Figure 4b
Ethnic Composition in Honduras

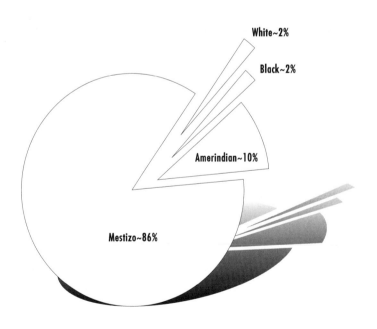

SOURCE: The Economist Intelligence Unit, "Country Profile: Guatemala, El Salvador, Honduras, 1991-92."

The Lenca inhabited the greater part of central Honduras at the time of the Spanish conquest, and today number about 50,000, concentrated in Intibucá, Lempira, and La Paz. The Chorti, a lowland Maya group, occupied the departments of Copán and Ocotepeque but migrated to the northern coast in the 17th and 18th centuries. Today the Chorti are almost extinct.[79] The Chorotega migrated south from Mexico and settled in Choluteca.

The Pipil indians came to Honduras in the 9th and 10th centuries, about the same time as the Chorotegas. The forest indians are related to the South American rainforest tribes. The Miskitos, numbering over 35,000, are the largest group of forest indians. Located in northeastern Honduras and across the border in Nicaragua, these Amerindians remained outside Spanish influence due to their isolated location.

The nearly 25,000 Miskito people of Honduras did not emerge as a distinct cultural-linguistic group until the mid-1600s. Closely related to the Sumu Indians, the Miskito people seem to have originally settled near Cabo de Gracias a Dios and then dispersed along the coast, displacing Pech and Sumu communities. Like the Miskitos, the few remaining communities of Sumu Indians were disrupted by the contra war during the 1980s. To avoid harassment, many Sumus have abandoned their language, leaving fewer than 1,000 ethnic Sumus divided into two subgroups—the Ulua and Tawahka. Most are subsistence farmers living along the Patuca River, and none have more than a sixth-grade education.[80]

At the time of the conquest, the Pech are believed to have inhabited as much as one-fourth of Honduras, but they have dwindled to between 700 and 1,800 persons, and are now confined to a few small communities in Olancho, Colón, Gracias a Dios, and Yoro. The Pech have resisted the national educational curriculum and have developed Pech language courses and Pech teachers. They have also battled against land grabbing by *mestizo* colonists and the National Agrarian Institute (INA).[81]

Ethnic Organizing

Indian people in Honduras have been organizing on a national level since the 1950s. The Autonomous Ethnic Organized Movement of Honduras was followed by the National Federation of Tribes for the Liberation of the Honduran Indian (FENATRILIH) and the Unity Committee of Indigenous People (CUPIH). Groups like FENATRILIH, founded in 1978, set out to improve the economic, political, and social conditions of the indian population with a special emphasis on protecting indian lands and facilitating agricultural credit and technical assistance.

Other organizations have attempted to form a national federation of all indian people to engage in political activity. The country's principal coordinating organization for these ethnic groups is the Honduran Advisory Council for Autonomous Ethnic Development (CAHDEA). Other individual groups include OFRANEH (Garifunas and other blacks), FETRIXY (Jicaque), ONILH (Lenca), MASTA (Miskito), FITH (Tawahka/Sumu), and FETRIPH (Pech).

Many issues concerning indian tribes as well as other ethnic minorities were discussed at the Third National Encounter of Ethnic Peoples in 1988. The conference, which assembled representatives from most indian tribes and Garifuna communities, demanded that the national government provide greater assistance to ethnic communities, especially in health care, education, and the building of rural access roads. While the ethnic groups represented at the conference were stressing the importance of maintaining their culture, they were also demanding that the government develop an immediate plan of action for the "total integration of this population into national life." [82] The conference also demanded a law by which "members of indigenous communities, as well as the Garifuna, be protected against political and religious intolerance, against socioeconomic exploitation, and racial discrimination." [83]

Refugees and the Internally Displaced

During the 1980s, Honduras was largely a host country rather than a source of refugees. Nicaraguans, Salvadorans, and Guatemalans all sought refuge in Honduras from the wars in their countries. In late 1991, Honduras announced its intention to sign both the 1952 Geneva Convention and the 1967 Protocol regarding refugees. Shortly thereafter, the government became one of the few in Latin America to offer a home to Haitian refugees, accepting a group of about 250 Haitians fleeing repression in the wake of the military coup there. Increasingly, however, Hondurans are leaving their country, mainly for economic reasons but also because of mounting human rights violations. One indication of this exodus is the growing number of Hondurans seeking political asylum in the United States.[84]

Central American Refugees

Honduras, bordering three countries at war, served as a haven for Guatemalans, Salvadorans, and Nicaraguans during the turbulent 1980s, with 60,000 refugees under the care of the United Nations High Commissioner for Refugees (UNHCR) by mid-decade. The subsiding of the contra war coupled with mass repatriations of Salvadorans resulted in a dwindling refugee population in the late 1980s. In addition to those refugees with official status, Honduras was host to an estimated 250,000 undocumented Central Americans—many of whom were also war refugees.

Guatemalans began spilling over into Honduras in the early 1980s when the country's counterinsurgency campaign was most fierce. At first the fleeing Guatemalans, mostly indians from Alta and Baja Verapaz, sought refuge in the individual homes of Hondurans. Later the UNHCR established a refugee camp called El Tesoro near the Guatemalan border. By mid-1991, all Guatemalan refugees in Honduras had returned home.

Salvadorans have been bandied about the Honduran border by war, poverty, and political tensions for decades. During the 1960s some 200,000 land-starved Salvadorans homesteaded in Honduras, but most were expelled prior to the 1969 "Soccer War" between the two countries. A festering source of tension between Honduras and El Salvador has been disputed territory bordering the Salvadoran department of Morazán.

In 1980 thousands of Salvadorans began fleeing into Honduras to escape the rampaging Salvadoran army and the intensifying civil war. Once inside Honduras, the Salvadorans sought refuge first in the homes of generous Hondurans, and later in UN-sponsored refugee camps. In cooperation with the United Nations, several local and foreign private organizations administered these camps, including Catholic Relief Services (CRS), CARE, World Vision, CARITAS of the Santa Rosa de Copán diocese, the Honduran Mennonite Church with volunteers from the U.S. Mennonite Central Committee, Medicins san Frontieres, and an evangelical relief and development agency called CEDEN.

Salvadorans in Honduras were under constant military siege by the Honduran army. Upon entering the country, some refugees were even killed by the Honduran military, which—despite longstanding tensions between the two countries—often participated with the Salvadoran military in joint operations against the FMLN and its supporters. On several occasions Honduran troops entered camps housing Salvadorans, brutalizing or killing refugees.

Beginning in 1987 Salvadoran refugees began repatriating. With threadbare assistance from the Honduran government's refugee agency CONARE and the UNHCR, the refugees themselves organized several large repatriations, many returning to their original communities. In early 1992, the last group of Salvadoran refugees arrived back in El Salvador. Between 1985 and 1992, approximately 30,000 Salvadoran refugees were also repatriated under UNHCR sponsorship.

In contrast with the tight rein at Salvadoran refugee camps, Nicaraguan camps experienced little or no military supervision by the Honduran government. The camps served as recruiting grounds for the contras and homes for the families of contras. Meetings between the contra leadership and U.S. military advisors took place openly in the camps. With the end of the contra war and the electoral defeat of the Sandinistas, by early 1991 the last of an estimated 43,000 Nicaraguan refugees had been repatriated.

A neglected byproduct of the contra war in Honduras was the displacement of some 22,000 Hondurans from small villages near the Nicaraguan border.[85] By 1984 at least 14 villages had been abandoned as frightened and angry Hondurans fled the border area. The displaced peasants blamed the contras for their exodus. "We haven't been able to live in peace for five years," deplored one group. "We lost everything; we aren't about to lose our lives and our children too. We cannot denounce these events because they accuse us of being Sandinista collaborators, but the contras are the responsible party." [86]

In 1986 the contras—with the complicity of the Honduran military—declared part of the Honduran department of El Paraíso to be "New Nicaragua." Groups of displaced Hondurans immediately began to complain to both the U.S. and Honduran governments. Some demanded the expulsion of the contras, while others asked to be relocated to another region.

As a result of the intensifying pressure and publicity, AID began providing development and relief funds to the ousted Hondurans. Food-for-work programs were initiated for their families, and special aid flowed to the thousands of uprooted peasants who had been small coffee growers in the region. Other groups like CARITAS, CRS, and the Red Cross also sponsored programs to assist the displaced.

PART 5

The Environment

© Bill Barrett

Environmental Crisis Erupts

A historical disregard for the environment has finally created an eco-logical crisis in Honduras—the consequences of which are just begin-ning to be understood. In the South, desertification is well under way and may be irreversible. The combination of woodcutting and unsus-tainable agricultural practices, particularly in the cotton and cattle industries, have denuded vast sections of southern Honduras.[1] The result has been decreasing rainfall, falling agricultural yields, and wi-dening food shortages. In Honduras' rush to exploit its timber reser-ves, roads have been bladed into tropical forests, opening up these areas not only to clearcutting but also to colonization by land-hungry peasants and the environmentally abusive cattle industry.

Although Honduras is not heavily populated, its land resources are becoming overtaxed. Mountains traverse most of the country, and the soil is not enriched with volcanic ash as it is in neighboring El Sal-vador. Rapid population growth—about 3.4 percent annually during the 1980s—is complicating the already serious land-use and land-ten-ure problems. By the year 2000 Honduras, with about seven million inhabitants (five times as many as in 1950), will be facing the kind of population pressure already felt in El Salvador and Guatemala. Many fear that current environmental problems—several of which stem from export promotion policies of the 1950s and 1960s—are bound to get worse before they get better. Although the current government pays lip service to environmental concerns, its export-led economic model is likely to engender new problems and perpetuate old ones.

Honduras is slowly waking up to the environmental crisis, but there are still very few environmental regulations. The few cloud for-ests remaining in Honduras continue to disappear at a rapid pace, and the country still serves as a regional export platform for parrots and other exotic wildlife. The landscape is already so denuded that the government's high hopes for Honduras to cash in on the booming international ecotourism business may prove difficult to fulfill.

Some blame for environmental degradation can be traced to the destructive practices of transnational corporations. But the more pervasive and intractable environmental problems are intricately bound up with issues of land tenure, unemployment, demography, and poverty. Conservation efforts almost inevitably represent an unacceptable burden for those who are barely eking out an existence. Thus, although the growing environmental consciousness is a positive sign, ultimately overcoming the country's environmental problems will require addressing some of the larger issues of social and economic justice.

Deforestation

Deforestation is not a new problem. When Hurricane Fifi struck in 1974, landslides on denuded slopes along the Caribbean Coast buried entire villages, leaving some 12,000 dead. Forest cover in Honduras shrunk from 63 percent in 1960 to 36 percent in 1980, and the country continued to lose 3.6 percent of its remaining forests annually during the 1980s.[2] Most of the primary hardwood forests that once covered parts of Honduras are now history, replaced by a secondary growth of pine.

Yet even this thin cover of pines is threatened by rapid deforestation. According to the Honduran Association for Ecology (AHE), pine forests are being logged commercially at a rate of 98,800 acres per year.[3] At the current loss rate, mature pine trees will be completely gone in ten years; all the country's woodlands will vanish in 20 years.[4] "Few stop to think that trees are more than simple sources of tables or fuel," lamented Francisco Martínez, project coordinator of AHE. "The woods are water, climate, protection for the soil, forest life, tourism, and life." [5]

Cattle ranching, the timber industry, peasant colonization, and forest fires are among the main causes of this rapid deforestation. According to traditional homesteading law, ranchers are given title of land they clear and graze. A powerful and reactionary sector, the large cattle ranchers have forced small farmers off the land and blocked all attempts at regulation. Cattle ranchers also regularly pay landless peasants to clear forested lands in order to make room for future pastures.

The timber industry however, is the major culprit. Beginning with the British and continuing with U.S. investors, Honduras' lumber industry has long exploited the country's forestry resources with little consideration for the long-term consequences of deforestation.

In 1974 the government nationalized the timber industry as part of Gen. López Arrellano's reform program. The stated purpose of the reform was to wrest control over forestry from foreigners and a few local industrialists, and to develop the country's woodland resources for the benefit of the entire nation. Timber cutting fell subject to licensing and the government established a monopoly on the export of sawn wood. Although bitterly resisted by private sawmill owners, the Forestry Development Corporation of Honduras (COHDEFOR) was created and several giant publicly owned sawmills were constructed, including CORFINO in Olancho, FIAFSA in Yoro, and CASISA in Siguatepeque.[6]

But the reform of the forestry industry did not yield the desired results. As with other public-sector investments in Honduras, the public was the net loser. Environmental destruction actually increased as vast new areas were opened up to exploitation. Lumber exports rose, but no corresponding forestry management program was established. Development loans from international lenders like the Inter-American Development Bank (IDB) were earmarked for new road construction into forest reserves and for the construction of sawmills rather than for forestry management.[7] Licenses were granted to private lumber companies, which took only the best wood, leaving more than half of the felled trees to rot on the ground.

It was not, however, the quickening pace of deforestation that sparked new pressure to privatize COHDEFOR, but rather the notorious corruption and inefficiency of the state enterprise. Between 1977 and 1985, COHDEFOR's investment program absorbed 10 percent of the expansion in the country's external debt. Rather than a source of income, the state's forestry industry proved to be a drain on the government's financial resources. The U.S. Agency for International Development (AID) eventually insisted that COHDEFOR and its associated sawmills be privatized—a process that began in 1985.

Although COHDEFOR has been corrupt, inefficient, and careless about the environment, there is little reason to believe that a privatized forestry industry will do much better. Many say that, given the exploitative history of private sawmills, the pace of environmental destruction will only quicken as a result of privatization. Wood exports have already been privatized, sawmills are being sold off to private investors at tremendous losses, and COHDEFOR has relaxed its licensing system. In an environmental gamble, private sawmills are being given exclusive control over tributary areas. Cutting quotas, though still in effect, are commonly ignored in the rush to abet exports and to meet the rising domestic demand for lumber. With the passage in 1990 of a new Municipalities Law, COHDEFOR ceded part of its remaining legal jurisdiction over forests, transferring regulation powers to small-town mayors and municipal governments. Environmentalists argue that small municipal governments have neither the resources nor the clout to oversee influential private concerns active in the timber industry.

Many feel the government's gamble is a loser for the environment. Rigoberto Meza of AHE complains that COHDEFOR is not enforcing the management plans stipulated in the tributary area agreements between loggers and the government.[8] And according to Rafael Alegría of the CNTC rural association, which includes many of the country's forest cooperatives, "Tributary areas amount to no more than the privatization of the forest."

Privatization has indeed been a boon for private sawmill owners and investors, who are picking up government mills at bargain prices. One aim of privatization is to improve the product quality and delivery times of the country's lumber exports, with a view toward maintaining a viable position in the increasingly competitive Caribbean market. Another objective is to cut government financial losses, although even after privatization is completed the government will be left with more than $240 million in external debt payments accumulated by COHDEFOR.

Stumpage fees—the charge levied on private cutters—are quite low, about one-quarter of U.S. levels. These are scheduled to rise, but lumber producers are notorious for their avoidance of government charges—from stumpage fees to income taxes and export levies. In December 1991, COHDEFOR abolished the 18 percent wood export tax, citing plans to recoup lost revenues through a hike in stumpage fees. Aside from better enforcement of present controls on private producers and the development of a stringent forestry management program, Honduras needs to augment the value of its wood exports by expanding its manufacturing industry. Currently manufactured wood exports are only a minor part of the total lumber picture. One such operation is the DERIMASA firm, which exports finished hardwood products to Germany for use in trim on BMW cars.

By the 1990s, environmental consciousness among the population had matured to the point where degradation of the nation's natural resources could no longer be carried out without provoking at least some degree of public backlash. Nowhere was this new attitude more forcefully demonstrated than in the case of a proposed massive timber concession for a U.S.-based company. In early 1992, following months of unprecedented public pressure and protest, the Honduran Congress voted against ratification of a timber exploitation contract with the Chicago-based Stone Container Corporation. This action stunned President Callejas, who had personally signed a letter of intent for the Stone contract in September 1991. The contract stipulated a 40-year exploration concession to Stone, allowing for unlimited extraction of timber from over one million hectares of pine forest reserve in

La Mosquitia—about 20 percent of all Honduras' forest land. Contract terms further stipulated that if Stone were unable to extract sufficient pulpable material from this area, it would have certain rights to exploit additional regions.

As additional "incentives," the contract obligated the Honduran government to construct a new airstrip in the main region set aside for timber extraction, upgrade existing port facilities at Puerto Castilla and Puerto Lempira, and provide Stone with electricity at reduced rates. Finally, the deal would have allowed Stone to terminate its contractual obligations at any time if the corporation deemed the operation unprofitable.

Environmental groups opposed to the concession argued that in addition to numerous technical flaws in the contract, large-scale deforestation resulting from the project would lead to devastating climate changes in Honduras, undermining the country's agricultural base. They also expressed concern over the effects that deforestation and erosion might have on the Río Plátano Reserve, a broadleaf forest area designated as a World Heritage Site by the United Nations Educational, Scientific, and Cultural Organization (UNESCO) and abutting the proposed Stone concession. A key argument souring Honduran legislators on the deal was Stone's poor track record in other countries where it operates, including pending lawsuits in the United States and Canada for air and land contamination.

Honduran political observers contend that the Stone case marked an important turning point for two reasons: it demonstrated that Honduran civil society has the capacity to force the government to change course on important issues, and for the first time it thrust environmental politics to the fore of the national political agenda. The coalition of forces that eventually defeated the Stone project was extremely broad. In addition to the usual array of popular organizations, human rights groups, and environmentalists, student and professional associations were central to the mobilization. Even the Honduran Association of Sawmill Operators rejected the proposal, citing a 1974 law requiring 51 percent local ownership of all forest or logging enterprises. Thousands of Tegucigalpa residents wore pine cones around their necks as a symbol of opposition, and middle-class families put "Save La Mosquitia" bumper stickers on their cars. In a crowning blow, the influential National Association of Industrialists (ANDI) denounced the agreement as a "new affront for the Honduran people and a severe blow to the economic, social and ecological interests of Honduras." [9]

The collapse of the Stone project forced the Callejas administration to reevaluate thoroughly its plans to promote the country's forestry reserves as one of the key "selling points" for Honduras in attracting foreign investment. By early 1992, a draft bill was circulating in Congress that would outlaw all hardwood exports.

Ravages of War

Honduran militarization, U.S. military maneuvers, and the contra war constitute other significant causes of environmental destruction. Contra occupation of the border area in the department of El Paraíso displaced some 16,000 Honduran families. According to the regional COHDEFOR office, the contras pillaged the area's environment—cutting wood for their camps and profiting from contraband lumber sales to Honduran lumber mills and tobacco farms.[10] U.S. environmental groups including the Environmental Policy Institute and the Environmental Project on Central America protested the use of U.S. "humanitarian aid" to buy chainsaws and sponsor chainsaw safety training courses for the contras. In a letter to Congress, the groups argued that "U.S. money could be more appropriately spent on reforestation efforts and to restore land that has been destroyed through U.S. military training and other support for the contras."[11] In addition to destruction caused directly by the contras, tens of thousands of Nicaraguan refugees residing in southern and southeastern Honduras cut down large quantities of trees for their own use.

Frequent U.S. military maneuvers in Honduras also contribute to deforestation. Fires from shooting exercises and a proliferation in the construction of airstrips, roads, and military bases led one COHDEFOR official to charge that the 1986 maneuvers alone destroyed 10 percent of the pine forests in the savannahs near the Nicaraguan border.[12] Congressional hearings revealed that over a thousand square kilometers of the Honduran forest were destroyed in the late 1980s as a result of U.S. military maneuvers and construction.[13] Added damage stems from road building by military engineering teams conducting civic-action operations in isolated areas of Yoro, Olancho, and other departments. These roads access new areas of the country for exploitation, thus escalating environmental decay. Furthermore, as one U.S. Army spokesperson revealed, military construction projects are "less environmentally constrained. If you're building a road, you don't have to worry about the width of the culverts, about the EPA, or about the environmentalists. Those are not concerns down here."[14]

Agriculture, Ranching, and Pesticides

Honduras is cursed with some of the poorest land in Central America. The country is largely mountainous, and is not graced by the mantle of rich volcanic earth blanketing large parts of Costa Rica, El Salvador, and Guatemala. Its tropical lowlands in the East are characterized by thin soils, and only 31 percent of its hillside lands are deeply fertile soil—compared with 76 percent in El Salvador. Only 11 percent of the land in Honduras is capable of supporting intensive annual crops, another 9 percent is suitable for perennial crops and pasture, and 13 percent is only capable of supporting perennial crops and forest plantation.[15]

Land-tenure and land-use patterns result in intense pressure on this limited, productive land base. The best lands are in the hands of a narrow group of large growers, who often leave their estates uncultivated or squander these fertile lands on pasture. According to the latest land-tenure statistics, 4 percent of the country's landowners control 56 percent of the farmland. Such skewed land ownership relegates peasant farmers to the worst lands and nudges them toward the uncultivated (but forested) agricultural frontiers.

The environmental impact of agroexport crops vary. The traditional method of coffee cultivation, locating coffee bushes beside shade trees, causes only moderate environmental damage. By contrast, intensive production promoted by AID—removing shade trees and intensifying agrochemical use—is more environmentally damaging. Multiplying cotton production since the 1950s has been particularly damaging because of the massive quantities of pesticides applied.

The use of DDT is still widespread in Honduras, and elevated levels of DDT residues have been found in the fat tissues of Hondurans living in Choluteca and other areas of southern Honduras. A 1981 study in Choluteca, a rice and cotton region, revealed that 10 percent of residents suffered from high levels of pesticide intoxication.[16] In 1989 at least 129 Hondurans died from pesticide poisoning. Environmental experts estimate that indiscriminate pesticide use results in as many as 150,000 poisonings per year.[17] Each year Honduras imports about $22 million in pesticides, but only 15 percent of the country's farmers receive any form of technical instruction in the proper use of these chemicals.[18] Not only are pesticides deadly for farmers, but the country's food supplies have also been found to contain unhealthy concentrations of these agrochemicals.

In mid-1991, following a fresh wave of protests by farm workers regarding illnesses caused by pesticides and complaints by U.S. agricultural officials regarding possible pesticide-contaminated bananas originating in Honduras, Tegucigalpa attempted to tighten controls. For example, the Natural Resources Ministry banned all imports of 14 pesticides, including Aldrin, Amitrole, Dieldrin, Dinozed, Parathion, and Mirex. Ministry of Health officials reported that in some areas of the country, at least half of all people hospitalized were suffering from toxic chemical exposure.[19]

The transnational fruit companies, which have been dumping toxic pesticides on their banana plantations for decades, are also considered major culprits. In mid-1992, after years of attempting to hide or ignore the problem, the Honduran government finally pointed an accusing finger directly at the Standard Fruit Company. According to a report based on investigations carried out by the Health Ministry's Pollution Control Center, intensive use of the pesticide Lindane on Standard's Atlantic Coast plantations has resulted in extensive health problems among plantation workers as well as local residents and wildlife. Minister of Health Cesar Castellanos explained that he had summoned representatives from Standard Fruit to a meeting to discuss implications of the report, but that they had failed to come.[20]

A related problem is the spread of malaria and dengue fever in coastal areas as mosquitoes become resistant to pesticides. Cutting two ways, pesticide poisoning is both an economic and a human problem. Because of the unregulated and excessive use of pesticides in Honduras, exports of beef and nontraditional crops like melons have been repeatedly refused at U.S. ports.

About 30 percent of Honduran land is currently dedicated to cattle ranching, including much of its meager fertile farmland.[21] Foreign-aid programs, including those of the U.S. Agency for International Development (AID), encourage the growth of this industry despite its contribution to the country's serious deforestation and erosion problems. Owing to the low quality of Honduran soils, cattle require more grazing land than in other Central American countries. The stocking rate in Honduras is .65 cattle per hectare (about 2 and one half acres) contrasted with a 2.36 rate in El Salvador.[22] With the best beef shipped to the United States, only stringy meat and less desirable body parts remain for the local market. Nevertheless, many restaurants in Honduras advertise that their beef is of "export quality."

The spread of cattle across the Honduran landscape is a major factor in the country's declining per capita grain production. To meet the escalating demand for basic grains from the country's soaring population, small farmers have cleared forested land. Impressive gains in productivity achieved during the 1960s have largely been squandered over the past two decades as the quality of the soil degenerates.

Overfishing has also provoked negative environmental and economic consequences. The conch population, for example, has been so depleted that there is no longer enough conch for either commercial exploitation or local consumption. The lobster and shrimp industries have also been severely affected. Moreover, Honduran fishermen arouse the ire of Belizeans for their practice of killing·the endangered manatees in Guatemalan and Belizean waters, and selling the meat of these large aquatic mammals in the Honduran market.

Urbanization and Colonization

Evidence of deteriorating circumstances in rural Honduras is readily found in the teeming slums of Tegucigalpa. Honduras is undergoing the most rapid urbanization in Central America—with urban population rising from 18 percent in 1950 to about 44 percent in 1990 and projected to reach 59 percent by 2010.[23] Forty years ago the capital was a quaint town of 75,000. Today there are over one million people living in this jungle of traffic jams, high crime, and human desperation. The pine-clad hills that once surrounded the capital city have long since been stripped bare to make room for tens of thousands of wooden shacks. For the most part, these hovels lack basic water and sanitation services. Electricity is generally available, but few can afford the monthly charges. A survey by the National Water and Sewer Service found that of the 392 neighborhoods in Tegucigalpa, 219 are considered "marginal" on account of their lack of basic services.[24]

Fewer than a third of the city's houses have their own drinking water, and the rank Choluteca River is the only sewage system for many. There is a booming water-for-sale business in Tegucigalpa whereby containers of water of questionable quality are sold to desperate slum dwellers. Shifting cultivation, roadbuilding, and deforestation are scarring the nearby Los Laureles watershed and causing a rapid build-up of sediment in the reservoir that provides the city with 60 percent of its drinking water. Elsewhere in the country, two new dams for hydroelectric power—El Cajón and El Níspero—are already hampered by siltation problems related to the deforestation of surrounding watersheds. Floods are a related problem. The peak runoff from steep watersheds is estimated at ten times more than when the mountains were heavily forested.[25]

Furthermore, environmental problems induced by urbanization are not confined to Tegucigalpa. Contamination of the Chamelecón and Blanco Rivers, which pass through San Pedro Sula, has polluted water supplies in surrounding villages and departments. Skin ailments are common among the poor, who are relegated to washing their clothes and bathing in these rivers. Most of the contamination flows from the many factories located inside city limits that dump their refuse into the rivers.[26] Another urban environmental problem is vehicular air pollution. Medical authorities have concluded that 60 percent of reported respiratory illnesses result from exhaust fumes.[27]

The rapid pace of urbanization and its consequent problems reflect the swelling number of landless and land-poor peasants who are forsaking rural areas. Another facet of the landlessness issue is the alarming rate of colonization of previously uninhabited regions, including the arid highlands and tropical eastern lowlands. The government has encouraged and at times aided this colonization process in the hope of defusing rural unrest. But the spread of land-hungry peasants into isolated forested areas is contributing to the country's deforestation as land is cleared for farms and pastures.

National Parks and Environmentalism

Honduras was the last country in Central America to establish a national park system. The Tigra Cloud Forest near Tegucigalpa was created in 1979. The country's only other major park, the Copán National Park, protecting Mayan ruins near the Guatemalan border, is administered separately from the newly created national park system.[28] The government has suggested placing 6 percent of the national territory into protected reserves but only some two-thirds of that has actually been designated as reserve lands.

The Río Plátano Reserve, one of the few reserves created, suffered as a result of the contra war. "Perhaps the most troubling news," deplored a 1988 COHDEFOR report, "is that the contra war is destroying the Río Plátano zone." With the influx of Nicaraguan Miskito refugees, the reserve's human population doubled at the height of the war. Threatening to further scar the reserve is a road intended to connect Puerto Lempira and Tegucigalpa.[29]

Conservation and development are often reluctant bedfellows. A case in point is the Biotopo Trifinio international reserve on the Honduras-El Salvador-Guatemala border. This project, in addition to its reserve status, will also be the site of controlled development, including proposed mining projects.[30] In 1991, Honduras received funding from the Inter-American Development Bank for development of ecotourism in the Bay Islands off the Atlantic Coast. Coral reefs skirting the Bay Islands are considered to be among the world's most biologically rich, and as such would be very sensitive to development of any kind.

Environmental consciousness is expanding in Honduras. One of several environmental organizations formed in the 1980s is the AID-funded Honduran Association for Ecology, which promotes its visionary project, "Toward a Green Honduras in the Year 2000." Probably more decisive in the long run, however, is the rising environmental consciousness among popular organizations such as peasant associations, which are now including environmental protection issues among their other concerns and demands. The most combative and progressive environmental group is the Committee for the Preservation of the Fauna and Flora of the Gulf of Fonseca (CODEFFAGOLF). Among its other projects, the group is organizing displaced and threatened communities along the gulf in an effort to protect their lands and mangrove forests from the depredations of new shrimp-farming ventures involving foreign capital and corrupt military figures.

In response to the rapidly deteriorating environmental situation in Honduras, during the late 1980s and early 1990s dozens of new groups were formed with the intent of pressuring the government to adopt more ecologically sound policies and of raising awareness on such issues among the population. In this regard, a national umbrella group called VIDA, comprising about 40 independent environmental groups, was instrumental in pressuring Congress to reject the Stone Container contract in early 1992.

Foreign Influence

© Bill Barrett

U.S. Foreign Policy

It was not until the Sandinista victory in 1979 that Honduras was placed high on the list of U.S. foreign policy priorities. But even before its rise to geopolitical importance, Honduras existed in the shadow of Washington. During the first half of this century U.S. diplomats looked after the interests of the two U.S. banana companies, United Fruit (presently United Brands) and Standard Fruit (Castle & Cooke), which accounted for over 80 percent of Honduran exports. To ensure that U.S. lives and property were adequately protected, U.S. warships were sent to Honduras several times in the early 1900s, and U.S. troops occupied the capital city in 1924.

U.S.-Honduran Relations, 1954-1980

After World War II, U.S. foreign policy broadened as Washington began to take a more active interest in the course of Latin American politics and economy. In the 1950s the Pentagon began shaping the Honduran military into a strong national institution capable of playing a leading role in national politics and of repressing leftist dissidence. The new dimensions of U.S. foreign policy interests in Honduras became apparent after 1954—a watershed year in Honduran politics and society.

Foreshadowing its role as a platform for U.S. militarization of the region, Honduras in 1954 allowed its territory to be used as a training ground for the CIA-supported, rightwing military force that overthrew the reformist government of Jacobo Arbenz in Guatemala. In that same year Washington signed a bilateral assistance pact with the Honduran military that laid the foundation for the close U.S.-Honduran military cooperation of the 1980s. It was also during the Honduran banana strike in 1954 that U.S. labor representatives associated with the State Department began infiltrating the Honduran labor movement and exerting a conservative, anticommunist influence that has long obstructed the advance of a unified, progressive popular movement in Honduras.

During the 1960s and the 1970s the Pentagon continued to be the main source of foreign support for the Honduran armed forces. On the economic front, the U.S. Agency for International Development (AID) provided grants and loans for the construction of hydroelectric dams, highways and rural roads, as well as for farm credit, agroexport promotion, public administration, grain marketing, private enterprise promotion, and public administration. Bolstered by U.S. funds and supplies, nongovernmental organizations like CARE, the American Institute for Free Labor Development (AIFLD), and Partners of the Americas began operations in Honduras.

Prior to the late 1970s there was little U.S. pressure for Honduras to shift from military to civilian rule. Suddenly, however, U.S. hegemony in Central America was threatened by the Sandinista challenge to Anastasio Somoza of Nicaragua and the rise of leftist movements in Guatemala and El Salvador. Bordering all three countries, Honduras gained new strategic importance for Washington and soon came to occupy a pivotal position in U.S. policy toward Central America.[1]

The outlines of U.S. foreign policy became apparent soon after the Sandinista victory in July 1979. Secretary of State for Inter-American Affairs Viron Vacky presented a major policy report to Congress in September 1979 in which he pointed out that "Honduras' geographical position gives it a key role in preventing regional conflicts and potential infiltrations." Even before the ouster of Somoza, however, the Carter administration had begun to pay closer attention to the political stability of Honduras. In 1978 the State Department began working with the military junta led by Gen. Policarpo Paz to facilitate a transition to civilian rule in 1980.

Instituting a policy that would later be repeated in El Salvador and Guatemala, the Carter administration adopted a dual program of political reform and militarization. With an election schedule in place and a promise by the military to cede direct control of the government to the political parties, the United States stepped up its commitment of economic and military aid to Honduras in 1980.[2] To bolster the Honduran military's capacity to patrol the Nicaraguan and Salvadoran borders, the Carter administration loaned the Honduran air force ten Huey helicopters. At the same time the U.S. Southern Command (SOUTHCOM) sent a Special Forces team to Honduras to instruct the armed forces in border security operations.[3]

The Carter administration moved quickly to help Honduras adapt to its new geopolitical role. It brokered a provisional agreement in October 1980 to settle the long-running border dispute between Honduras and El Salvador. This agreement provided for joint border patrols and granted the Salvadoran army access to the pockets of disputed border territory (known as *bolsones*) where Salvadoran guerrillas were camped. The expanding cooperation between the two armies had severe consequences for the thousands of Salvadoran refugees fleeing into Honduras. In one bloody incident some 600 Salvadorans were killed, mostly by Honduran troops, as they attempted to cross the Sumpul River into Honduras. Besides taking an active role in the Salvadoran conflict, the Honduran armed forces were also pressured by the United States to patrol the Nicaraguan border to prevent the alleged smuggling of weapons through Honduras into El Salvador.

Foreign Policy during the Reagan Era

The Carter policy of political reform seasoned with generous doses of militarization established the foundation for massive injections of military and economic aid by the Reagan administration. Like Carter, President Reagan recognized that a civilian government in Honduras was essential to the credibility of U.S. claims that its main foreign policy goal in Central America was to shore up democratic governments. Under Reagan the strategic significance of Honduras increased as the country became the launching ground for the Nicaraguan contra war. In the early 1980s the role assigned to Honduras in the regional crisis expanded from containment to counterrevolution.[4] The U.S. diplomatic corps, swelling to over 1,300, became one of the largest in the world.

Delineating Washington's expectations of its alliance with Tegucigalpa, Assistant Secretary of State Elliot Abrams explained:

> Our political objectives for Honduras are clear: to strengthen democracy and democratic institutions, to elicit full cooperation against nondemocratic forces in the region, to encourage regional cooperation and solidarity, and to obtain the greatest Honduran support possible for our objectives in the region and elsewhere. Our economic objectives must bolster and reinforce our overall objectives, which can and would be undermined if political and social progress is not achieved.[5]

In the 1980s U.S. foreign policy did succeed in eliciting Honduran cooperation for its program of counterrevolution and militarization. During the years 1980-89, Honduras received over $1.6 billion in direct U.S. military and economic aid. Largely as a result of this aid, Honduras became, as President Suazo had once reminded President Reagan, Washington's "closest ally" in Central America.

Interdependence between the two countries deepened during the 1980s. Large sums of U.S. economic assistance kept the economy afloat, and large allocations of U.S. military aid kept the armed forces acquiescent in the face of the "democratization" process and the expanding contra presence. For its part, Washington relied on Honduras for close cooperation in its war of destabilization against Nicaragua. Honduras became the base for a U.S. military build-up—allowing the Pentagon to construct an extensive infrastructure of air fields, bases, and radar sites in the country.

This interdependent relationship continued into the 1990s. With the end of the contra war, the electoral victory of UNO in Nicaragua, and consolidation of the peace process in El Salvador, Honduras lost much of its immediate geopolitical importance for Washington. U.S. aid levels were consequently curtailed, especially military assistance. Nonetheless, the threat of leftist challenges in El Salvador and Guatemala, the continuing strong presence of the Sandinistas in Nicaragua, and the strategic military infrastructure established during the 1980s incline Washington toward maintaining Honduras as a base for regional operations and intervention for many years to come.

Strains in the Alliance

The alliance between Honduras and Washington was strained during the 1980s by Honduran demands for still more assistance. As the political and social costs of the contra and U.S. military presence rose, Honduran leaders became less grateful for the proffered aid and more convinced that the country was not receiving a fair shake. Government and military officials grew increasingly unhappy with their share in this shameful *quid pro quo* deal.

The occupation of Honduras by U.S. troops met little opposition during the first half of the decade. The situation began to change, however, in 1986 following the U.S. airlift into Honduras of 3,200 rapid-deployment troops in response to a Nicaraguan offensive against the Honduras-based contras. Popular organizations began to demand the removal of U.S. troops and bases, while media commentators and politicians expressed concern that the country's dignity and sovereignty were being trampled upon by the United States. U.S. troops became the target of bombings and ambushes. Instigation of most of the attacks was either claimed by the country's small guerrilla groups or blamed on them. Significantly, however, the U.S. embassy did not dismiss the possibility that the Honduran military itself was responsible for at least one bombing.

Growing popular and official resentment over repeated U.S. impositions also rose to explosive proportions regarding drug trafficking in Honduras. By the mid-1980s, Honduras had become an important transshipment point for drugs en route from Colombia to the United States. In 1987 the U.S. Drug Enforcement Administration (DEA) reopened its office in Honduras, closed since 1981 apparently as a favor to the military high command. The subsequent abduction by DEA agents of Honduran drug kingpin Juan Ramón Matta rubbed a raw nerve among Hondurans. In April 1988, during a student protest march over the Matta abduction, an annex at the U.S. embassy compound was attacked and set afire while Honduran security force members turned a blind eye. Students were outraged that the United States had once again violated Honduran sovereignty, while forces within the military and police were apparently angered by new U.S. initiatives to interfere with what was for many corrupt officers a profitable drug trade.

The alliance faces a rocky future in the 1990s. U.S. budget constraints, the end of the Cold War, the Sandinista electoral defeat, and a rising chorus of funding demands from other countries will all make it more difficult for Washington to allocate sufficient funds to keep Honduras content. As U.S. aid declines and as the likely flow of dollars slows, nationalistic and anti-U.S. tensions will sharpen.[6] These tensions will also be aggravated by the unpopular economic policies imposed by the Callejas administration as a result of U.S. and International Monetary Fund (IMF) pressure.

U.S. Policies Destabilize

Democracy, development, and stability have been the oft-repeated U.S. goals in Honduras. But after more than a decade of aid and intervention, these goals still seem distant. In fact, rather than moving Honduras forward, U.S. policies and programs in Honduras appear to have sown the seeds of economic and political instability. This failure can be attributed in part to the contradictory and misdirected character of U.S. economic and military assistance. But it also has to do with the fact that from the beginning Washington's interest in Honduras has been mainly a product of U.S. foreign-policy concerns in Nicaragua, El Salvador, and Guatemala.

At the same time that Washington voiced its support for democratization, it proceeded to militarize Honduras by fortifying its army and police, occupying it with U.S. troops, and establishing a counterrevolutionary army on its soil. Likewise, Washington contributed to the marginalization of civilian government authorities by repeatedly negotiating directly with the military on major substantive issues. As a result Honduras evolved into an even more repressive and polarized country where a weak civilian government rules in the shadow of a military that is stronger than ever.

The provision of economic aid has been mostly counterproductive. Large injections of balance-of-payments assistance did temporarily ease the financial crisis but resulted in Honduras becoming an aid junky increasingly dependent on a foreign-assistance fix. Instead of directing funds to programs that would address the basic needs and development concerns of the poor majority, AID favored the elite private sector with U.S. dollars (see U.S. Economic Aid). While corrupt colonels, politicians, and businesspeople soaked up U.S. aid, socioeconomic conditions for the majority of Hondurans deteriorated. Indeed, despite a five-fold increase in U.S. economic assistance between 1981 and 1990, per capita income for the population actually declined. Laments one foreign relief worker: "In Honduras, people have fallen from a state of poverty to total misery." [7]

Attracted to Honduras by its lack of internal political turmoil, Washington proceeded to support the military and the business elite, while obligating the government to adopt political and economic positions contrary to the interests of workers, peasants, and the middle class. In so doing, the United States has shaped a more polarized and repressive nation and contributed to the country's long-term instability.

The Bush administration repeated and extended the mistakes of its predecessor. Rather than backing away from a one-sided commitment to the private sector, President Bush strengthened this bond. The U.S. embassy openly allied itself with the Honduran Council of Private Enterprise (COHEP) and the narrow business interests of the governing National Party.[8] The only exception to this pattern was in the realms of military reform and respect for human rights. In these areas, during the early 1990s, the U.S. embassy stood as a key force counterbalancing resistance to change within the armed forces.

U.S. Trade and Investment

Honduras has long been a country dominated by the economic presence of the United States. The banana plantations of Standard Fruit (Castle & Cooke) and United Fruit (United Brands) have been dominating factors in the Honduran economy since the late 1890s. More than simply a banana republic, Honduras has also attracted U.S. investors and traders in mining, manufacturing, services, and diversified agricultural production.

Ninety percent of foreign investment in Honduras comes from the United States, which is also the country's leading trading partner—supplying roughly 40 percent of its imports and purchasing over half of its exports.[9] The leading exports to the United States are fruit (bananas and citrus), coffee, seafood (shrimp), vegetables, and beef. Honduras buys machinery, agricultural chemicals, and basic grains from the United States (Figure 6a).

The book value of U.S. investment in Honduras is estimated to be $250 million, and the top three investors are United Brands, Castle & Cooke, and American Pacific Mining.[10] About 300 U.S. companies do business in Honduras, including 60 of the top 500 corporations in the United States.[11]

All three major U.S. banana companies have operations in Honduras. Although United Fruit and Standard Fruit's plantations date back almost one hundred years, RJR Nabisco (Del Monte) is a newcomer to the banana business. Castle & Cooke, owner of Standard Fruit, also produces pineapples and African palm oil and is experimenting with the production of winter vegetables. United Brands operates African palm estates and cattle ranches in addition to its banana plantations.

Three major U.S. banks—Citicorp, BankAmerica, and Chase Manhattan—conduct business in Honduras. Citicorp has interests in Banco de Honduras while Chase Manhattan owns part of Banco Atlántida. Among the other major industries dominated by U.S. investment are oil refining (Texaco), mining (American Pacific/AMAX), beef and poultry production, insurance, shrimp cultivation, and animal-feed production. The industrial parks in Puerto Cortés and Choloma have attracted a score of U.S. manufacturers (including Christian Dior), which produce apparel and other goods for the U.S. market.

Because of their domination of certain economic sectors, U.S. corporations have been able to exact extraordinary concessions from the government. The banana companies have repeatedly threatened to lay off hundreds of workers or completely close down operations if the government did not lower export taxes. On one occasion in 1984 Standard Fruit agreed to retain 500 workers whom it had threatened with layoffs after the government agreed to suspend the company's tax liability for one year and ignore its overdue property taxes.[12] A similar agreement was later signed with United Brands.

U.S. companies also use their economic leverage to break unions. Standard Fruit tried to break one union by switching its pineapple production to another corporate subsidiary. AMAX, the corporate giant that owned Rosario Mining, closed down its operations in 1987 in order to break the union, opening up a half year later under the administration of another subsidiary called the American Pacific Holding Company. The "new" mining firm was then eligible for a series of incentives and tax breaks that AID had pushed through to encourage foreign investment. During the subsidized firm's first 18 months, six Honduran miners died as a result of unsafe working conditions. A new workers' union charged that safety problems arose after the former union was destroyed by the shutdown and corporate shuffling.[13]

Figure 6a
Honduras' Trade with the United States

In percent.

	Imports	Exports
1985	36.1	55.1
1986	37.3	50.6
1987	39.1	51.1
1988	42.3	51.7
1989	39.5	50.7
1990	39.5	52.8
1991	40.5	53.8
1992	54.2	52.4

SOURCE: IMF, *Direction of Trade Statistics Yearbook* (Washington, DC, 1993), and IMF, "Direction of Trade Statistics," September 1993.

Texaco, the country's only refinery, has also used its monopoly position to force the government to keep taxes low and prices high.

Pressured by AID, the Honduran government has increased the incentives offered to foreign investors in the 1980s. Designed primarily to stimulate nontraditional export production by foreign investors, new measures include partial or total exemption from export taxes, the right of foreign investors to hold dollar-denominated accounts in the country, and easy capital repatriation. Honduran capitalists, resenting the privileges afforded U.S. investors, succeeded in reducing major tax breaks that were suggested in the 1989 foreign investment law supported by AID.

Honduran businesses have also resisted U.S. efforts to liberalize all foreign trade. AID insists that trade liberalization (dropping all tariff barriers) would make Honduran industry more competitive, but local businesspeople have protested that a growing influx of foreign goods is already killing domestic industries. Not only do new consumer products threaten local businesses, but even used clothing and shoes from the United States are flooding into the local market.

Most new U.S. investment in Honduras has been attracted by the provisions of the Caribbean Basin Initiative (CBI) and assorted other U.S. government programs to promote export production. Several new business-promotion organizations funded by AID, including the Foundation for Investment and Export Development (FIDE) and the National Council to Promote Exports and Investment (CONAFEXI), offer generous lines of subsidized credit and marketing assistance to companies exporting to the United States. As a result of these efforts, U.S. imports of apparel from Honduras more than doubled while total U.S. imports of manufactured goods from Honduras jumped by 90 percent between 1983 and 1988.[14]

U.S. Economic Aid

During the 1980s Honduras ranked among the top ten recipients of U.S. economic assistance in the world (Figure 6b). Well over half of this aid came in the form of Economic Support Funds (ESF) for balance-of-payments upkeep. Between 1982 and 1990 Honduras received $711 million in ESF, $355 million in development assistance, and $173 million in U.S. food aid. Not only did the country experience an unprecedented influx of economic aid during the 1980s, but for the most part this aid came in the form of direct grants rather than loans. Between 1985 and 1990 over 85 percent of U.S. economic aid to Honduras consisted of grants, although grants had composed only 39 percent of the economic-aid package between 1977 and 1983.[15]

The U.S. Agency for International Development (AID), which dispenses all this aid, has attained a central position in the Honduran society and economy.[16] At first glance, no sector of the society seems untouched. Everyone and every organization appears to be on the AID dole. Political parties, judges, military/civic-action teams, business associations and businesspeople themselves, journalists, unions, development groups, charitable organizations, churches, ranchers, and, of course, government ministries and ministers depend on regular AID handouts.

As pervasive as AID seems to be in Honduras, the positive developmental impact of these dollars is difficult to find. Socioeconomic conditions continue to worsen, the economy shows few signs of stabilizing, and the gap between rich and poor has widened. This absence of development is not surprising, given the focus and objectives of the AID strategy in Honduras. Waste and corruption have also been major problems in Honduras. Jaime Rosenthal, a former vice-president under Azcona, charged that 30 percent of U.S. economic aid was lost to corruption and another 50 percent was misdirected, going to the business elite rather than to programs to help the poor.[17]

The dramatic escalation of AID funds for Honduras came not as a response to poverty and underdevelopment but rather as a complement to U.S. political and military goals in the region. As such, this aid has served as a payoff for Honduran acquiescence to U.S. foreign policy strategy for Central America.

AID has not used its economic-aid package to help Honduras tackle its deep structural problems such as land-tenure patterns and declining per capita grain production. Nor has it insisted that the government and oligarchy develop strategies to meet the basic health, educational, and income needs of the country's impoverished majority. Instead AID has concentrated on implementing macroeconomic and private-sector solutions that aggravate and accentuate the deep social and economic divisions in Honduras.

Figure 6b
U.S. Economic Aid to Honduras

In millions of U.S. $.

	DA	ESF	PL480 I & III	PL480 II	Peace Corps	Total
1977	7.8	0	0	2.8	1.5	12.1
1978	13.0	0	0	2.4	1.7	17.1
1979	22.0	0	2.0	2.8	2.1	28.9
1980	45.8	0	2.0	3.2	1.9	52.9
1981	25.7	0	3.6	4.6	2.4	36.3
1982	31.1	36.8	7.0	3.1	2.6	80.6
1983	31.3	56.0	10.0	5.5	3.2	106.0
1984	31.0	40.0	15.0	5.2	3.8	95.0
1985	54.4	150.2	15.0	4.4	5.0	229.0
1986	45.3	66.5	15.0	4.6	5.2	136.6
1987	42.7	131.8	12.7	5.4	5.2	197.8
1988	44.9	85.0	12.0	8.4	6.5	156.8
1989	38.0	15.0	18.0	10.2	6.3	87.5
1990	36.5	130.1	12.0	9.6	4.0	192.2
1991	38.3	60.9	14.0	6.3	3.4	122.9
1992*	35.0	30.0	14.0	9.5	2.8	91.6
1993	26.0	9.7	13.0	5.7	2.7	57.1
1994**	27.5	7.5	0	6.0	2.8	43.9

*Total includes $0.256 in other economic aid.

**Requested.

SOURCES: AID Congressional Presentation Summary Tables FY1994; U.S. Overseas Loans and Grants: Obligations and Loan Authorizations.

In order to win good will for the United States and soften the dislocations caused by its stabilization program, AID has spread a small portion of its development assistance to the popular sectors including some NGOs, women's organizations, unions, and peasant groups. Yet even here AID has ignored the real development and educational needs of these sectors. Instead the agency has focused on bolstering the most conservative popular organizations with nonconfrontive projects that stress individual and export-oriented solutions. Ignored are the more progressive and representative popular organizations that emphasize community-based and structural solutions to the country's pressing socioeconomic problems.

AID has not only deepened Honduras' economic dependency but has also further debilitated the country's governmental and nongovernmental sectors. Through its agricultural, health, educational, finance, and other development programs, AID has created a "shadow government" in Honduras. Outside consultants have been placed in most ministries, and the government has grown accustomed to turning to AID and the U.S. embassy for consultation and approval of most economic and political decisions. The same U.S. influence and control has come to pervade the nongovernmental sector as well—from the smallest social service organizations to the country's largest business associations. Washington has bought friends and immediate influence and has established structures and operating methods guaranteeing that Honduras will remain the type of society that Washington wants—irrespective of which individual politicians, bureaucrats, and businesspeople come and go.

The Pace of Economic Stabilization

Half of U.S. economic aid to Honduras during the 1980s came in the form of Economic Support Fund (ESF) grants, used primarily to relieve the country's foreign-exchange crunch. Honduras qualifies for such a large commitment of ESF aid because the Pentagon and the State Department (both of which sign off on ESF allocations) consider Honduras to be critical to U.S. security interests. The PL480 Title I food-aid program functions similarly in that it relieves the country from using scarce foreign exchange to buy U.S. wheat. About $42 million in wheat donations scheduled for allocation over a three-year period beginning in 1992 equate to about 80 percent of domestic consumption requirements.

At the same time that ESF and Title I ease the country's balance-of-payments crisis, they also provide the government and the private sector with a source of local currency to fund AID-approved programs. This secondary impact of the ESF and Title I food-aid programs works this way: private-sector importers and wheat mills use local currency (*lempiras*) to buy U.S. dollars and U.S. wheat from the government. This local currency is then divvied up among government ministries, private development groups, and AID itself, according to agreements AID arranges with the government.[18]

Besides their value as balance-of-payments aid and as generators of local currency, ESF (and to a lesser extent Title I assistance) are used by AID to demand economic-policy reforms from the Honduran government. U.S. economic assistance comes with certain conditions, many of which are stipulated in the aid agreements themselves, with others hammered out in what AID calls "policy dialogues." Sometimes caveats arise in the form of directives from the U.S. ambassador. Such was the case in late 1981 when Ambassador Negroponte presented the newly inaugurated President Suazo with a 12-point economic-stabilization program that was incorporated almost word for word into the new government's Plan of Action. The "Azcona Plan" for economic development, unveiled four years later, was also largely written by AID. When Azcona balked at implementing some of the more politically unpopular aspects of the plan at a pace acceptable to the United States, AID withheld $70 million in economic support funds. Those funds were released shortly after the newly inaugurated Callejas administration implemented its Plan de Ajuste, yet another AID-authored project.

AID's formula for economic stabilization in Honduras amounts to the same package of neoliberal remedies that the United States has been imposing throughout Latin America and the third world. The plan's main components are privatization of state-owned enterprises, currency devaluation, budget cutbacks, liberalization of trade, and promotion of nontraditional exports. It is a plan that parallels the structural adjustment programs that the International Monetary Fund (IMF) and the World Bank have been trying to institute in Honduras since the early 1980s.

The basic thrusts of AID's economic-stabilization plan are 1) to impose austerity measures on the Honduran economy that will cut budget deficits and allow the government to meet its debt payments, and 2) to place private investment in export production at the center of the country's development strategy. According to this strategy, once the economy is stabilized and exports begin picking up, the benefits of growth will trickle down to the poor. But as AID has acknowledged:

> . . . implementation of a stabilization program will probably lower living standards and may well increase unrest among the country's already impoverished people in the short term. The painful and wrenching adjustments that will take place during

the retrenchment will temporarily dash the hopes of many for improved living standards. Low-income rural families will see their earnings diminish to the extent that the cost of transportation, imported agricultural inputs, and consumer goods rise in relation to the prices they can obtain for their products. The urban unemployed are the most likely to give up hope and look for solutions that threaten political stability. . . . Thus, some of our assistance must be aimed at helping the government minimize social unrest during this difficult period.[19]

AID has had mixed success in forcing Honduras to implement its stabilization plan. Austerity measures have been put into effect, the currency has been devalued, and increased resources and incentives have been directed to the private sector. But as of mid-1992, AID was still complaining about high budget deficits and the slow pace of privatization.

Recognizing that full implementation of AID's stabilization measures would substantially aggravate social unrest, President Suazo and, to a lesser extent, President Azcona resisted AID pressure to devaluate the *lempira* and reduce budget deficits. They were able to do this by playing off Washington's political and military strategy for Honduras against its economic one. It was more important to the U.S. embassy that Honduras remain a compliant partner in U.S. militarization and support for the contras than that it fully comply with AID's stabilization demands. When AID attempted to withhold further assistance, higher authorities in the Pentagon and State Department urged the release of that aid.

AID has had more luck in pursuing its structural adjustment remedies with the Callejas administration, both due to a closer ideological affinity and because Callejas has fewer bargaining chips than his predecessors. Nonetheless, even Callejas has in some cases hedged on AID and multilateral economic requests for fear of igniting popular unrest. Resistance to devaluation, tariff reductions, and austerity measures also remain strong among many sectors of the business community which recognize that externally imposed economic stabilization plans might in fact drive the economy into a cycle of recession and inflation.

Private-Sector Support

Outside the government, the private sector is the favored recipient of AID funds.[20] AID's economic assistance goes either directly to business associations or to development and social service organizations that sponsor private-sector solutions to social and economic problems. The business community is also the main beneficiary of AID-generated credit and of policy reforms stipulated in economic-assistance agreements with the government.

Nearly two dozen business associations and promotional groups receive AID funds, either directly as part of Development Assistance and ESF grants or indirectly from local currency generated by balance-of-payments support. Among the most important are the Honduran Council of Private Enterprise (COHEP), Federation of Agroexport Producers (FEPROEXAH), Foundation for Investment and Export (FIDE), National Association of Honduran Exporters (ANEXHON), National Association of Industrialists (ANDI), Associated Managers and Entrepreneurs of Honduras (GEMAH), National Development Foundation of Honduras (FUNDAHEH), and the Honduran American Chamber of Commerce (HAMCHAM). At least half of the business associations currently receiving support were founded by AID in the early 1980s.[21]

Other AID private-sector funding goes to such groups as the Cattle Fund (created by AID to promote beef exports) and the Honduran Foundation for Agricultural Research-FHIA (the former research department of United Fruit, converted by an AID grant into a research center for banana, citrus, and nontraditional agroexport crops).

This devotion to private-sector solutions even extends to population control. AID is funding a Private Sector Population Program that is using the techniques of "social marketing" to sell and distribute birth control devices. AID is also funding the social-marketing approach in schooling and popular education through AVANCE, an elite AID-created, mass-education organization. AVANCE sponsors radio programs, a newspaper, and other popular-education ventures, and believes it can play a role in reforming the Honduran population by "fostering the values needed to make you efficient in your work and give you the capacity to create your own businesses and initiatives."

AID pressured the National Congress to adopt two measures—the Export Promotion Law of 1983 and the Temporary Import Law of 1984—designed to promote nontraditional exports and assembly manufacturing. But nontraditional crops have failed to respond to new incentives.[22] During the 1980s most of the gains in the nontraditional agroexport sector were in palm oil and citrus—two products not supported by AID programs.[23]

Other examples of AID's extensive private-sector-support programs include: funding an array of NGOs promoting microenterprises; backing new export-processing zones, industrial parks, and initiatives to "strengthen the private forestry industry"; and encouraging local and foreign investors to purchase state enterprises through its Privatization of State-Owned Enterprises Project.

In his evaluation of AID programs in Honduras, Philip Shepherd of Florida International University observed that AID "clothes its aid in the language of reform, broadly shared development, and democracy. This is either wishful thinking or cynical perversion of the English language." He concluded:

> The greatest obstacle to successful U.S. aid in Honduras is the elitist and reactionary nature of the U.S. aid program itself. U.S. aid is *not* being directed toward the majority of poor Hondurans. Instead both U.S. aid and other economic policies are serving to prop up an increasingly creaky structure of incompetent, corrupt, and venal elites.[24]

Democracy-Strengthening Assistance

In the 1980s the U.S. government launched a new category of economic aid called "democracy-building" or "democracy-strengthening" assistance. Funds for these democracy projects are channeled through AID and the National Endowment for Democracy (NED), a government-funded private organization founded in 1983. In Honduras, democracy-strengthening projects have ranged from managing the voter-registration and election process to training political leaders.

AID has financed virtually the entire electoral process in Honduras. It funds the National Registry of Persons and the National Elections Tribunal—the two institutions responsible for the registration of voters and management of the electoral process. The November 1989 presidential election was entirely paid for by U.S. taxpayers, including the paper for the ballots, the printing of the ballots, marking pens for the ballots, construction of voting tables, curtains for the voting booths, international observers, the election-return system and monitoring center, and the labor to manage the elections.

AID paid not only for the mechanics of the election but also for the three-part civic-awareness campaign that preceded the voting. Part one was a six-month general education campaign in 1988 "designed to raise the awareness of the public about the advantages of the democratic system." This was followed in 1989 by an AID-sponsored voter-registration drive and a second education campaign, this one devoted to presenting "key issues and the presidential candidates' positions." Finally, civic interest was piqued by a series of radio and television debates as well as newspaper summaries of the candidates' positions.[25]

For all the AID funding and hyperbole about free elections, the integrity of the November 1989 electoral process was undermined by a high rate of abstention (despite costly get-out-the-vote drives) and a highly inaccurate voter registry. The failure of the government and of AID to implement the proposed revamping of the voter registry resulted in post-election charges of manipulation and fraud by losing parties. Nonetheless, AID's sponsorship of the electoral process in Honduras conferred an international stamp of approval on the presidential election.

The country's judicial and legislative institutions have also been included in AID's democracy strengthening. Judges and legislators are being trained by AID consultants and are being provided with a wealth of written materials and information services. Although AID notes that the Congress and Supreme Court have been traditionally weak institutions, its institution-strengthening projects do not address or even mention the principal cause of their debility and lack of independence—the overriding power of the armed forces.

Yet another component of AID's multifaceted approach is called Democratic Leadership Training. Through national leadership conferences and more specialized courses, AID has set out to influence the country's most powerful figures. According to AID: "Training services will be provided for all levels of political leadership, from local to national. The political leadership will also benefit from improved support services, such as information systems and improved administrative backup and support." [26] A further effort to influence future leaders is the Central America Peace Scholarships Program, through which thousands of Hondurans have been schooled or trained in the United States.[27]

AID's leadership-training efforts extend beyond the political parties to selected unions, women's organizations, the media, peasant organizations, and business groups. Key members of these organizations are trained so that they will "promote the diffusion of democratic principles into these organizations." [28] In accordance with AID's commitment to "develop human rights organizations," the agency has directed ESF local-currency funds to the governmental Interagency Committe for Human Rights (COINDEH) created in 1987[29] (see Human Rights). AID funds are also channeled through U.S. private organizations such as the Overseas Education Fund (OEF) and the American Institute for Free Labor Development (AIFLD) to enable them to conduct their own political-education courses.

In addition to AID funding, AIFLD in Honduras receives NED funds for civic-awareness promotion and political education among the country's union and peasant sectors. Other NED funding passes through the National Republican Institute for International Affairs (NRI) to the Center for Economic, Political, and Social Studies in Honduras. This center authored the policy platform of the National

Party and sponsored a self-serving national radio program on the history of Honduras and the National Party.[30]

Peace Corps, Labor Unions, and Humanitarian Assistance

Honduras hosts the largest Peace Corps contingent in the world. The first Peace Corps volunteers came to Honduras in 1962. As of the early 1990s, over 360 volunteers were working in health, education, agricultural, environmental, and business programs. One of the most ineffective and inappropriate endeavors is an adult education program in which the volunteers, most of whom are themselves just learning the language, teach reading and writing to illiterate adults. The Peace Corps efforts are often coordinated with AID projects, particularly in small-business promotion.

AIFLD, in addition to its previously mentioned NED funding, receives AID Mission support for its Honduran program. Since the 1954 banana strike U.S. organized labor in association with AID and the State Department have exerted a conservative, pro-U.S. influence among Honduran workers and peasants. The main vehicle for this effort—ever since its creation by the State Department and the AFL-CIO in 1962—has been AIFLD. In Honduras, AIFLD has worked through the National Association of Honduran Peasants (ANACH) and the Confederation of Honduran Workers (CTH). In recent years AIFLD's influence has been waning as Honduran peasant associations and labor unions, including ones that it has funded, have grown more progressive.[31]

Rather than supporting efforts to unionize agricultural workers, AIFLD has consistently focused on programs to encourage an "entrepreneurial approach" among individual small farmers.[32] AIFLD sends Honduran labor and peasant leaders to training courses in "democratic unionism" in the United States, Panama, and Israel, as well as sponsoring in-country political education and training seminars.

U.S. Military Aid

Following El Salvador, Honduras was the leading recipient of U.S. military aid to Latin American countries in the 1980s. During the decade almost a half-billion dollars in direct military assistance and training was provided to Honduras (Figure 6c). Yet its military aid had more to do with wars raging in neighboring countries, particularly Nicaragua and El Salvador, than with any security threat faced by Honduras. The aid essentially served as a payoff to the Honduran armed forces for their cooperation in U.S. counterrevolutionary efforts in Nicaragua and El Salvador.

Cooperation between the U.S. military and the Honduran armed forces dates back to the 1920s when U.S. advisers assisted the country's air force. Occasionally, U.S. warships were sent to Honduran ports in a show of U.S. strength or in order to "protect U.S. interests" in times of political turmoil. In the year following their 1924 occupation of Tegucigalpa, U.S. Marines once again marched into the capital to sort out a presidential succession dispute. In 1934, the Military Aviation School was founded, with a U.S. officer serving as its first commander.

Prior to the 1950s the Honduran military had little sense of itself as a national institution. As a result of post-World War II efforts of the U.S. Department of Defense (DOD) to establish strong alliances with Latin American armies, the Honduran military began to professionalize. The country's first military academy was established in 1952 under U.S. tutelage. With the 1954 signing of the Bilateral Military Assistance Agreement between Washington and Honduras, the professionalization and strengthening of the country's military was hastened.[33] Military advisors were dispatched to Honduras and remained in the country through 1967.[34]

During the 1950s Honduran officers also began receiving training at the U.S. Army School of the Americas in the Panama Canal Zone. Between 1950 and 1961, 391 officers and 691 recruits received training in Panama.[35] Having acquired a new sense of importance and strength, the armed forces seized control of the government in 1956. The country was returned to civilian rule in 1957, but the coup marked the beginning of a central role for the military in Honduras.

Between 1946 and 1980 Honduras received a total of $32.6 million in U.S. military loans and grants. Beginning in 1980 U.S. military assistance to Honduras soared, rising from about $4 million in fiscal year 1980 to $77 million in 1984. According to the 1990 Department of Defense budget presentation:

> Security assistance to Honduras is a tangible demonstration of the U.S. commitment to the defense and development of this key ally. The military program is critical to modernizing the Honduran armed forces in order to provide a credible deterrent to the Sandinista threat. This assistance also contributes significantly to the professionalization of the armed forces, a crucial factor in strengthening of Honduran democracy. An important goal of security assistance is to promote respect for human rights through improved training.[36] (recruiting; brother fights brothers)

The rapid growth in U.S. military interest in Honduras in the 1980s was facilitated by a 1982 amendment to the 1954 bilateral accord. The new agreement specifically allowed the United States to upgrade three major airfields and an unspecified number of smaller airstrips. The agreement was expanded again in 1988 to allow the U.S. military to build a major radar station on the North Coast and to allow it a greater degree of control over the joint maneuvers program.

Few doubted that military aid to Honduras would be reduced when Washington reassessed priorities in view of the new regional environment of the 1990s. Indeed, from the high of $77 million in 1984, U.S. military assistance plummeted to just $2.5 million in the Clinton administration's request for 1994. Despite the drop in aid levels, however, U.S. officials were quick to insist that the permanent personnel presence and the maneuvers program would not be terminated anytime soon.

Components of U.S. Military and Police Aid

The three elements of the military aid program are: Foreign Military Financing (FMF), Military Assistance Program (MAP), and International Military Education Training (IMET). During the 1980s most U.S. military aid (89 percent) was allocated under the MAP grant program.

During the same decade the only Latin American country to receive more military training than Honduras under the IMET program was El Salvador. IMET provided military education to 9,500 Honduran military officials in the United States and other locations from 1980 to 1989.[37] In addition to the IMET exercises at the U.S. Army School of the Americas (in Panama and, after 1985, at Ft. Benning, Georgia), Honduran troops are also being instructed by Mobile Training Teams (MTTs) of U.S. Special Forces (Green Berets) that enter the country for short periods to drill entire units in counterinsurgency tactics and other military skills. MTTs have been working in Honduras since August 1981.[38]

Outside of the three main categories of military aid (MAP, FMF, IMET), the Honduran military has benefited from an array of other U.S. military-aid programs. Under the Overseas Security Assistance Management Program (OSAMP), the United States stations managerial military personnel in Honduras. In the 1980s nearly $2 million

Figure 6c

U.S. Military Aid to Honduras

In millions of U.S. $.

	IMET	FMF	MAP	Total
1977	0.6	2.5	#	3.10
1978	0.7	2.5	#	3.20
1979	0.3	2	#	2.30
1980	0.4	3.5	#	3.90
1981	0.5	8.4	0	8.90
1982	1.3	19	11.0	31 30
1983	0.8	9	38.5	48.30
1984	0.9	0	76.5	77.40
1985	1.1	0	66.3	67.40
1986	1	0	60.1	61.10
1987	1.2	0	60	61.20
1988	1.2	0	40	41.20
1989	1.1	0	40	41.10
1990	1.053	20.2	0	21.25
1991	1.569	31.9	0	33.47
1992	1.375	5	0	6.38
1993*	1.1	1.5	0	2.60
1994**	1	1.5	0	2.50

*Estimated **Request #Less than $50,000

SOURCES: Congressional Presentation for Security Assistance Programs, FY 88-94, AID Congressional Presentation Summary Tables FY 1992 and FY 1993; U.S. Overseas Loans and Grants: Obligations and Loan Authorizations.

was authorized each year for this management program. Honduras has also profited from DOD military construction grants, which finance the construction and maintenance of foreign military bases. Once built, the base is turned over to the host country, but the U.S. military retains access and perusal rights to the facility. In 1987 and 1988 over $4.1 million was spent each year for U.S. military construction in Honduras.[39]

In 1985 Congress authorized an exemption for Honduras and El Salvador from the ban on U.S. aid to foreign police forces. In Honduras, $2.8 million was authorized for the program to supply the Public Security Force (FUSEP) and other national police with training, riot control gear, weapons, vehicles, and communications equipment.[40] Aid to the Honduran police has also been provided under the Anti-Terrorism Program, managed by the State Department's Bureau of Diplomatic Security. Additional police training has been sponsored by the International Criminal Investigative Training Assistance Program (ICITAP) run by the U.S. Justice Department.

Further sources of military-related aid include the DOD's Humanitarian Assistance Program, Exercise-Related Construction (see Military Maneuvering), and Commercial Sales. In addition to acquiring U.S. arms through the MAP and FMF programs, Honduras also purchases weapons commercially from U.S. exporters. During the 1980s these purchases ranged from a low of $0.9 million in 1987 to a high of $3.9 million in 1988.[41] The U.S.-guided militarization of Honduras is enhanced by numerous joint military exercises that have occurred on Honduran soil since 1981. During the 1980s, equipment and weapons used during the maneuvers rarely returned to the United States but were instead left for use by the Honduran military and the contras.[42]

In 1983 the DOD formulated a Honduran Force Modernization Plan designed to augment the strength and mobility of the Honduran armed forces.[43] Among the plan's specific objectives were developing an effective counterinsurgency capacity, bolstering the army's ability to patrol the Salvadoran border, and building a deterrent force for national defense. Extensive U.S. support was also offered for psychological operations, intelligence, and civil affairs. The most expensive component of the U.S. military-aid package has been DOD assistance for the Honduran air force. In 1987 the United States agreed to replace the country's Super Mystere jet fleet with 12 highly sophisticated F-5 jet fighters.[44] The United States has also provided two C-130 transport aircraft for remote-operations support and is upgrading the country's fleet of 15 A-37 aircraft.[45]

U.S. Military Facilities in Honduras

More than simply a recipient of generous U.S. military aid and training, Honduras in the 1980s became a U.S. military outpost. Newly constructed air bases, radar stations, and airstrips form part of this U.S. military infrastructure. The Enrique Soto Cano Air Base (formerly Palmerola) outside Comayagua, constructed in 1983, is operated by the Honduran air force but functions as the nerve center of U.S. military operations in Honduras. Stationed at the huge base is Joint Task Force Bravo (JTFB), a contingent of 1,100 U.S. troops and about half that number of Honduran soldiers. JTFB, a joint U.S. Army and Air Force command center, coordinates U.S. military operations as well as the joint operations of U.S. and Honduran forces. Excluding military salaries and expenses for intelligence missions originating at the base, yearly operating costs amount to $25 million.[46]

Besides overseeing troop maneuvers within the Honduran borders, the Soto Cano Air Base coordinates reconnaissance flights over Nicaragua and El Salvador. JTFB also manages an extensive military/civic-action program, including regular medical and food-distribution efforts. As part of its educational outreach, local children are invited on base "to inspect the U.S. military's largest aircraft." [47] In early 1992, even as Washington was urging reforms in the Honduran military, the Pentagon insisted that the U.S. troop presence at the Soto Cano base must continue "indefinitely."

Since the early 1980s the U.S. military has operated two major radar stations. At Cerro La Mole, between Tegucigalpa and Comayagua, there is a long-range early-warning system purportedly erected to signal Hondurans of a Nicaraguan invasion. A second station was constructed in late 1983 during joint maneuvers on Tigre Island in the Gulf of Fonseca. In 1988 Washington signed a Mutual Cooperation Agreement with the Honduran government opening the door for construction of a still larger radar station on the North Coast, a facility designed to assist in the control of narcotrafficking activities in the Caribbean Basin.

Numerous airstrips, most of them originally designed to serve the contras, were built by U.S. military engineers both along the North Coast and along the Nicaraguan border. These airstrips, the most famous being El Aguacate, were constructed during joint military maneuvers but continue to be maintained by the U.S. military. Special congressional appropriations have also permitted the expansion and maintenance of large airfields at Palmerola and La Ceiba air bases.[48]

In 1983 the U.S. military established the Regional Military Training Center (CREM) on the North Coast near Trujillo primarily to train Honduran and Salvadoran soldiers. After two years of operation, CREM had trained 5,600 Salvadoran and 5,900 Honduran troops in addition to several dozen Civil/Rural Guard officers from Costa Rica.[49] The center was closed in June 1985 owing to strong objections by the Honduran top brass at having the Salvadoran military trained on Honduran soil. After CREM's closure the U.S. military adopted a new strategy of establishing national training in each country. Toward this end, the Honduran Military Training Academy was opened in Olancho in 1988.

Military Maneuvering

Joint U.S. maneuvers with the Honduran military have been conducted since 1965, but the frequency and scale of these training exercises escalated in the 1980s. Using DOD general funds, the Pentagon launched a series of more than six dozen military maneuvers that brought tens of thousands of U.S. regular forces and National Guardsmen to Honduras. The maneuvers, according to the DOD, are intended to: 1) help develop Honduras' defenses; 2) improve the readiness skills of U.S. forces in overseas deployment; and 3) demonstrate U.S. commitment to the democratic nations of the region.[50] In practice, these exercises adapted U.S. invasion forces to the Central American climate and terrain, and augmented the military infrastructure along the Nicaragua border. Related objectives included providing a framework of logistical support for the contras and sending a powerful psychological message to U.S. adversaries.

Three short maneuvers took place in 1981-82 along the Nicaraguan border. Since these limited maneuvers did not raise serious objections in Congress, the U.S. Southern Command under newly appointed Gen. Paul Gorman launched military exercises of unprecedented magnitude and duration beginning in 1983 with Big Pine II, which lasted six months.[51]

Since 1983 Honduras has experienced an almost unbroken series of joint maneuvers. Besides playing out invasion and defense strategy, the maneuvers have been designed to facilitate the militarization process in Honduras. As part of the military games and training exercises, a network of roads has been built, a series of airfields constructed, barracks erected, tank traps dug, radar stations established, and ocean ports upgraded.[52]

Troops from the United States have far outnumbered those Honduran soldiers who have participated in the maneuvers. On several occasions U.S. troops in Honduras for maneuvers have assisted the Honduran military with national defense concerns. In 1983 U.S. advisors assisted Honduran counterinsurgency units in the pursuit and interrogation of captured Honduran guerrillas, including a U.S. priest who was part of the guerrilla force.[53] In 1985 and 1986 U.S. units in Honduras for maneuvers were called upon to ferry Honduran troops to the Nicaragua border to defend against a possible invasion. Then, in 1988, 3,200 U.S. troops were airlifted to Honduras to protect the country against another fictitious Nicaraguan invasion. This expeditionary force touched off cries within Honduras that the country's national sovereignty was being violated by the U.S. military build-up.

The U.S. military presence has not been without its human costs to the United States. Accidents and shootings between 1983 and 1990 resulted in the deaths of 47 U.S. military personnel. Several bombings, some claimed by leftist guerrillas, wounded at least three dozen U.S. soldiers, and dozens more have been seriously injured as a result of accidents.[54]

Despite the new regional climate and widespread popular pressures to end the costly maneuvers program, U.S. and Honduran military officials insisted in 1992 that there were no plans to scrap the exercises. January saw the first phase of Big Pine 1992, a five-phase maneuver involving a series of joint U.S.-Honduran engineering projects. Increasingly, the U.S. military presence in general, and the joint-maneuvers program in particular, have been justified in the name of the antinarcotics-trafficking effort.

Winning Hearts and Minds: Civic Action

The Pentagon has long promoted military/civic-action and nation-building programs as part of its military aid and training in Honduras. In the 1960s the U.S. military guided the establishment of a civil-affairs office within the Honduran military command and encouraged the army to take a more active role in the country's internal matters through educational, infrastructure, and social-service projects. These programs fostered "as a purpose and intended result the strengthening and continuance of the military role in the country." [55]

In the 1970s, on the heels of the U.S. experience in Vietnam, Pentagon support for civic action diminished. But with intensified U.S. involvement in Central America in the 1980s, civic-action programs once again came into vogue. Not only did the U.S. military renew its support for the Honduran army's civil-affairs division, but it also mounted its own civic-action programs.

U.S. military/civic-action programs in Honduras are of two types: those sponsored year-round by Joint Task Force Bravo, and those that accompany joint U.S.-Honduran military maneuvers. The most common civic-action programs are road building and medical care, but other activities include well digging, the building of schools and clinics, and various distribution projects. Road-building projects are undertaken mostly by National Guard engineers while medical programs are the responsibility of a wide range of specialized Army and National Guard units.

The medical outreach programs include: Immunization Readiness Training Exercise (IMRETE), Medical Readiness Training Exercise (MEDRETE, formerly known as MEDCAPS), Dental Readiness Training Exercise (DENTRETE), Veterinary Readiness Training Exercise (VETRETE), and clinic services offered several times a week at the Soto Cano Air Base.[56] According to Maj. Bernard Eugene Harvey, the purpose of these medical programs, aside from their training value to U.S. medical personnel, is to make the U.S. military "presence as palatable as possible to the Honduran people." [57]

From its headquarters at the Soto Cano Air Base, Joint Task Force Bravo sponsors a wide range of programs, mostly in areas surrounding the base. Typically a MEDRETE team is airlifted into a rural village, teeth are pulled, aspirin and antidiarrheal medicine is distributed, and immunization shots are given to hundreds of Honduran peasants lined up to see the U.S. military doctors. These events generally succeed in generating good will for the U.S. military. From a medical standpoint, however, the MEDRETE programs have been criticized for being one-time affairs that provide inadequate treatment and lack the necessary follow-up. The Pentagon has acknowledged this weakness and is attempting to remedy it with longer-term medical projects.[58]

Besides its military/civic-action programs, the United States, both through the DOD and AID, has since 1985 been bolstering the Civil Affairs (C-5) capabilities of the Honduran military. The United States began "motivating the Honduran military to engage in Military Civic Action as part of a national development plan." [59] Under the tenure of Gen. López, the military command sponsored a series of joint military and civilian seminars on civic-action programs. Along these lines, Military Technical Projects (PROMITEC) was created in the late 1980s to plan and execute civic-action projects and accompanying psychological operations.[60]

AID's Office of Disaster Assistance has supported new military initiatives in disaster assistance and civil defense, and has worked to reestablish the Permanent National Emergency Committee (COPEN), originally established by the Honduran military in 1975. COPEN, which coordinates disaster assistance and other civic-action programs, is directed by the chief of Civil Affairs. During the late 1980s, aside from providing direct aid to COPEN, AID supplied disaster assistance to the Honduran military for several programs along the Nicaraguan border.

With U.S. support, COPEN and the Civil Affairs command have established a network of military-controlled civil-defense committees throughout the country. COPEN serves as the national coordinating institution for regional committees known as CODERs and local civil-defense committees called CODELs. Both COPEN and Civil Affairs have received training from the U.S. Army's 361st Brigade of Military Civic Action. Supplies for the Honduran military's civic-action programs come from AID and U.S. private organizations, including World Opportunities International, Friends of the Americas, and Adolph Coors Brewery.[61]

Reference Notes

Introduction

1. For an excellent discussion of the limitation of the "formal democracy" in Honduras see: Mark B. Rosenberg and Philip L. Shepherd, eds., *Honduras Confronts Its Future: Contending Perspectives on Critical Issues* (Boulder, CO: Lynne Rienner Publishers, 1986), pp. 22-53 and 230-34. Also see: Victor Meza, ed., *Honduras: Pieza Clave de la Política de Estados Unidos en Centro América* (Tegucigalpa: CEDOH, 1986).
2. Interview by Medea Benjamin, Food First.
3. The declarations of Judge Miguel Angel Izaguirre led to the creation of the Special Investigative Commission on Drug Trafficking (CIEN). CEDOH, *Boletín Informativo*, December 1989.

Part 1: Politics

1. Jack Anderson, "Why Another Somoza?" *Washington Post*, March 28, 1980.
2. In October 1981 Honduran military and political leaders came to a behind-the-scenes agreement regarding ground rules for the transition to civilian rule. The civilians committed themselves to noninterference in military affairs, including foreign policy matters relating to national security and the country's borders as well as investigations into corruption under previous military regimes. The military also retained veto power over cabinet appointments. Richard Lapper and James Painter, *Honduras: State for Sale* (London: Latin America Bureau, 1985), p. 81.
3. Victor Meza, "The Military: Willing to Deal," *NACLA Report on the Americas*, January-February 1988, p. 14.
4. Unless otherwise cited, all material in this section is based on James A. Morris' excellent study of Honduran politics. See "The State and Elections" in James A. Morris, *Honduras: Caudillo Politics and Military Rulers* (Boulder, CO: Westview Press, 1984), pp. 60-73.
5. Cited in Lapper and Painter, *Honduras: State for Sale*, p. 98.
6. Perhaps the two most important manifestations of this tendency were the Riccy Mabel Martínez case (see Human Rights), the first time civilian courts attempted to prosecute armed forces members, and the February 1992 rejection by Congress of a contract signed by President Callejas with the U.S.-based Stone Container Corporation (see Environment).
7. More details on the history of Honduran political parties and their internal factions can be found in Morris, *Honduras: Caudillo Politics*, pp. 74-78; Margarita Oseguera de Ochoa, *Honduras hoy: Sociedad y crisis regional* (Tegucigalpa: CEDOH/CRIES, 1987), pp. 98-112;

Lapper and Painter, *Honduras: State for Sale*, pp. 7-10; and "Elecciones Otra Vez," *Boletín Informativo*, CEDOH, October 1989, pp. 8-12.

8. "¿Un Cristiani para Honduras?" *Pensamiento Propio*, November 1989, p. 36.

9. "Falló el Acarreo a las Urnas," *Pensamiento Propio*, December 1989, pp. 2-3.

10. "¿Un Cristiani para Honduras?" p. 36.

11. American Friends Service Committee, "Honduras into the 1990s," April 1, 1990.

12. Cited in "Taming the Tiger: Hondurans Attempt to Rein in the Military," *Mesoamerica*, January 1992.

13. This argument is developed in greater detail in Rosenberg and Shepherd, *Honduras Confronts Its Future*, pp. 23-53, 230-34.

14. Good accounts of the elections held in Honduras since 1980 can be found in Leyda Barbieri, "Honduran Elections and Democracy: Withered by Washington" (Washington DC, Washington Office on Latin America, February 1986), and Morris J. Blachman, William M. LeoGrande, and Kenneth Sharpe, *Confronting Revolution: Security Through Diplomacy in Central America* (New York: Pantheon Books, 1986), pp. 129-30, 151-52.

15. CEDOH, *Boletín Informativo*, December 1989, p. 1.

16. For more details, see Lapper and Painter, *Honduras: State for Sale*, p. 81.

17. Details on the constitutional crisis of 1985 can be found in: Alison Acker, *Honduras: The Making of a Banana Republic* (Boston: South End Press, 1988), pp. 124-25; Lapper and Painter, *Honduras: State for Sale*, pp. 113-15; and *Central America Bulletin*, August 1989, p. 4.

18. For more details on the Pact of National Unity, see Oseguera de Ochoa, *Honduras Hoy*, pp. 148-50.

19. Accounts of the irregularities reported in the 1989 elections can be found in: *Central America Report*, November 17, 1989; *Regionews from Managua*, October 1, 1989, pp. 9-10; *Latin American Regional Reports—Mexico and Central America*, November 30, 1989, p. 7; and "Falló el Acarreo a las Urnas," pp. 2-3.

20. These declarations and further details on accusations of irregularities can be found in *Miami Herald*, December 3, 1989; *Latin America Regional Reports—Mexico and Central America*, November 30, 1989, p. 7; and *Inforpress Centroamericana*, December 7, 1989, pp. 15-16.

21. In addition to a desire among the electorate to throw out the incumbent party, possible electoral fraud, and the difficulties caused to the Liberals by delays in disbursement of aid funds, there is a fourth factor that reportedly had a significant impact on the National Party victory. Liberal Party presidential candidate Carlos Flores Facussé, who had served as a vice-president under President Suazo Córdova, comes from a family of Arab descent. Arab and Lebanese Hondurans are deprecatingly referred to in Honduras as *turcos*. Analysts say that many Liberals, particularly among the urban poor, simply refused to vote for a *turco* and decided to abstain or vote for Callejas, despite their traditional party preference.

22. An outstanding analysis of the roots of Honduran foreign policy and the major issues confronting the country from 1975 to 1985 is found in Ernesto Paz, "The Foreign Policy and National Security of Honduras," in Rosenberg and Shepherd, *Honduras Confronts Its Future*, pp. 181-209.

23. The most blatant example of this was the unconstitutional installation of the CREM, a base set up in Honduras by the United States in 1983 for training Salvadoran troops.

24. For more information on APROH, see Rosenberg and Shepherd, *Honduras Confronts Its Future*, p. 187; Lapper and Painter, *Honduras: State for Sale*, pp. 101-2; Scott Anderson and John Lee Anderson, *Inside the League* (New York: Dodd, Mead, and Co. Inc., 1986), pp. 217-41; and Instituto de Investigaciones Socioeconomicas de Honduras (INSEH), *Anos 90: Retoques y Permanencia de la Derecha*, September 1990.

25. In addition to Callejas, former APROH members in high posts include Benjamín Villanueva, Oswaldo Ramos Soto, Gilberto Goldstein, and Emín Abufele.

26. For details on the 1969 war and its aftermath, see Morris, *Honduras: Caudillo Politics*, pp. 110-13.

27. *Central America Report*, March 27, 1992.

28. For more information on the ICJ ruling and its implications, see Manuel Torres Calderon, "Mapa Nuevo," *Pensamiento Propio*, September 1992, pp. 30-31.
29. See Oseguera de Ochoa, *Honduras Hoy*, pp. 86-9.
30. *Honduras Update,* October 1987, p. 2.
31. *Central America Report*, August 19, 1988.
32. Excerpts from the text were reproduced in CEDOH, *Boletín Informativo*, July 1988, p. 13.
33. CEDOH, Americas Watch, "Human Rights in Honduras: Signs of the 'Argentine Method,'" December 1982, pp. 5-6.
34. *Boletín Informativo*, October 1984, cited in Acker, *Honduras: The Making of a Banana Republic*, p. 122.
35. Meza, "The Military: Willing to Deal," p. 16.
36. For one account of the court proceedings, see Americas Watch, "Honduras: Without the Will" (1989), pp. 69-77.
37. Ibid., pp. 2-3.
38. Cited in "Human Rights Ombudsman Releases Landmark Report on Political Disappearances," *NotiSur—Latin American Political Affairs*, January 7, 1994.
39. Americas Watch, "Honduras: Without the Will" (1989), pp. 59-60.
40. See *Miami Herald*, November 14, 1989, and U.S. Department of State, *Country Reports on Human Rights Practices for 1988* (Washington, DC: February 1989), pp. 610-22.
41. Americas Watch, "Honduras: Without the Will," p. 8.
42. *Central America Report*, March 13, 1992.
43. Cited in The Economist Intelligence Unit, *Country Report: Guatemala, El Salvador, Honduras*, No. 2, 1992, p. 34.
44. Ibid.
45. Cited in *Central America Update*, April 3, 1992.

Part 2: Military

1. Tom Barry and Debra Preusch, *The Central America Fact Book* (New York: Grove Press, 1986), p. 112.
2. For a comprehensive account of the military's role in Honduras during the 1980s, see Meza, "The Military: Willing to Deal," pp. 14-21.
3. Cited in Blachman, et al., *Confronting Revolution*, p. 135.
4. The lower figure is cited in *The Military Balance, 1988-1989* (London: The International Institute for Strategic Studies, 1989), p. 198. The higher figure was cited for 1988 in "Informe especial: Distensión no pasa por centroamérica," *Inforpress Centroamericana*, December 7, 1989.
5. Cited in U.S. embassy, "Handbook on Honduras: Democracy, Defense, Development, Diplomacy and Drug Control" (Tegucigalpa: Fall 1988).
6. Raúl Sohr, *Centroamérica en Guerra* (Mexico City: Alianza Estudios, 1989), cited in *Inforpress Centroamericana*, December 7, 1989.
7. George Thomas Kurian, *Encyclopedia of the Third World, Third Edition* (New York: Facts on File, 1987). This source cites 25 combat aircraft, to which must be added the 12 F-5 fighters acquired in 1989. Total of 120 aircraft cited in U.S. embassy, "Handbook on Honduras."
8. U.S. embassy, "Handbook on Honduras."
9. Cited in Robert H. Holden, "Honduras Seeks to Fill a Post-contra Political Space," *In These Times*, October 10, 1990.
10. See *NACLA Report on the Americas*, January-February 1988, p. 30.
11. For more details on the involvement of Honduran officials in international drug trafficking, see Jacqueline Sharkey, "The Contra-Drug Trade Off," *Common Cause*, September-October 1988, pp. 23-33; Eric Shultz, "Top Civilians Involved in Drugs, Says Ex-Judge, with Military Backing," *Honduras Update*, June-July 1988, pp. 14-6; and *Central America Report*, May 27, 1988, p. 158.

12. Cited in "Honduras: A U.S. Base for Intervention" (Philadelphia: NARMIC/American Friends Service Committee, March 1989), p. 6.

13. Cited in "La batalla de los negocios," *Pensamiento Propio*, June 1993, p. 2.

14. Cited in "Honduras: U.S. Diplomat Criticizes Military Investments in Business Ventures," *NotiSur — Latin American Political Affairs*, July 16, 1993.

15. The main sources consulted regarding the national-security doctrine and militarization of Honduras were: *NACLA Report on the Americas*, January-February 1988; *Honduras: Fuerzas armadas 1988, Contrainsurgencia interna y disuasión regional* (Mexico: Instituto de Investigaciones Socioeconómicas de Honduras, 1988); Oseguera de Ochoa, *Honduras Hoy*, pp. 53-63; and "Military Impact Indicators," *Honduras Update*, March 1987, pp. 1-3.

16. See Rosenberg and Shepherd, *Honduras Confronts Its Future*, p. 189, and *Honduras: A Country Study* (Washington, DC: U.S. Government Printing Office, 1984), p. 236.

17. A detailed account of Alvarez' rise to power and his links to the Argentine military, the Moonies, and the World Anti-Communist League can be found in Anderson and Lee Anderson, *Inside the League*, pp. 217-41.

18. This effort included not only providing secure bases for the contras in Honduras and occasional military backup for contra incursions and retreats across the border, but also the direct participation of Honduran military personnel in attacks and sabotage operations inside Nicaragua. See "Military Insubordination," *Washington Report on the Hemisphere*, January 21, 1987.

19. For details on the current Honduran interpretations of national-security doctrine, see the text of a speech delivered by Regalado in January 1989 in CEDOH, "Seguridad nacional y conflictos internos," *Boletín Informativo*, February 1989, pp. 6-7.

20. See CEDOH, *Boletín Informativo*, October 1989, pp. 4-5.

21. Cited in Roger Burbach, "Restive Honduran Military—Ready to Bite the Hand That Feeds It," *Pacific News Service*, January 23-29, 1989.

22. Cited in "Taming the Tiger: The Battle to End Military Impunity in Honduras," *Mesoamerica*, February 1992.

23. Cited in "Taming the Tiger: Hondurans Attempt to Rein in the Military."

24. Accessible accounts of the activities of Battalion 3/16 include George Black, "Dirty Hands in Honduras: The Many Killers of Father Carney," *The Nation*, January 23, 1988; *New York Times*, June 5, 1988; and Julia Preston, "Honduras Accused of Death Squad Operations," *Washington Post*, November 1, 1988.

25. Additional information on these groups can be found in Lapper and Painter, *Honduras: State for Sale*, pp. 9-10; Helen Schooley, ed., *Conflict in Central America* (Essex, UK: Longman Group Ltd., 1987), p. 165; and Oseguera de Ochoa, *Honduras Hoy*, pp. 139-42.

Part 3: Economy

1. *CEPAL Review*, April 1984.

2. The poverty statistics are based on government household survey data, cited in "Honduras: On Financial Support for Government's Economic Reform Program," *Central America Update*, April 17, 1992.

3. The two most graphic examples of the dismal failure of this approach are CONADI, the state development corporation set up in 1974 to provide low-cost investment funds to the private sector, and COHDEFOR, the state's forestry development corporation. Both were subsequently dissolved and sold to private investors, local and foreign. Their massive debts have been absorbed by the government.

4. Comisión Económica para América Latina y el Caribe, *Estudio economica de América y el Caribe 1990: Honduras*, January 1992, p.14.

5. Tiempo, February 1, 1989, cited in CEDOH, *Boletín Informativo*, February 1989, p. 2. Many investors cite regional political instability as a major disincentive to opening new businesses in Honduras.

6. Comisión Económica para América Latina y el Caribe, *Estudio economica*, p. 25.

Reference Notes

7. Unless otherwise cited, statistics in the following summary came from three sources: a study by the Honduran Association of Economists, summarized in "Structural Adjustment Provokes Recession," *Central America Report*, August 9, 1991; the United Nations Economic Commission for Latin America and the Caribbean (ECLAC) report on 1991 economic performance in Honduras, summarized in "Stabilization Efforts Undermine Investment Growth," *Central America Report*, March 6, 1992; and a report by the Callejas' government on its first year in office, summarized in "Callejas Government, One Year Later," *Central America Report*, February 15, 1991. A more thorough examination of performance under the structural adjustment program, including proposed alternatives, is contained in Rafael Del-Cid, Hugo Noé Pino, and Alides Hernández, *Honduras: Crisis económica y proceso de democratización política* (Tegucigalpa: Centro de Documentación de Honduras, 1990).

8. Report by the Honduran Association of Economists, cited in "Honduras: On Economic Performance in 1990," *Central America Update*, July 19, 1991.

9. Figures on average real wages cited in Inter-American Development Bank, *Economic and Social Progress in Latin America: 1989*, p. 14.

10. Cited in "Honduras: Catholic Bishop Accuses President of Appointing Thieves to High-Level Government Positions," *Central America Update*, November 30, 1990.

11. The performance in the 1980s of Honduras' top four nontraditional exports, which together account for more than 25 percent of income from all nontraditionals, was mixed: exports of palm oil did well, those of pineapple and fruit conserves developed modestly, while those of manufactured wood products plunged. Eva Paus, ed., *Struggle Against Dependence: Nontraditional Export Growth in Central America and the Caribbean* (Boulder CO: Westview Press, 1988), p. 125.

12. *Business Latin America*, November 27, 1989, p. 379.

13. Reported at a COHEP-sponsored seminar on privatization held in June 1989. See *Central America Report*, June 24, 1989.

14. CARICOM, established in 1973, includes Anguilla, Antigua, Bahamas, Barbados, Belize, Dominica, Grenada, Guyana, Jamaica, Montserrat, St. Kitts & Nevis, St. Lucia, St. Vincent, and Trinidad & Tobago.

15. In 1988 some 59 percent of the population lived in rural areas, down from 65 percent in 1980 and 70 percent in 1974.

16. Kurian, *Encyclopedia of the Third World*, p. 855.

17. This information is taken from Honduras background material supplied to Peace Corps volunteers, 1985, pp. 15-17.

18. Kurian, *Encyclopedia of the Third World*, p. 855.

19. *Crónica*, April 7, 1988.

20. Cited in *Latin America News Update*, August 1990.

21. For details on the 1990 "Banana War," see *Central America Report*, June 1, 1990 and June 29, 1990.

22. *Central America Report*, June 29, 1990.

23. U.S. Agricultural Attaché Report, #HO-9002, April 4, 1989, pp. 5-6.

24. Food and Agriculture Organization, *Food Security in Latin America and the Caribbean*, June 1984; Tom Barry, *Roots of Rebellion: Land and Hunger in Central America* (Boston: South End Press, 1987).

25. Cited in Susan C. Stonich, "The Dynamics of Social Processes and Environmental Destruction: A Central American Case Study," *Population and Development Review*, 15, No. 2 (June 1989), p. 281.

26. Hondupress, April 18, 1989.

27. For a full treatment of the objectives and consequences of the U.S. food-aid program see Rachel Garst and Tom Barry, *Feeding the Crisis: U.S. Food Aid and Agricultural Policy in Central America* (Lincoln: University of Nebraska Press, 1990).

28. Roger Norton and Carlos Benito, Winrock International for AID-Honduras, "Evaluation of the PL480 Title I Program in Honduras," 1987.

29. *El Heraldo*, November 2, 1988.

30. CEDOH, *Boletín Informativo*, November 1988.

31. Cited in Stonich, "The Dynamics of Social Processes and Environmental Destruction," p. 280-81.
32. For one good analysis of the agrarian-reform program, see Medea Benjamin, "*Campesinos*: Between Carrot and Stick," *NACLA Report on the Americas*, January-February 1988, pp. 22-30. Another extensive analysis of Honduran agrarian reform is found in Raul Ruben, "Una reforma agraria con perspectivas economicas: Notas sobre el sector reformado en Honduras," in *Revista Centroamericana de Economia*, January-April 1991, Vol. 12, No. 34, pp. 47-78.
33. CEDOH, *Boletín Informativo*, May 1989, p. 5.
34. See *Central America Report*, January 31, 1992, and March 13, 1992; *Central America Update*, March 27, 1992.
35. Cited in *Central America Report*, January 31, 1992.
36. Cited in *Central America Update*, March 27, 1992.
37. Cited in *Central America Update*, February 1, 1991.
38. CEDOH, *Boletín Informativo*, special edition on 25 years of agrarian reform, September 1987.
39. *Envío*, August 1989, p. 17.
40. According to one author, 77 percent of credit finances export crops and livestock, while only 13 percent supports basic grains. See Mario Ponce, "Honduras: Agricultural Policy and Perspectives," in Rosenberg and Shepherd, *Honduras Confronts Its Future*, p. 146.
41. *NACLA Report on the Americas*, January-February 1988, p. 30.
42. For additional information on Honduran *maquilas* and Asian investment, see "El modelo Asiático no es una solución," *Pensamiento Propio*, September 1988; "Bienvenidos, Tigers!" *Forbes*, May 27, 1991, pp. 190-91; and "Asian Tigers Leap Into Central America," *Business Latin America*, December 16, 1991, pp. 401-2.
43. In December 1990, the Honduran Congress approved a decree that allows foreigners to become naturalized Hondurans by purchasing a Honduran passport for $25,000 ($3,000 for each additional family member). According to government spokespersons, the move was geared to attracting Asian investors, especially Hong Kong Chinese. See CEDOH, *Boletín Informativo*, December 1990, and The Economist Intelligence Unit, *Country Report: Guatemala, El Salvador, Honduras*, No. 2, 1992, pp. 39-40.
44. *El Heraldo*, May 12, 1989, cited in CEDOH, *Boletín Informativo*, May 1989, p. 5.

Part 4: Social Forces and Institutions

1. Henry W. Berger, *Union Diplomacy: American Labor's Foreign Policy* (1966), p. 364.
2. See Tom Barry and Debra Preusch, *AIFLD in Central America: Agents as Organizers* (Albuquerque: Resource Center, 1990), p. 40.
3. For more information see Benjamin Santo, *Datos para el estudio del movimiento Social Cristiano* (Tegucigalpa: Instituto de Investigaciones Socio-Económicas, 1981).
4. *Directory and Analysis: Private Organizations with U.S. Connections-Honduras* (Albuquerque: Resource Center, 1988), p. 5.
5. CEDOH, *Boletín Informativo*, November 1988.
6. U.S. embassy, *Foreign Labor Trends: Honduras* (Tegucigalpa: U.S. Department of Labor, 1987).
7. Robert H. Holden, "In U.S.-Funded Honduras, Misery Trickles Down," *National Catholic Reporter*, December 1, 1989.
8. Guillermo Molina Chocano, "Problemas de la democracia en Honduras," in Mark B. Rosenberg and Philip L. Shepherd, eds., *Honduras: Realidad nacional y crisis regional* (Tegucigalpa: CEDOH, 1986), p. 38.
9. Cited in Holden, "Honduras Seeks to Fill a Post-contra Political Space."
10. Two comprehensive accounts of Honduran trade unions are: Mario Posas, "El movimiento sindical Hondureño durante la década de los Ochenta," CEDOH, *Boletín Informativo*, October 1989; and Neale J. Pearson, "Honduras," in Gerald Michael Greenfield and Sheldan

Reference Notes

L. Maran, eds., *Latin American Labor Organizations* (New York: Greenwood Press, 1987), pp. 463-94.

11. For more information on this strike and on *solidarismo* in Honduras, see CEDOH, *Boletín Informativo*, October 1989, pp. 11-13; and *Central America Report*, December 9, 1988, pp. 382-3.

12. Cited in U.S. Department of Labor, "Foreign Labor Trends: Honduras, 1990-1991," 1991, p. 6.

13. Ministry of Public Education, cited in *Tiempo*, June 14, 1989.

14. National Census of Population and Dwellings, 1988, sponsored with the support of the UN Population Fund.

15. These statistics were cited by Education Minister Jaime Martínez, in *La Tribuna*, January 4, 1991.

16. U.S. Agency for International Development, *Honduras: Country Development Strategy Statement FY1986* (Washington, DC: AID, May 1984), p. 23.

17. Philip L. Shepherd, "The Honduran Economic Crisis and U.S. Economic Assistance: A Critique of Reaganomics for Honduras," unpublished manuscript, p. 170.

18. *Tribuna*, January 23, 1989.

19. Acker, *Honduras: The Making of a Banana Republic*, p. 100.

20. *Central America Report*, September 1, 1989.

21. Ibid.

22. U.S. embassy, "Honduras," January 1, 1989.

23. Ibid.

24. Comité de los Periodistas de los Estados Unidos, *La Prensa Hondureña: Un periodismo del silencio* (Tegucigalpa: Escuela de Periodismo de UNAH, 1984).

25. Ibid.

26. Ibid.

27. Council on Hemispheric Affairs, *Survey of Press Freedom in Latin America 1985-1986* (Washington, DC: 1986).

28. Comité de los Periodistas de los Estados Unidos, *La Prensa Hondureña*.

29. Information on USIS programs supplied to authors by the United States Information Agency (USIA).

30. Rosa Morazán, "Malnutrition: The Child's Side of the Crisis," *Hondupress*, December 15, 1989; Kurian, *Encyclopedia of the Third World*.

31. Morazán, "Malnutrition," citing UNICEF study.

32. U.S. A.I.D. "Latin America and the Caribbean: Selected Economic and Social Data," Washington, DC, 1993.

33. U.S. Agency for International Development, *Congressional Presentation FY1990, Annex II, Latin America and the Caribbean* (Washington, DC: AID, 1989).

34. *Tiempo*, May 11, 1988, quoting Minister of Health Rubén Villeda Bermúdez.

35. Medea Benjamin, "Hunger in Honduras," *Links*, Spring 1987.

36. Cited in *Central America Report*, February 15, 1991.

37. *Primer Censo Nacional de Talla en Escolares de Primer Grado* (Ministerio de Educación Pública, 1987).

38. Barry, *Roots of Rebellion*, p. 16, citing CEPAL and AID statistics.

39. *Tribuna*, November 8, 1988.

40. World Bank, "Sound Investment in Guatemala, El Salvador and Honduras, 1991," p. 42.

41. Mary Jo McConahay, "Highest Incidence of AIDS in Region," *Pacific News Service*, February 2, 1988.

42. Ibid.

43. The 1990 PAHO data indicates an average 28.8 per million AIDS cases in Central America, and 22.7 per million in Latin America. Health Situation and Trend Assessment Program, PAHO/WHO Global Program on AIDS/Americas, "AIDS Surveillance in the Americas," PAHO, September 16, 1991, cited in "Incidences of Acquired Immune Deficiency Syndrome (AIDS) in Central America, by Country, 1986-91," *Central America Update*, October 30, 1991.

44. Ibid.

45. Sandra Avila and Luis Sierra, "War Without Bullets," *Links*, Summer 1987.

46. *Centroamérica Hoy*, May 17, 1989.
47. Dr. Carlos Godoy Arteaga, *El sistema unico de salud y seguridad social* (Tegucigalpa: 1988), p. 9.
48. This section on religion is excerpted from *Directory and Analysis: Private Organizations*.
49. *Tribuna*, August 21, 1989.
50. For a history of the Catholic Church in Honduras see: José María Tojeira, *Panorama histórico de la iglesia en Honduras* (Tegucigalpa: CEDOH, 1986).
51. Gustavo Blanco and Jaime Valverde, *Honduras: Iglesia y Cambio Social* (San José: DEI, 1987). The discussion of the trends within the Catholic Church is drawn largely from this excellent work.
52. World Vision, "Analysis de la realidad nacional de Honduras," 1988.
53. Ibid.
54. *Directory and Analysis: Private Organizations.*
55. Interviews by Tom Barry with NGO directors, Tegucigalpa, December 1985.
56. Acker, *Honduras: The Making of a Banana Republic.*
57. Melba Reyes, "Situación de la mujer en Honduras," *Paz y Soberanía*, March 6, 1988.
58. Cited in CEDOH, "La mujer y la Política en Honduras," *Boletín Informativo*, February 1991, p. 14. The statistics were compiled as part of a research project undertaken by the Center for Women's Studies—Honduras.
59. Elvia Alvarado with Medea Benjamin, ed., *Don't Be Afraid Gringo: A Honduran Woman Speaks from the Heart* (San Francisco: Institute for Food and Development Policy, 1987).
60. Cited in Dolly Pomerleau, "Women in Honduras," *Honduras: A Look at the Reality* (Hyattsville, MD: Quixote Center, July 1984).
61. Reyes, "Situación de la Mujer."
62. Nancy Peckenham and Annie Street, "Women: Honduras' Marginalized Majority," in *Honduras: Portrait of a Captive Nation* (New York: Praeger, 1985).
63. *Hondupress*, December 6, 1989.
64. The report, based on government statistics, was published in the Managua magazine *Gente*, cited in *Central America Update*, March 29, 1991.
65. Reyes, "Situación de la mujer."
66. For elaboration, see Peckenham and Street, "Marginalized Majority."
67. Ibid. Also see Graciela García, *Páginas de lucha* (Tegucigalpa: Editorial Guaymuras, 1981).
68. Salley Yudleman, *Una apertura a la esperanza: Estudio de cinco organizaciones femeninas de desarrollo de América Latina y el Caribe* (Inter-American Foundation, 1988), p. 33-7.
69. *Directory and Analysis: Private Organizations.*
70. Peckenham and Street, "Marginalized Majority."
71. Nancie L. Gonzalez, *Sojourners of the Caribbean: Ethnogenesis and Ethnohistory of the Garifuna* (Urbana and Chicago: University of Illinois Press, 1988), pp. 51, 59.
72. Ibid.
73. Melanie Counce and William Davidson, "Indians of Central America," *Cultural Survival Quarterly*, 1989, Vol. 13, No. 3, pp. 38-39.
74. Gonzalez, *Sojourners of the Caribbean.*
75. Linda Newson, *The Cost of Conquest: Indian Decline in Honduras Under Spanish Rule* (Boulder, CO: Westview Press, 1986).
76. The higher estimate comes from the Consejo Asesor Hondureño para el Desarrollo de las Etnias Autóctonas (CAHDEA), while the lower estimate was reported in Counce and Davidson, "Indians of Central America."
77. Newson, *The Cost of Conquest.*
78. Kurian, *Encyclopedia of the Third World*, p. 849.
79. *Tiempo*, July 4, 1988.
80. Ibid.
81. *Tiempo*, July 16, 1988.
82. *Tiempo*, January 3, 1989.
83. "Declaración de los grupos etnicos," *Boletín Informativo*, November 1989.

84. Of the 27,500 asylum requests processed by the U.S. Immigration and Naturalization Service (INS) in Texas during the last half of 1988, 11 percent were by Hondurans. *Washington Report on the Hemisphere*, February 1, 1989.
85. United Nations High Commissioner for Refugees, "Information Paper," International Conference on Central American Refugees, Guatemala City, May 29-31, 1989.
86. *Desplazados de Guerra Hondureños* (Tegucigalpa: CEDOH, October 1988).

Part 5: The Environment

1. An extensive examination of the factors that contributed to the environmental problems facing southern Honduras can be found in Stonich, "The Dynamics of Social Processes and Environmental Destruction," pp. 269-96.
2. H. Jeffrey Leonard, *Natural Resources and Economic Development in Central America* (New Brunswick, NJ: Transaction Books/International Institute for Environment and Development, 1987), pp. 99, 120.
3. Cited in *Central America Report*, August 10, 1990.
4. JRB Associates, *Honduras: Environmental Profile* (Washington, DC: AID, 1982).
5. Manuel Torres Calderon, "Forests Going, Deserts Coming," *Latin America News Update*, August 1989.
6. David Pickles, "Honduran Forestry Lumbers into Crisis," *Financial Times*, April 28, 1989.
7. Jim Barborak, "Tough Times Ahead for Honduras" (Centro Agronómico Tropical de Investigación y Enseñanza-CATIE, undated draft).
8. Pickles, "Honduran Forestry."
9. ANDI pronouncement published on October 22, 1991, cited in Alcídes Hernández, "La política económica y la situación de sector forestal," CEDOH, *Boletín Informativo*, No. 57, December 1991.
10. Denise Stanley, "Contras Contribute to Ecological Destruction in Honduras," *Earth Island Journal*, Summer 1989.
11. "U.S. Buying Chainsaws for Contras in Honduras," *Not Man Apart*, June-September 1989.
12. UPI, Tegucigalpa, May 10, 1986.
13. Hearings before a subcommittee of the House of Representatives Committee on Appropriations, *Foreign Operations, Export Financing, and Related Appropriations for 1989*, 2nd sess., 1988.
14. *Washington Post*, April 5, 1986.
15. Leonard, *Natural Resources*, pp. 16, 18.
16. Ibid., pp. 146, 149.
17. The figure was released during a May 30, 1991, seminar in Tegucigalpa on pesticide use. Cited in "Honduras: On 'Indiscriminate' Use of Pesticides," *Central America Update*, May 31, 1991.
18. *Hondupress*, October 5, 1981.
19. Cited in "Costa Rica and Honduras Ban Toxic Pesticides," *Central America Update*, June 12, 1991.
20. Inter Press Service, June 30, 1992.
21. Leonard, *Natural Resources*, p. 99.
22. Ibid., p. 90.
23. United Nations, "Prospects of World Urbanization," 1988.
24. *Hondupress*, September 28, 1989.
25. Leonard, *Natural Resources*, p. 135.
26. *Hondupress*, October 17, 1989.
27. *Central America Report*, January 19, 1990.
28. Bill Weinberg, "War on the Land: The Politics of Ecology and the Ecology of Politics in Central America," unpublished manuscript.
29. Ibid.; *Cultural Survival Quarterly*, Vol. 11, No. 3, 1987, pp. 38-45.

30. For an inventory of Honduran parks and reserves, proposed and actual, see: Gustavo Cruz, *Guía de los parques nacionales* (Tegucigalpa: Honduran Association for Ecology, 1986).

Part 6: Foreign Influence

1. Robert E. Sanchez, "Honduras: U.S. Foreign Assistance Facts," *A Congressional Research Service Brief*, May 20, 1988.
2. Military assistance rose from $2.3 million in fiscal year 1979 to $3.9 million in 1980, and economic assistance leapt from about $29 million to about $53 million.
3. Lapper and Painter, *Honduras: State for Sale*, p. 78.
4. Philip L. Shepherd, "The Case of the Invisible Aid," *NACLA Report on the Americas*, January-February 1988, p. 33; Philip Shepherd, "Honduras," in Blachman, et al., *Confronting Revolution*.
5. AID-Honduras, "Briefing Book" (Tegucigalpa: January 1988).
6. For discussion of Honduran nationalism see David Ronfeldt, *U.S. Involvement in Central America: Three Views from Honduras* (RAND Corporation, July 1989).
7. Cited in Burbach, "Restive Honduran Military."
8. During the early 1980s COHEP resisted the complete implementation of AID's neoliberal remedies and AID directed the bulk of its private-sector support assistance through a new breed of export-oriented business associations, most of which were created by AID. Yet AID never broke the hegemony of COHEP. An eventual realignment between AID and COHEP opened the way for AID funding of COHEP beginning in 1988. For more background see Tom Barry, *Rain of Dollars* (Albuquerque: Resource Center, 1986), and Benjamin Crosby, "Crisis y fragmentación: Relaciones entre los sectores público-privado en Centroamérica" (Latin American and Caribbean Center, Florida International University, May 1985).
9. U.S. Department of Commerce, *Foreign Economic Trends and Their Implications for the United States* (Washington, DC: U.S. Department of Commerce, June 1989).
10. U.S. embassy, "Business Fact Sheets: Honduras," June 1989.
11. *Resource Center Compilation of Corporations* (Albuquerque: Resource Center, 1986).
12. *Tiempo*, December 6 and 27, 1984.
13. *Hondupress*, April 11, 1989.
14. *CBI Business Bulletin*, November-December 1988.
15. AID, *U.S. Overseas Loans and Grants, Obligations and Loan Authorizations*, July 1, 1945-September 30, 1987.
16. For a more thorough examination of AID in Honduras and Central America see Tom Barry and Debra Preusch, *The Soft War: The Uses and Abuses of U.S. Economic Aid in Central America* (New York: Grove Press, 1988), and Shepherd, "The Honduran Economic Crisis."
17. *Tiempo*, March 11, 1987.
18. AID-estimated ESF local-currency expenditures for 1988 were divided into four categories: $26.3 million for Public Development Activities, $37.5 million in Private Sector Programs, $11.7 million for the Public Sector Recurrent Budget, and $6.8 million for the AID Trust Fund. Figures from AID's "FY1990 Annual Budget Submission."
19. U.S. Agency for International Development, *Honduras: Country Development Strategy Statement FY1986* (Washington, DC: AID, May 1984), p. 5.
20. Planning Minister Francisco Figueroa revealed in 1987 that 50 percent of the local currency created by ESF payments went directly to the private sector and that the government did not exercise any control over these grants. *Tribuna*, March 24, 1987.
21. Crosby, "Crisis y fragmentación."
22. Kathleen Heffernan, "Honduras," in Paus, *Struggle Against Dependence*. As of 1985 nontraditional exports were 25 percent below their 1980 level as a percentage of total export value.
23. U.S. Agency for International Development, *AID Policy Determination 71*.

Reference Notes

24. Shepherd, "The Honduran Economic Crisis," p. v.
25. U.S. Agency for International Development, *Honduras Project Paper: Strengthening Democratic Institutions*, 1987, Project No. 522-0296.
26. Ibid., p. 72.
27. U.S. Agency for International Development, *Congressional Presentation, FY1990, Annex III* (Washington, DC: AID, 1989), p. 107.
28. Ibid., p. 15.
29. Interview with Roberto Figueroa, U.S. embassy, February 14, 1990.
30. David Corn, "Foreign Aid for the Right," *The Nation*, December 18, 1989.
31. Barry and Preusch, *AIFLD in Central America*.
32. AIFLD Report, December 1985.
33. Article I of the 1954 agreement reads: "Each government will make or continue to make available to the other . . . such equipment, materials, services, or other military assistance as the government furnishing such assistance may authorize and in accordance with such terms and conditions as may be agreed." Cited in *Honduras: A U.S. Base for Intervention* (Philadelphia: NARMIC/American Friends Service Committee, March 1989), p. 1.
34. U.S. Department of Defense, "Training U.S. National Guard Engineers in Honduras: 'General Terencio Sierra,' " 1986, p. 1.
35. Erick Weaver, "La diplomacia del banano: El desarrollo de las relaciones entre los Estados Unidos y Honduras," in Meza, *Honduras: Pieza Clave*.
36. U.S. Department of Defense, *Congressional Presentation for Security Assistance Programs FY1990* (Washington, DC, 1989), p. 160.
37. Between 1946 and 1986, some 3,100 Honduran officers and enlisted men received training at the U.S. Army School of the Americas.
38. U.S. Department of Defense, "Training U.S. National Guard."
39. U.S. General Accounting Office, *Security Assistance: Update*, pp. 52, 54.
40. Ibid., p. 59.
41. Ibid., p. 87. The 1987 figure is a DOD estimate.
42. Philip Shepherd, "El trágico curso y las consequencias de la política Norteamericana en Honduras," in Meza, *Honduras: Pieza Clave*, p. 127. Sen. James Sasser (D-TN) criticized the military exercises as "an open back door" to fortify the Honduran military, observing that the construction activities were often unnecessary for the success of the maneuvers. "Report on Honduras," *Congressional Record*, February 8, 1984, pp. 1122-25.
43. The DOD plan for Honduras called for an annual U.S. military-aid commitment of $100 million for each of four years. U.S. embassy, "U.S. Military Activities in Honduras" (Tegucigalpa, February 1984).
44. The $74.5 million military-assistance package included ten FE-5 fighter jets and two F-5 training aircraft. These Mach 1.1 supersonic jets are superior to any other aircraft in Central America and replace the Super Mysteres, which had been the most sophisticated in the region. See: "Statement of Edward L. King before the Subcommittee on Arms Control, International Security, and Science," May 19, 1987.
45. U.S. embassy, "Handbook on Honduras."
46. U.S. General Accounting Office, *Honduras: U.S. Military Presence at Soto Cano Air Base* (Washington, DC, March 1989), p. 9.
47. Joint Task Force Bravo, "Fact Sheet J-5," June 1, 1987.
48. U.S. Department of Defense, "Training U.S. National Guard."
49. Ibid.
50. Ibid.
51. Shepherd, "El trágico curso y las consequencias," p. 131.
52. *Honduras: A U.S. Base for Intervention*, pp. 2-3.
53. George Black and Anne Nelson, "Mysterious Death of Father Carney," *The Nation*, August 4, 1984.
54. CEDOH, "Incidentes y costo humano de la presencia militar de los Estados Unidos en Honduras," *Boletín Informativo*, August 1989.
55. Willard F. Barber and Neale Ranning, *Internal Security and Military Power* (Columbus: Ohio State University Press, 1966), p. 127. For more information on early military/civic-action programs see: Tom Barry, *Low Intensity Conflict: The New Battlefield in Central*

America (Albuquerque: Resource Center, 1986), pp. 41-45, and C.M. Simpson, *Inside the Green Berets: The Story of the U.S. Army Special Forces* (New York: Berkeley Books, 1984).

56. *National Guard Update*, January-February 1989.

57. Maj. Bernard Eugene Harvey, USAF, "Military Civic Action in Honduras 1982-1985: Tactical Success, Strategic Uncertainty," CLIC Papers, Army-Air Force Center for Low Intensity Conflict, October 1988. For a critical analysis of the Harvey paper, see: Eric Shultz, "Medical Counterinsurgency in Honduras," *Honduras Update*, November-December 1988.

58. Harvey, "Military Civic Action in Honduras."

59. Ibid., p. 2.

60. Interview with Juan Sieca Fonseca, Honduran Army Public Relations Officer, March 16, 1989.

61. Interview with COPEN director, July 1987; *Proyecciones Militares*, No. 83, January 1989.

Bibliography

The following periodicals are useful sources of information and analysis on Honduras:

Boletín Informativo, Centro de Documentación de Honduras (Tegucigalpa), monthly, Spanish.
Hondupress, Honduran Press Agency (Boulder, CO, and Managua), biweekly, English.
NACLA Report on the Americas, North American Congress on Latin America, bi-monthly, English.
Pensamiento Propio, Coordinadora Regional de Investigaciones Económicas y Sociales (Managua), monthly, Spanish.

The following books contain valuable background on many issues important to understanding Honduras:

Alison Acker, *Honduras: The Making of a Banana Republic* (Boston: South End Press, 1988).
Elvia Alvarado with Medea Benjamin, *Don't Be Afraid, Gringo: A Honduran Woman Speaks from the Heart* (San Francisco: Institute for Food and Development Policy, 1987).
Longino Becerra, *Cuando las tarantulas atacan* (Tegucigalpa: Baktun Editorial).
Morris J. Blachman, William M. LeoGrande, and Kenneth Sharpe, *Confronting Revolution: Security Through Diplomacy in Central America* (New York: Pantheon Books, 1986).
Filander Diaz Chávez, *Carías, el último caudillo frutero* (Tegucigalpa: Editorial Guaymuras, 1982).
Richard Lapper and James Painter, *Honduras: State for Sale* (London: Latin America Bureau, 1985).

James A. Morris, *Honduras: Caudillo Politics and Military Rulers* (Boulder, CO: Westview Press, 1984).

Linda A. Newson, *The Cost of Conquest: Indian Decline in Honduras under Spanish Rule* (Boulder, CO: Westview Press, 1986).

Margarita Oseguera de Ochoa, *Honduras Hoy: Sociedad y Crisis Regional* (Tegucigalpa: CEDOH/CRIES, 1987).

Nancy Peckenham and Annie Street, eds., *Honduras: Portrait of a Captive Nation* (New York: Praeger Publishers, 1985).

Mario Posas, *Luchas del movimiento obrero hondureño* (San José, Costa Rica: Editorial Universitaria Centroamericana—EDUCA, 1981).

Mario Posas, *Modalidades del proceso de la democratización en Honduras* (Tegucigalpa: Editorial Universitaria, 1989).

Mark B. Rosenberg and Philip L. Shepherd, eds., *Honduras Contronts its Future: Contending Perspectives on Critical Issues* (Boulder, CO: Lynne Rienner Publishers Inc., 1986).

Donald E. Schulz, *The United States, Honduras, and the Crisis in Central America* (Boulder, CO: Westview Press, 1993).

Chronology

1502	Christopher Columbus lands on northern coast of Honduras.
1821	Honduras declares independence from Spain as part of Central American Federation.
1839	Honduras becomes independent republic.
1848	New constitution promulgated.
1855	Liberals removed from power.
1865	New constitution promulgated.
1876	Liberals regain power under Marco Aurelio Soto.
1880	New constitution promulgated.
	Tegucigalpa named national capital.
1891	Conservatives elected to power.
1894	New constitution promulgated.
1896	U.S. troops land in Honduras.
1899	First banana concession granted to Vaccaro brothers, later to become Standard Fruit Company.
1902	Founding members of National Party (PN) split off from Liberal Party (PL).
1905	U.S. troops land in Honduras for first of five times during next 20 years.
1907	Policarpio Bonilla overthrown and replaced by Dávila.
	U.S. banana merchant Sam Zemurray forms Cuyamel Fruit Company.
1910	Dávila deposed by U.S. mercenaries and replaced by Manuel Bonilla.
1912	Trujillo Railroad Company wins contract to build railway, beginning United Fruit Company's involvement in Honduras.
1921	First Congress of Workers convenes and organizes Honduras Workers Federation.
1923	Presidential elections won by Gen. Tiburcio Carías Andino, who is prevented from taking office.
1924	Carías' forces take Tegucigalpa; new elections won by Paz Baraona.

Inside Honduras

1925	New constitution promulgated.
1926	Formation of Federation of Workers Societies of the North.
1929	United Fruit purchases Cuyamel for $32 million.
	Formation of Honduran Syndical Organization.
1932	Carías begins 16-year dictatorship.
1936	New constitution promulgated.
1948	Carías steps down; Nationalist Party candidate Juan Manuel Gálvez elected president.
1952	Founding of Francisco Morazán military college.
1954	Elections won by Ramón Villeda Morales of Liberal Party; Vice-President Julio Lozano Díaz seizes power.
	Successful strike by banana workers leads to widespread organizing among other workers.
	Communist Party reorganized.
1955	United Fruit workers form Union of Tela Railroad Company Workers.
1956	Constituent elections overturned by coup; military junta led by Roque J. Rodríguez assumes power.
1957	Villeda Morales elected president; new constitution promulgated; new labor codes and social security law adopted.
1959	Abortive military coup.
1960	Resolution of Atlantic Coast border dispute with Nicaragua.
1961	Introduction of agrarian reform program.
1963	Shortly before finishing his term, Villeda ousted by army coup led by Col. Osvaldo López Arellano.
1965	New constitution promulgated.
	Peasant leader Lorenzo Zelaya killed.
1969	Four-day "Soccer War" with El Salvador over mistreatment of Salvadorans in Honduras and related issues.
1971	Ramón Ernesto Cruz elected president.
	Pact of National Unity divides congressional seats evenly between National and Liberal Parties.
1972	Cruz deposed; López returns to power.
1974	Hurricane Fifi leaves 12,000 dead and 150,000 homeless.
1975	"Bananagate" scandal: United Brands pays "high government official" $1.25 million bribe for reduction in banana taxes and saves $7.5 million.
	López is overthrown and Juan Alberto Melgar Castro takes power.
	Army and local landowners kill 15 peasant demonstrators, including two priests.
1976	Border conflicts with El Salvador; OAS intervenes.
1977	Las Isletas banana cooperative destroyed by soldiers who arrive in Standard Fruit's railroad cars.
1978	Melgar ousted after drug-related allegations surface; Gen. Policarpio Paz García assumes power.

Chronology

1979	President Carter strengthens ties to Honduras after fall of Somoza in Nicaragua.

1980   Constituent Assembly elections.

"Soccer War" officially ends after signing of treaty with El Salvador.

1981   Liberal Party candidate Roberto Suazo Córdova elected president—first civilian president in more than two decades. Gen. Gustavo Alvarez retains power as chief of staff.

John Dimitri Negroponte becomes U.S. ambassador to Honduras.

First U.S. military advisors arrive in Honduras; joint U.S.-Honduran naval and air maneuvers.

1982   Gen. Alvarez instigates change in constitution that reduces presidential authority; Constituent Assembly approves Honduras' 14th constitution.

Foreign Ministers of Honduras, Costa Rica, and El Salvador form Central American Democratic Community.

Feb.   Reagan administration pledges 50 percent hike in military aid to Honduras.

Four clandestine cemeteries discovered.

April   Strikes and land occupations declared "subversive acts" in new decree.

June   Honduran army participates in joint operations with Salvadoran army against FMLN guerrillas.

July   Joint U.S.-Honduran military maneuvers along Nicaraguan border.

Aug.   Honduran armed forces on full alert after border clashes with Nicaragua.

Strike by 30,000 teachers.

Nov.   *Newsweek* reveals Negroponte in control of contra operations against Nicaragua.

1983   U.S. training base opens at Puerto Castilla.

Joint U.S.-Honduran Big Pine I and II military and naval maneuvers begin.

Contadora group meets for first time to develop dialogue and negotiation in Central America; parties to peace accords include Costa Rica, El Salvador, Guatemala, Honduras, and Nicaragua.

1984   Alvarez ousted by younger officers and goes into exile; Gen. Walter López Reyes named commander in chief of armed forces.

Grenadier I joint military exercises along Salvadoran border with U.S., Honduran, and Salvadoran troops.

60,000 demonstrators in Tegucigalpa and 40,000 in San Pedro Sula protest U.S. presence in Honduras.

Honduran government halts U.S. training of Salvadoran soldiers at Puerto Castilla.

Army publishes report on human rights violations blaming left and rightwing non-Hondurans.

Kissinger Commission recommends $8 billion developmental aid to Central America and increased military assistance to Honduras, El Salvador, and Guatemala.

U.S. military aid has soared 20-fold since 1980.

Nicaragua agrees to sign Contadora treaty, but Costa Rica, El Salvador, and Honduras refuse to sign.

1985	Liberal Party candidate José Azcona Hoyo declared winner of presidential elections although National Party candidate gains most votes.

Constitutional crisis over appointment of judges.

Nicaraguan contras linked to 200 death squad killings in Honduras.

MISURA contra leader Steadman Fagoth expelled.

Formation of National Union of Rural Workers (CNTC).

Big Pine III, Universal Trek '85, and Cabañas '85 joint military exercises.

Honduran army enters Colomoncagua refugee camp, killing two Salvadoran refugees and abducting ten others.

1986	López Reyes resigns as head of military and is replaced by Regalado Hernández.

Blazing Trail joint exercises.

Third revised Contadora treaty presented. Costa Rica, El Salvador, and Honduras refuse to sign.

1987	Mass repatriation of refugees from Mesa Grande camps in Honduras.
Feb.	Costa Rican President Arias assumes leadership role in regional peace initiatives; meets with representatives from El Salvador, Guatemala, and Honduras in Esquipulas, Guatemala.
Aug.	Presidents of Costa Rica, El Salvador, Guatemala, Honduras, and Nicaragua sign Esquipulas II Peace Accords.
1988	Honduras requests UN peacekeeping force to patrol its borders with El Salvador and Nicaragua.
March	Arias accuses El Salvador, Guatemala, Honduras, and Nicaragua of not complying fully with Esquipulas accords; criticizes presence of U.S. troops in Honduras.
1989	Esquipulas peace talks held in El Salvador after four postponements.
Oct.	Major union federations and popular organizations come together in "Plataforma de Lucha" coalition.
Nov.	National Party (PN) presidential candidate Rafael Leonardo Callejas wins elections and PN candidates capture 71 of 128 seats in Congress.
1990	President Callejas implements structural adjustment program led by a reduction in value of *lempira* by half.
March	Thousands of contras abandon their bases in Honduras in wake of electoral victory by National Opposition Union (UNO) in Nicaragua.

Chronology

1991	Congress approves amnesty law, paving way for eventual return of exiled political leaders and guerrillas.
1992	Last of 30,000 Salvadoran refugees repatriated under sponsorship of UN High Comissioner for Refugees.
March	Congress passes Agricultural Modernization Law, removing teeth from agrarian reform legislation in effect since 1962.
Sept.	International Court of Justice (ICJ) rules on longstanding El Salvador-Honduras border dispute. Ruling seen as victory for Honduran diplomacy.
Oct.	Gen. Luis Alonso Discua consummates his reelection to the post of armed forces chief. Discua, who will serve until 1996, was the first military leader in more than three decades to succeed in a reelection bid.
1993	
April	Blue ribbon commission recommends major reforms to bring military establishment under civilian control, including dissolution of military-controlled National Investigations Division (DNI).
Aug.	Judge issues sentences against two military officers for 1991 rape-murder of Riccy Mabel Martínez. The verdicts mark the first time military personnel have been prosecuted and sentenced by civilian courts.
Sept.	Congress authorizes legalization of Democratic Unification Party (PUD), an alliance of several former guerrilla groups.
Nov.	Liberal Party candidate Carlos Roberto Reina elected president with 52 percent of votes.
1994	
Jan.	Human Rights Ombudsman Leo Valladores issues report on the fate of 184 people disappeared between 1979 and 1990.

SOURCES: Tom Barry and Debra Preusch, *The Central America Fact Book* (New York: Grove Press, 1986); Helen Schooley, ed., *Conflict in Central America* (Essex, UK: Longman Group Ltd., 1987); *Encyclopedia of the Third World* (New York: Facts on File, 1987); Nora Hamilton, *Crisis in Central America: Regional Dynamics and U.S. Policy in the 1980s* (Boulder, CO: Westview Press, 1988); Gerald Greenfield and Sheldon Maran, eds., *Labor Organizations in Latin America* (New York: Greenwood Press, 1987); Richard Lapper and James Painter, *Honduras: State for Sale* (London: Latin America Bureau, 1985).

For More Information

Resources

Centro de Documentación de Honduras (CEDOH)/
 Boletín Informativo
Apartado Postal 1882
Tegucigalpa, Honduras

Human Rights

Human Rights Watch
485 Fifth Ave.
New York, NY 10017-6104

Amnesty International
322 8th Avenue
New York, NY 10001

Comité para la Defensa de los Derechos Humanos (CODEH)
Apartado Postal 1256
Tegucigalpa, Honduras

Comité de Familiares de Desaparecidos en Honduras
 (COFADEH)
Apartado Postal 1243
Tegucigalpa, Honduras

Tours

Global Exchange
2017 Mission Street, #303
San Francisco, CA 94110

Official

Embassy of Honduras
3007 Tilden Street NW
Washington, DC 20008
(202) 966-7702

Embassy of the United States in Honduras
APO Miami, FL 34022

U.S. State Department
Citizen's Emergency Center/Travel Information
Main State Building
Washington, DC 20520
(202) 647-5225

The Resource Center

The Inter-Hemispheric Education Resource Center is a private, non-profit, research and policy institute located in Albuquerque, New Mexico. Founded in 1979, the Resource Center produces books, policy reports, audiovisuals, and other educational materials about U.S. foreign policy, as well as sponsoring popular education projects. For more information and a catalog of publications, please write to the Resource Center, Box 4506, Albuquerque, New Mexico 87196.

Board of Directors

Become an RC member!

I want to support your work concerning U.S. influence in the sharing of global resources.

☐ $25 Basic Membership: You receive free annual subscriptions to our two quarterly publications: *Resource Center Bulletin* and *BorderLines*.

☐ $50 Amigo Membership: You receive free annual subscriptions to our quarterlies as well as all our special reports (such as our recent reports on the democratization process in Mexico).

☐ $100 Compañero Membership: You receive our two quarterlies, all our special reports, and a 33% discount on all RC book purchases.

☐ $250 Comadre/Compadre Membership: Patrons of $250 or more receive all the benefits of a compañero membership as well as all new RC materials free.

☐ $1,000 RC Sustainer: You receive all our publications as they are released, and are invited to take your pick of existing materials from our catalog.

Charge my ☐ VISA ☐ MasterCard

Account # _____

Expiration date _____ Daytime Phone_____

Name_____

Street Address_____

City_____ State_____Zip_____

The Resource Center is a nonprofit organization.
All donations are tax deductible.

To receive our catalogs, phone us at (505) 842-8288, or fax (505) 246-1601. Our address is:

Resource Center
Box 4506
Albuquerque, NM 87196

Other books on Latin America from the Resource Center Press

The Inside Central America Series and Country Guides–
Everything you need to know about each nation's
economy, politics, environment and society.

Inside Belize
1995 Paperback, ISBN 0-911213-39-2, $10.95

Inside Costa Rica
1995 Paperback, ISBN 0-911213-51-1, $10.95

Inside El Salvador
1995 Paperback, ISBN 0-911213-53-8, $10.95

Inside Guatemala
1995 Paperback, ISBN 0-911213-52-X, $10.95

Inside Panama
1995 Paperback, ISBN 0-911213-50-3, $10.95

Nicaragua: A Country Guide
1990 Paperback, ISBN 0-911213-29-5, $9.95

Mexico: A Country Guide
The Essential Source on Mexican Society,
Economy and Politics
1992 Paperback, ISBN 0-911213-35-X, $14.95

The Great Divide
The Challenge of U.S.-Mexico Relations
Grove/Atlantic Press
1994, Clothbound, 464 pages
ISBN 0-8021-1559-4
$24.00